The Regional Italian Kitchen

NIKA HAZELTON

The Regional Italian Kitchen

Drawings by Honi Werner

CASTLE BOOKS

This edition published in 1995 by
CASTLE BOOKS
A division of Book Sales, Inc.
P.O. Box 7100
Edison, NJ 08818-7100

Published by arrangement with M. Evans and Co., Inc.,
216 East 49th Street, New York, NY 10017-1502.

Library of Congress Cataloging-in-Publication Data

Hazelton, Nika Standen.
   The regional Italian kitchen.
   Includes index.
   1. Cookery, Italian. I. Title.
TX723.H37   641.5'945   78-3717

ISBN 0-7858-0459-5

MANUFACTURED IN THE UNITED STATES OF AMERICA

For
Lois and Vincent Romei
and
Alessandro Morandotti
Best of Friends

Contents

Introduction

Italy today is an up-to-date, modern country with its full share of automobiles, latest appliances, supermarkets, modern kitchens, and a shortage of domestic help. Food has not escaped the onslaught of the twentieth century: most restaurants feature an all-Italy menu (pasta and veal, guaranteed to please all comers); lunch counters, the *tavola calda* (literally, the "hot table"), are set up in cafés, and along with espresso, you can have a sandwich or a quick dish of pasta or vegetables instead of sitting down to the time-honored, leisurely three-course meal.

Yet the tradition of superb and varied regional cooking has never been lost. Since the days when Italy was largely agricultural and the food was solid, flavorful, peasant cooking, this tradition has always been kept alive in the home. Even today, the cook still cooks basically what she has always cooked and what her mother cooked though her food will be less substantial and much lighter. Italians are individualists, fiercely attached to their native localities and to the cooking of their region. When left to myself, for instance, I cook Tuscan or Roman food, the remembered dishes of my Italian homes.

The recipes in this book have come from such home cooks. Some go back to my Italian childhood, some are from relatives, dispersed to all parts of the Italian peninsula. Others were gathered in my travels, given to me by friends, discovered in old cookbooks or in eating places in every region of Italy that still feature *la cucina casalinga,* home cooking of the region.

This is not a systematic or historical account of the traditional food of the Italian provinces, nor does it duplicate recipes found in most Italian cookbooks (ravioli, cannelloni, salt cod, and so forth). Rather, it concentrates on recipes not generally known in America. However, the dishes are not complicated or costly, and they don't require special ingredients. It is my hope that they will bring new tastes and variety to ordinary everyday cooking, while expressing to some degree the marvelous tastes and variety of the regions of Italy.

Like all cookbooks, this one reflects my tastes and those of the people I cook for, as well as my personal opinions based on the experience of traveling throughout Italy and keeping house each year in Tuscany among terraces of olives and vines.

Italian Regional Food

Broadly speaking, Italy is divided into two main culinary areas, with the basic flavor of each determined by the cooking fats used. The northern part uses butter, and olive oil is in secondary use. The southern part is the olive oil region, and butter is not often used, although a certain amount of lard in the cooking of the South gives it a characteristic flavor (for instance, in Roman cooking).

Beyond this simple division, the regional food of Italy has been influenced by several factors that give each area its special taste: geography, history, economy. All the conquerors of different parts of the country have left their mark on the culture and the food of the regions—Etruscans, Romans, Arabs, Lombards, Goths, Normans, Spaniards, French, Austrians. The northern parts of Italy, with their abundant natural resources and economic advantages and their closeness to other parts of Europe, especially France and Austria, feature food that is much lighter, subtler, and more varied than that of the regions to the south, in the heel of Italy. The food of the South reflects its Greek origins, and in Sicily we still see the influence of the Arab conquest in the stuffed meats and vegetables, the sweets, the absence of pork. In the North, the herbs are sage and rosemary, applied with a light hand, and tomato sauces have a modest role in traditional cooking. In the South, garlic, basil, oregano and olives appear, and the tomato is ubiquitous. The bread and pasta foundation of all Italian cooking was laid by the Romans, who were large-scale wheat cultivators.

Most Italian regional cooking is "more or less" cooking, where specific quantities or even specific ingredients are not necessary to the same dish, and the same dish, incidentally, may have different names, even within the same region. Italian food varies from region to region not so much in the basic dishes as in the way they are put together and seasoned. Italy produces basically the same food products throughout the country: grains, vegetables, fruits, cheese, poultry, pork products and, along the coasts and in the lakes of the North, fish. Traditionally, meat did not figure largely in this country, for it had not been favored with much pasture land. Meat was the longed-for Sunday and holiday food. Now, because of the country's comparative prosperity, Italy can import larger quantities of meat from abroad, and it is no longer a luxury food.

All these many influences produced a cookery throughout the country that stresses the individual flavors of the food and simple, very careful cooking. It also stresses fresh ingredients, freshly prepared. "Italian food is *not* plastic," said a friend who visited Italy for the first time and was thrilled by the fresh seasonal foods.

Finally, all of Italy is one great vineyard, and wine is not simply a drink; it is part of the daily food of the country.

Piedmont

The cooking of Piedmont is substantial but restrained, and dignified like a citizen of the region. It is excellent, serious cooking, resembling French cookery (Piedmont and France border on each other). There is a courtliness to the food of Turin (the city of the former Italian royal family), which is credited with having invented the *grissino*, the bread stick, and where chicken is cooked *à la marengo*, as in France (Napoleon had been in Turin).

The ample game of the mountains is marinated in red wine and spices; the famed braised beef, made with Barolo, one of the great wines of the region, is as carefully constructed as its French cousin, beef Bourguignonne. The *bolliti*, the boiled meats also found in other parts of Italy, in Piedmont are a majestic assembly of beef and fowl, tongue, veal shanks and sausage cooked in broth rather than water. The vegetables are outstanding, and are often eaten raw, dipped into the *bagna cauda* sauce. The mountain pastures produce excellent butter, milk and cream and many cheeses, among them the lovely Fontina.

The fragrance of Piedmont is that of the white Alba truffle, far more delicious than the black truffle of France (and, alas, as impossible to afford in a dish of spaghetti with butter and cheese or over scrambled eggs).

Marvelous chocolate desserts are part of Turin's tradition, since King Emanuele Filiberto of Savoy introduced cocoa. A sweet *alla torinese* means chocolate, and sometimes chestnuts. Zabaglione is another dessert from more polite days.

The red wines of Piedmont are Italy's greatest wines. They are gentlemanly, carefully produced wines that need aging like all great reds. Barbera, Barolo, Gattinara and Ghemme are noble names. Asti Spumante needs no explanation. To top it all, vermouth was invented in Turin.

Lombardy

The elegant cooking of Lombardy is that of Milan, an elegant city indeed. The rich pastures of Lombardy, Italy's best, provide the region with first-class butter, and the cream and milk also make Italy's best cheeses. Rice from the Po valley is common here, too, but is generally eaten by itself, as in Risotto alla Milanese. A risotto enriched with mushrooms or chicken livers, chicken or turkey breasts lightly sautéed in butter, guinea hen baked in clay to retain its natural flavors, are all found to perfection here. The *marrons glacés* and the superlative candied fruits of the Milanese pastry and confectioners' shops are so freshly made, so juicy, that to me they are the height of luxurious eating.

In Bergamo they eat *polenta osei*, little songbirds plucked but not drawn, heads left on, and cooked on skewers with sage leaves and thin slices of pork and bacon. In Cremona there is good salami and *mostarda di frutta*, fruits preserved in a mustardy sugar syrup to liven up sausages and boiled meats (also available in Italian grocery stores in America). In Saronno, they make the famous *amaretti*, slightly bitter, dry almond macaroons (also available here in gourmet shops).

Frecciarossa (a brand name) and Sangue di Giuda (Jude's Blood) are well-known red wines from the hills above the great plain watered by the Po River. The red Lombard wines I love are the medium-bodied ones from the Valtellina, a long, narrow and high valley that links Italy and Switzerland and looks like a piece of Spain: Sassella, Grumello, and the fiercely named (but not tasting so) Inferno.

Trentino, Alto Adige

The cooking of the Trentino–Alto Adige, the latter part of the Austrian Tyrol until the end of World War I, the first long under earlier Austrian domination, is not, I feel, truly Italian. The food typical of these regions is, on the whole, Austrian food or heavily influenced by the culinary traditions of the Austro-Hungarian Empire of early days. While the region is Italian, its food is not within the gastronomical Italian tradition, and thus I have omitted a discussion of the area.

The region produces excellent red and white wines from the Pinot, Merlot, Cabernet, Pinot Bianco and Riesling grapes.

Veneto, Friuli, Venezia Giulia

The most elegant food in Italy, to my taste, comes from this region (along with Tuscany and parts of Lombardy). Venetian cooking makes great use of rice, since rice grows in the wetlands of the Po valley. It is combined with other ingredients such as fowl, fish, seafood and vegetables. In a good Venetian restaurant, if you order a rice dish, you will be warned that you will have to wait; rice that is not cooked freshly is not worth eating and *non aspetta*—it does not wait for the diner. Fish that is simply cooked (fried, grilled or broiled) is the mainstay of Venice, but there is much more to be found in the region. The cities of Verona, Padua and Treviso have lovely marketplaces, where the foods are displayed with elegance, and the gnocchi and filled pastas and the bean soups are fastidiously cooked. In the Friuli and the Venezia Giulia, the mountainous areas of the region, the food has been influenced by the cooking of Austria and Yugoslavia, countries that touch the borders of Italy there.

The best-known wines of the region are the white Soave and Prosecco di Conegliano, and the red Valpolicella and Bardolino. The red Amarone and the Recioto are bigger, more important wines.

Liguria

In the tenth century the coast of Liguria was subject to the Saracens, who left behind place names and some of their dishes. At the same time, Sicily, far to the south, had fallen to the Arabs, and thus shares an unexpected culinary link with Liguria. To this day, Arab cookery likes foods that are stuffed or layered with many different ingredients, and the same is true of the cooking of Genoa, one of the principal cities of Liguria. In Liguria we find a variety of ravioli stuffed with meat, herbs and cheese; savory pies of vegetables and/or meats enriched with hard-cooked eggs, currants and pine nuts; stuffed lettuces and stuffed eggplants. Perhaps the lack of pork products, compared to the abundance of sausages in almost all of Italy, is also due to the old Islamic ties (true as well of Sicily).

Ligurian cooking must be the greenest in all of Italy, with the use of wild and domesticated greens, used with meats, fish (the fish market of Genoa is an incredible tapestry of colors, shapes and textures), eggs, bread crumbs and herbs, made piquant with anchovies and rich with pine nuts or walnuts. The most famous of these green dishes is *pesto*, a sauce made from fresh basil, garlic, the delicious olive oil of the Ligurian coast, cheese and, often, nuts. It is spooned into soups, over trenette (very thin noodles) and other pastas, raviolis and gnocchi, onto vegetables—anything at all, if you like the taste of basil.

Liguria produces relatively little wine. But the wine of the Cinqueterre, villages between the cliffs and the sea west of La Spezia, is a joy to drink, as is the elegant dry red Dolceacqua, made not far from San Remo.

Emilia-Romagna

The cooking of Bologna, the chief city of the Emilia-Romagna region, is said to be Italy's finest. It is certainly the best advertised, especially where pasta, sausages and cheese are concerned; Parmesan cheese and Parma ham are from the region. To my taste, the cooking is too rich, with meat sauces and cream, butter and cheese spread over stuffed pastas, the famed tortellini, and their cousins, cappelletti, agnolini and ravioli. There is also a bewildering variety of superb smoked hams and sausages, including mortadella (baloney, from Bologna, to us). There is no question that Bologna, called *la grassa*, "the fat one," is the eating capital of Italy, secure in her architectural beauty and the richness of her foods.

The wines of the region are good, but not outstanding. Red Lambrusco, the best known, goes well with the region's rich food, but generally does not travel well.

Tuscany

The elegance of Tuscan food is exemplified by the simplicity (which equals perfection) of its most famous dish, Florence's *bistecca Fiorentina,* made with superlative meat and skilled hands on the grill or at the spit, a Renaissance cooking method still much used in Tuscany.

Tuscany uses both oil and butter: the delicious light oil of Lucca and the butter of the fertile valleys which graze the excellent Val di Chiana cattle are used in the delicious dishes of Florence. Tuscan cooking does not like the taste of fats; the hams and sausages are lean, as are the meats. Pasta dishes that need sauces, however simple, are few, and bread takes their place. The food is fragrant with sage and rosemary, marjoram, leeks, celery, which are incorporated into the dish rather than into a sauce.

When in New York, I ache with nostalgia for the country cooking of our Tuscan cook Isolina—her unforgettable oven-roasted rabbit, her spit-roasted chickens redolent of rosemary, her frittatas with fresh herbs from our garden, her light, fragrant tomato sauce, and most of all her bean dishes. Tuscans have so many bean dishes that they are called "bean eaters." All of the bean dishes are worth eating, whether made from fresh *fagioli* or kidney, navy and other beans that Americans know best as dried beans.

On the coast, Livorno is one of the centers of the Italian fishing industry, and the people make extraordinary fish soups that include an amazing variety of fish and seafood. Among the sweets of the region, which are dry rather than luscious, is the Panforte di Siena, a flat fruitcake as delicious today as it was centuries ago when Siena was a powerful, independent city.

The best Chianti are the aged *riserva* that come in Bordeaux-shaped bottles. Equally good are the red wines of Montepulciano, the Brunello from Montalcino, and the white Vernaccia of San Gimignano, lovely wines from lovely old cities.

Umbria

Umbria, hilly rather than mountainous, has tamed much of her nature with olive trees that surround the golden cities of the region: Perugia, Gubbio, Assisi, Spoleto, where you step right into the Middle Ages. The region uses almost exclusively local, seasonal products in a simple, straightforward cookery, specializing in oven and spit-roasts. Spit-roasted pig, fragrant with herbs, known as *la porchetta*, is said to be even better in Umbria than in Tuscany; I find it equally good in both regions. The pigs are always fat and fragrant with rosemary and sage, and served in thick slices between slices of bread. Norcia is especially renowned for its hams and pork products; to this day, pork butchers in Rome are called *norcini*, men from Norcia.

The black truffles of Norcia and Spoleto and other parts of Umbria (to my mind, not as fragrant as the white truffles of Piedmont) enjoy great fame beyond the frontiers of Italy, and when the truffles of Périgord run scarce, the French truffle merchants buy up the Umbrian crop.

The golden wine of Orvieto, a hill city with a most beautiful cathedral, is as justly famous as its home town. It is made both dry and *abboccato*, the first well balanced, with a flowery bouquet, the second light and slightly sweet but with no hint of cloying.

The Marche

In the Marche, there are two kinds of cookery, that from the coast and that from the interior (pork, chicken and wild birds, vegetables). The stars of the coastal fish cookery are the fish soups from the important fishing ports. One of these soups, the *brodetto d'Ancona*, requires no less than thirteen varieties of fish and seafood. The cookery of the interior resembles that of Emilia-Romagna, Umbria and Abruzzi, which border the Marche. It is the peaceful cooking of a prosperous and hardworking countryside: pastas stuffed and layered in the Romagna manner but less exuberant. The love for stuffed dishes extends to chickens, meat and fish, all good, flavorful family dishes.

The pale, straw-colored Verdicchio is a dry but full-bodied white wine of the region. At its best, it is one of the most satisfactory table wines of Italy.

Lazio (Rome)

In a way, there is no such thing as an original Roman cuisine. The city has been the recipient of food specialties from all parts of Italy. Roman cooking is *trattoria* and family cooking, and Romans love to eat, and love to eat out. There must be more restaurants, *trattorie*, cafés and pastry shops in Rome than in any other city of Italy.

Much of the flavor of Roman cooking comes from the *battuto*, a mixture of some kind of pork fat, such as the fat from prosciutto (religiously kept for this purpose in Roman households) or lard, or *pancetta*, an Italian form of bacon, with garlic, parsley, a little celery and onion, and frequently other herbs. All these ingredients are minced together into a paste, the start of much Roman and Lazio cooking.

The cooking is robust and spicy, although not nearly as much so as that of southern Italy, where Rome learned its ways with anchovies, vinegar, garlic, capers and *peperoncini*. From the South too comes pizza; from the Abruzzi and central Italy, the way of thickening the natural juices of a meat dish with egg yolks beaten with lemon, called *brodettare*. From there, too, comes the Roman *alla cacciatora*, the hunters' ways with chicken, lamb and veal. It does not include much tomato, but is fragrant with garlic, rosemary, white wine, anchovies and hot pepper. From northern Italy come the veal dishes sautéed in butter and the good olive oil of Lazio, the peas with prosciutto, and from Tuscany, the bean dishes. Roman vegetable dishes are either simple, as in boiled greens dressed with oil and vinegar, or interesting composites, marrying vegetables and meat or stuffing vegetables.

The classic meat of Rome is lamb, *abbacchio*, traditionally an animal no less than twenty days and no more than a month old; now the range is more flexible, but the lamb is never a robust, teenage animal. Roasted lamb, lamb *cacciatora*, lamb in any way is still delicious in Rome, especially at Eastertime.

Rome has excellent mozzarella from the former Paludi Pontine, the ancient swamps finally drained under Mussolini, which gave Lazio rich pasture and agricultural lands.

The wines of Rome and the Lazio are essentially good, sturdy table wines from Frascati and the hills around Rome. Modern vinification methods have made it possible for some of them to travel to America.

Abruzzi, Molise

In this region, the mountains stretch from the Adriatic into the highest point of the Apennines. The traditional cooking is a more rustic version of that of Umbria—mountain cooking. The interior is wild, very beautiful country with high pastures and dense forests, and pigs graze along with sheep. The first make a lean, tasty mountain ham, better than any I've eaten, even in Bologna; the latter are the meat of the region, made into stews seasoned with oil, onion and rosemary, cooked with egg and lemon as they do in Greece. And I remember the wonderful, fresh ricotta of the high mountains, sold to us by the solitary shepherds who make it.

The important fishing ports of the Adriatic Coast, such as Pescara, supply much of central Italy's fish. They are famous for their majestic fish stews and soups, which are matters of great local pride and often heated discussions. *Maccheroni alla chitarra* are the one pasta specialty of the Abruzzi. These are long, thin egg noodles, cut with the *chitarra*, a rectangular wooden frame strung with steel strings like a guitar (hence the name). Thin sheets of dough are laid on the strings and pressed with a rolling pin into the long strands.

A much more interesting and fiery idiosyncrasy of Abruzzi cookery is the use of *peperoncini*, small, very hot red peppers sold threaded on a string. You find them in practically all dishes of fish, meat and vegetables and wonder that there are none in the few sweets of the region. They are a fitting match for the hot temperament of the natives.

The pale red Montepulciano d'Abruzzo (not to be confused with the Montepulciano of Tuscany) and the white Trebbiano d'Abruzzo are pleasant, unpretentious wines that go well with the local foods.

The Campania

The Campania, dominated by the capital city of Naples, does not use butter in traditional cooking, or milk or cream (true also of Sicily). There were no pastures, and what little milk was produced went to making cheese. When I was a very small girl, we used to summer partly at Anacapri on the Isle of Capri. We went early in the season, and on the boat with us each year was the "Anacapri cow," imported each summer to provide the likes of us with milk. Thanks to modern progress, there is no longer a lack of dairy products in southern Italy, but the tradition of using almonds and almond milk instead remains. Pine nuts and almonds, both indigenous to southern Italy, are used to enrich both savory and sweet dishes.

All Neapolitan cooking is almost baroque in taste, color and decoration. There are two cookeries, actually: the popular and the ceremonial. The first is based upon pasta, tomato sauce, fish and vegetables, what we think of as typically Neapolitan cooking. But Naples was also for centuries under the domination of the Spanish Bourbon kings and of France, and this produced a local cuisine that combines the techniques of France and Spain in dishes far more vivacious than in either of these countries. Many of these dishes survive as traditional feast day foods: timbales and *gattos* (from *gâteaux*), savory mixtures of chicken livers, little meatballs, sausages, hard-cooked eggs, peas and mozzarella, encased in rice or in pasta dough for Christmas; the stuffed lasagna for Carnival; lamb stuffed with egg for Easter. In a poor city like Naples, complicated and rich food on feast days makes up for the simplicity of the daily pasta dressed with oil and garlic, the fried fish, the bit of cheese with bread.

The best and very good wine of the region is that of Ischia, made by the Ambra family.

Puglia, Basilicata, Calabria

It may be cavalier to join the three regions of Italy's South into a gastronomic unity when regional pride is so strong. But Puglia (the heel), Basilicata (the instep) and Calabria (the toe) have a common geography and history. Phoenicians, Greeks, Arabs and Spaniards have all left traces of their cultures in the foods of the regions, especially in the fish cookery of the coastline. The extraordinary fish and shellfish are boiled or fried or stewed with tomatoes and vegetables or made into fish soups. In Taranto I once enjoyed a dish of tiny fried fish, mixed with bread crumbs and marinated in vinegar to which had been added a touch of saffron. This was one of the many *scapece*, the Spanish *escabeche*.

All this part of southern Italy is pasta country par excellence. Along with superb vegetables and fruits, excellent hard wheat is grown in the fertile heel and coastal lands of Puglia, and until recently almost all pasta was made at home daily.

Piquancy, even if only a little lemon juice or a drop of vinegar, is found in all of the food of southern Italy. When meats were tough, sauces containing variously wine, anchovies, herbs, olives, spices, raisins and pine nuts were used. They also served to relieve the tedium of the pasta, fish and vegetable diet, the basic eating.

In the rugged interior, the cooking is that of the shepherds, although it is spicier and more aromatic than in Umbria or Abruzzi. Lamb, kid, piglet, stuffed with herbs and cheese and ground-up innards, are still spit-roasted on special occasions. Pork is made into hams and sausages. The shepherds make good Pecorino and marvelous, snowy-white ricotta.

It may be an Arab legacy that left Puglia, Basilicata and Calabria with a sweet tooth and a fondness for sweets that resemble those of Sicily. These are made with almonds, honey, ricotta sweetened with fruits and nuts; cookies are fried or baked. The baked figs, stuffed with almonds and flavored with fennel seed and packed in baskets, can occasionally be found in Italian groceries in the United States.

All the regions, but especially Calabria, produce a good deal of mostly red wine. The wines are heavy compared to those of northern Italy, but they are dry, with the exception of the dessert wines. The whites travel north to Turin as the basis for the city's famous vermouths, the reds are used for blending.

Sicily

The layered pasta dishes and pizzas of Sicily, the stuffed vegetables, and fish and meat rolls make Sicilian cooking redolent of its great Arab past. Even more than in Liguria, fish is the protein of the region, from the beef-red meat of the giant tuna to the sea date, a yellowish-gray mollusk, about two inches long. Sardines stuffed with pine nuts, currants, anchovies and bread crumbs, cooked with lemon and oil, or with vinegar, or else fried and then dressed with a tomato sauce with capers and olives, are typical of local cooking.

I remember a dish of spaghetti cooked with the wild fennel of the Sicilian mountains, dressed with a sauce of fresh anchovies cooked with oil and lemon, topped with toasted bread crumbs, an extraordinary flavor combination. Always there is the recurrent note of added piquancy with anchovies and capers, sliced hard-cooked eggs, diced salami, grated cheese, seasonings and herbs. Or there are simple, perfectly fried foods, olive oil being plentiful and fuel scarce, which results in many fried dishes.

Sicilian food is exuberant, and nowhere more so than in the

sweets. From the days of the Arabs the Sicilians have had a great reputation as pastry cooks. They make very sugary sweetmeats, carved and scrolled, brightly colored, as in the sugar figures of knights, paladins and ladies, taken from the traditional puppet theaters. The loveliest, I think, is the fruit *alla martorana,* which I first had at Agrigento, ravishing shells, fruits and flowers made from tinted almond paste by the cloistered nuns of the Holy Ghost Convent.

Among the many Sicilian wines I like especially Corvo (a brand name found in the United States) and the wines from Alcamo, the Aetna and Belice. The wine drunk in Sicily is not the coarse, rough, sweet stuff people think of as Sicilian but good, dry table wines, although without the subtleties of a great Piedmontese wine. They are a pleasure to drink.

Sardinia

I have not yet visited Sardinia, but I am told that away from tourist resorts, the food still preserves its traditional quality. The interior of Sardinia is a land of barren mountains and plains, where shepherds graze their sheep. Much justly famous Pecorino cheese and ricotta come from Sardinia, when the traditional foods are spit-roasted lamb, aromatic with wild herbs, and pigs cooked in a barbecue pit. Once there were many wild pigs on the island; now they have been replaced by domesticated pigs.

Although the Sardinians are not a seagoing people, they do fish along their high and rocky coasts. I have been told of great local fish soups, aromatic with saffron, a herb liked by Sardinians, laurel, and even pungent wild fennel that flavors so many Sardinian (and Sicilian) fish, meat and vegetable dishes.

The sweets are surprisingly delicate: meringues, called *sospiri* (sighs), nougat, orange-rind candies, ricotta- and macaroon-filled fried fritters, almond cakes. They are not only delicious but charmingly decorated with pastel sugar scrolls, flowers and pistachio designs.

The amber-colored Vernaccia is Sardinia's best-known wine, and famous beyond its native shores. Aging intensifies its bouquet (the scent of almond blossom), and its dry, somewhat bitter flavor. Also famous are the muscatels and the Malvasia, once known in England as Malmsey.

The
Regional
Italian
Kitchen

Antipasto and Salad

Antipasti e Insalate

The word *antipasto* means "what comes before the meal." It is a starter and should be kept small and interesting, to titillate the appetite but not spoil it for what follows. Italians are orderly eaters, who like a beginning, middle and end to their meals whenever possible, so that the antipasto plays an important role as the appetizing prelude.

Antipasto can be very simple or very elaborate, depending on the occasion; it follows no set rules, being a product of local, regional and seasonal ingredients. Antipasto is either cold or hot (the former is far more common), and it is divided into meat, fish and vegetable dishes and combinations. Meat *antipasti* include the great Italian hams (Parma ham is just one), the salami, of which there are hundreds, and the specialty from Bologna, mortadella, a cut as different from American baloney as sable is from skunk. The cornerstone of fish *antipasti* is tuna canned in oil, followed by sardines and anchovies. Along the Italian coasts fish *antipasti* will include shellfish, crustaceans and mollusks, either alone or in tasty cold combinations. Vegetables, prepared as salads, are an integral part of most *antipasti*.

There is no virtue in preparing all of the antipasto foods in one's own kitchen. No one in Italy would think of doing this. The Italian *salumerie*, combinations of grocery and delicatessen, bulge with antipasto goodies, not only in Italy but in this country as well. Admittedly, the Italian ones are more glorious, with their displays of cold meats and salads gleaming with aspics and decorated with vegetables in lovely baroque swirls, dozens of pickles and marinated vegetables such as mushrooms, artichokes, olives, eggplant and other delights. Salami of every kind and size hang from the ceilings, and the fresh mozzarella reposes in a bowl of fresh water to keep it white, fresh and cold. Since it is possible to buy as little as one *etto*, that is 100 grams or roughly 3½ ounces, of everything, it is not hard to bring variety into one's antipasto course.

A family antipasto can consist of nothing more than a platter of thin slices of Parma ham, or stuffed eggs topped with mayonnaise on tomato slices, or slices of peppers topped with anchovies. In season, it might consist of ham or ripe figs with melon, a combination highly prized even in restaurants where the antipasto carts offer a dazzling choice of tidbits. Other popular *antipasti*, especially in Rome, are stuffed vegetables, tomatoes, artichokes or zucchini, and hot *crostini*, savory toasts, or hot mozzarella sandwiches.

The choice is wide, and governed by one principle: be moderate in your antipasto or you won't enjoy your meal.

Antipasto Platter for the Home

Antipasto di Casa

Use this as a guide for home entertaining. The platter should look neat and decorative, with color contrasts in the foods.

Use a large round or oblong platter, and work from the platter's center outwards.

In the center, place the drained contents of a can of Italian tuna fish preserved in olive oil. Surround the tuna with a band of lemon mayonnaise, preferably piped through a pastry tube. Next comes a round of stuffed egg halves, or egg slices topped with 2 crossed anchovy fillets topped by 2 or 3 capers and a tiny parsley sprig. The eggs may be separated from each other by strips of green, red and/or yellow peppers which have been marinated in olive oil. Another circle might consist of little heaps of marinated mushrooms, artichoke hearts, and bean salad separated by sardines. The next circle should be prosciutto and cooked ham rolled up into cornets, with radishes and parsley sprigs tucked in between the meats. The final round might be sliced tomatoes alternating with little mounds of Eggplant Marinara or Caponata (see Index).

Melon or Fresh Figs with Prosciutto   4 servings

Melone o Fichi col Prosciutto   All-Italian

1 medium-size ripe
   melon (honeydew,
   cantaloupe,
   Crenshaw, or
   Persian)

½ pound prosciutto,
   sliced thin
   freshly ground black
   pepper

Peel melon and cut it into ¾-inch-thick wedges, allowing 2 wedges for each serving. Place wedges on a plate. Cover them with 2 to 4 slices of prosciutto, or wrap each wedge in 1 or 2 slices of prosciuto.

Or use 2 ripe figs for each serving. Cut figs open diagonally to form 4 petals held together by their stem; or peel the figs. Place figs on a plate and arrange prosciutto slices on or around them.

Serve either melon or figs with prosciutto with a twist or two of pepper, freshly ground at the table.

Garlic Black Olives   6 servings

Olive all'Aglio   All-Italian

1 pound canned black
   ripe olives, drained
   olive oil

3 large garlic cloves,
   halved
   about 1 cup cracked ice

Place olives in a small bowl. Cover to the depth of ½ inch with olive oil. Add garlic and stir in the ice. Cover and let stand at room temperature for 3 hours. Drain and serve speared on food picks.

Mozzarella with Tomatoes and Anchovies

6 or 12 servings

Mozzarella Fresca con Pomodori e Acciughe from Rome and Naples

Serve as a luncheon dish with a green salad for 6, or as an appetizer for 12. Fresh mozzarella is found in Italian groceries.

1 pound fresh
mozzarella,
approximately
12 slices of ripe red
tomatoes,
approximately ½
inch thick
24 flat anchovy fillets,
drained

4 teaspoons dried basil or
oregano, or 8 large
leaves of fresh basil,
minced
4 to 6 tablespoons olive
oil
freshly ground pepper

Cut the mozzarella into 12 slices and trim them to be even in size. Arrange mozzarella on a serving platter, top each slice with a tomato slice, and place 2 anchovy fillets on each tomato slice. Sprinkle each serving with a little basil or oregano and olive oil. Season with pepper to taste. Serve at room temperature.

Bread, Olive Oil and Tomato Appetizer   6 servings

La Panzanella   from Tuscany

In the past, Tuscan peasants baked only once a week, which meant that there was bound to be leftover bread. The *panzanella* recipe uses the stale dry bread in a tasty and easy manner and has become a favorite among sophisticated Florentines and foreigners. The flavor of the dish depends on the freshness of the tomatoes; it is best made in the U.S. in the summertime, when tomatoes are really ripe. Similar dishes are found throughout central and southern Italy. The bread to use is the slightly gray, whole-wheat Italian bread baked in round or long loaves and found in Italian bakeries, or any coarse, unsweetened homemade country bread. The following recipe is a method rather than a rule; *panzanella* is put together according to taste.

1 pound stale Italian whole-wheat bread, approximately	1 large sweet onion, sliced thin
ice water	⅓ to ½ cup fresh basil leaves, chopped, or to taste
⅓ cup olive oil	
2 tablespoons wine vinegar	6 medium-size ripe tomatoes, chopped into coarse pieces
salt	
freshly ground pepper	

Cut bread into thick slices and trim off the crusts. Put slices into a bowl and add enough ice water to cover, plus 1 or 2 inches. Soak the bread for about 15 minutes, crumbling it with your hands as soon as it gets soft. You will have thick, coarse crumbs. Squeeze the bread dry with your hands, then put it into a clean kitchen towel and squeeze it dry. Put bread into a serving dish and refrigerate for 30 minutes or longer, to chill it thoroughly. Combine oil, vinegar, and salt and pepper to taste to make a French dressing. At serving time, lay the onion slices over bread and top with basil and tomatoes. Pour the dressing over the *panzanella* and toss well. Serve immediately.

NOTE: You may have to increase the amounts of French dressing depending on the bread used; the whole dish should be well seasoned, but not soupy.

Cold Tuna and Potato Mold
6 to 8 servings

Sformato Freddo di Tonno e Patate
from Tuscany

While this dish may not sound appealing, it is attractive to look at and good to eat. I don't know its true origins, but since I've always had it at the house of a Tuscan friend, Tuscany shall claim it.

13 ounces canned tuna packed in olive oil, preferably imported from Italy
2 large Idaho potatoes (to make 2 cups mashed potatoes)
1 cup heavy cream

1 tablespoon grated onion
salt
freshly ground pepper
1 cup lemony mayonnaise
watercress

Drain tuna and grate it or shred it very fine. Boil potatoes in their skins and peel them while still hot. Mash hot potatoes thoroughly, beat in cream and grated onion, then the tuna. Taste for saltiness; if necessary, add a little more salt, and pepper to taste. Rinse a fish mold or other 4-cup mold with cold water and chill. Spoon in the mixture, pressing it down. Chill. At serving time, unmold on a platter. Drizzle the mayonnaise over the fish mixture and decorate with watercress. If desired, serve with more mayonnaise on the side; this mayonnaise should be more liquid.

Vegetable Casserole from Palermo
6 servings

Fritteda alla Palermitana
from Sicily

The ingredients of this dish may be increased or decreased at will; however, the balance should be kept because it determines the flavor. Use as a first course or main dish.

½ cup olive oil
2 small onions, sliced very thin
2 garlic cloves, minced
4 large or 5 small artichokes, sliced (see p. 248)
2 cups sliced celery hearts, white part only
2 cups shelled fava beans or lima beans, or 10 ounces frozen lima beans

2 cups shelled peas, or 10 ounces frozen peas
⅓ cup water
salt
freshly ground pepper
½ teaspoon dried thyme
1 teaspoon sugar
¼ cup white vinegar

Heat olive oil in a heavy saucepan or casserole. Add onions and garlic. Cook, stirring constantly, for about 4 minutes, or until onions are soft. Add artichoke slices. Cook covered over low heat, stirring occasionally, for about 5 minutes. Add celery and cook for 5 more minutes. Add fava or lima beans, the peas and the water. Season with salt and pepper to taste and stir in the thyme. Cook covered over low heat for 10 more minutes, or until vegetables are just tender; do not overcook. Stir sugar into vinegar and stir the mixture into the vegetables. Cook over medium heat without a cover for about 3 minutes. Serve warm or cool but not chilled.

Eggplant Marinara

6 to 8 servings

Melanzane alla Marinara

from Southern Italy

2 eggplants, about 1½
pounds each
boiling water
½ cup white vinegar
1 tablespoon salt
1 teaspoon freshly
ground pepper
2 garlic cloves, minced
1 teaspoon crumbled
dried oregano
½ teaspoon dried basil

¾ cup olive oil
½ cup seedless golden
raisins, plumped in
warm water and
drained
½ cup pine nuts (pignoli)
3 whole canned sweet
red peppers
(pimiento), cut into
½-inch dice

Trim eggplants and cut them into 1-inch cubes, leaving on the skin. Place eggplant in a large saucepan and add boiling water to cover. Cook without a cover over medium heat for 3 to 5 minutes. Cubes should be soft but retain their shape. Drain thoroughly. Combine vinegar, salt, pepper, garlic, oregano and basil, and mix well. Put drained eggplant cubes into a deep bowl (not aluminum). Pour the vinegar mixture over the eggplant and toss with a fork to mix. Cover with plastic wrap and marinate overnight, or for at least 8 hours. One hour before serving, add olive oil, raisins, pine nuts and canned red peppers. Toss thoroughly to mix. Refrigerate until serving time.

Peppers, Onions and Tomatoes   6 servings

Peperonata   from Southern Italy

Versions of this dish are found from Rome on south, some with fewer peppers, others with fewer onions or with trimmings, such as black olives, capers and anchovies. They all taste good, hot or cold, as an antipasto or a side dish, and especially for lunch with a piece of fresh Italian bread and a glass of wine. For a decorative touch use a mixture of green, yellow and red peppers.

¼ cup olive oil
3 large onions, cut into thin slices
1 pound ripe tomatoes, seeded and chopped, or 2 cups drained canned Italian-style tomatoes

salt
freshly ground pepper
¼ cup minced fresh basil leaves, or 1 tablespoon dried basil
6 medium-size sweet peppers, cut into strips

Heat olive oil in a heavy casserole. Add onions and cook over medium heat, stirring constantly, for 3 to 4 minutes, or until onions are soft but not brown. Add tomatoes, salt and pepper to taste, and the basil. Cook without a cover over low heat for about 10 minutes. Add peppers and mix well. Simmer covered for 10 more minutes, or until the peppers are tender.

Marinated Mushrooms
6 servings

Antipasto di Funghi   All-Italian

3 tablespoons olive oil
3 garlic cloves, crushed
1 pound mushrooms, cut
   into medium-thick
   slices
2 bay leaves
2 tablespoons minced
   fresh tarragon leaves,
   or 2 teaspoons dried

½ cup dry white wine
juice of 1 lemon
salt
freshly ground pepper
¼ cup minced parsley

Heat olive oil in a large deep frying pan. Add garlic and cook until garlic is browned; discard garlic. Add mushrooms, bay leaves and tarragon. Cook over medium heat, stirring constantly, for about 3 minutes. Add wine and lemon juice and season with salt and pepper to taste. Simmer without a cover over medium heat, stirring frequently. Turn into a bowl and chill. Before serving, pour off most of the liquid in which the mushrooms cooked, and sprinkle mushrooms with the parsley.

Pickled Eggplant   8 to 12 servings

Caponata   from Sicily

There is no English word for the most famous Sicilian appetizer, which is sold in cans or jars under its own name or under its diminutive: *caponatina*. Preserve it in sterilized jars or in the refrigerator, where it will keep for weeks.

4 medium-size eggplants
1½ cups olive oil
4 large onions, cut into thin slices
1 cup drained canned Italian plum tomatoes, strained through a sieve or puréed in blender
4 celery stalks, peeled and cut into ½-inch dice
½ cup drained capers
½ cup minced parsley

16 black olives, pitted and chopped
2 tablespoons pine nuts (pignoli)
½ cup red-wine vinegar
¼ cup sugar
½ teaspoon salt
½ teaspoon freshly ground pepper
⅛ teaspoon hot red pepper flakes, or to taste
lettuce leaves

Peel eggplants and cut them into 1-inch pieces. Heat 1 cup of the olive oil in a large, heavy frying pan. Cook eggplant in one layer over medium heat, stirring constantly, until it is soft and browned; do not overcook. Put cooked eggplant in a bowl and cook remaining eggplant, adding it to the first lot. Add remaining oil to the frying pan. Add onions and cook, stirring constantly, for 3 to 5 minutes, or until onions are soft. Add tomatoes and celery. Cook, stirring frequently, until celery is soft. If necessary to prevent scorching, add a little water. Add capers, parsley, olives, pine nuts and the fried eggplant, and mix well. Remove from heat. Heat vinegar and sugar in a small saucepan; stir until sugar is dissolved. Pour over the vegetables. Season with salt, pepper and hot pepper flakes. Return to lowest possible heat. Simmer covered, stirring frequently, for about 20 minutes. If necessary to prevent scorching, add a little water, 1 tablespoon at a time; the *caponata* should be soft but not soupy. Cool before serving on lettuce leaves.

Pickled Vegetables
1 quart

Verdure Marinate
from Sicily

¼ cup wine vinegar
¾ cup olive oil
1 tablespoon sugar
1 large garlic clove,
mashed
1 teaspoon salt
¼ teaspoon hot red
pepper flakes, or to
taste
¾ cup green pitted olives
½ cup pitted black olives
¾ cup 1-inch pieces of
cauliflower

½ cup diced carrots
½ cup thin slices of celery
½ cup 1-inch pieces of
eggplant
½ cup small white onions
½ cup 1-inch pieces of
zucchini
½ cup ½-inch pieces of
green or red sweet
pepper
2 tablespoons capers

Combine vinegar, olive oil, sugar, garlic, salt and hot pepper flakes and bring to the boiling point. Cool. Add remaining ingredients and toss thoroughly. Chill for at least 48 hours.

NOTE: This may be served as part of a mixed antipasto.

Lemon-Stuffed Eggs

6 servings

Uova Farcite al Limone

from Tuscany

6 hard-cooked eggs, peeled
¼ teaspoon grated lemon rind
3 tablespoons olive oil or mayonnaise

1 tablespoon fresh lemon juice
salt
freshly ground pepper
dash of Tabasco
36 capers, drained

Cut eggs lengthwise into halves. Lift out the yolks, and mash them with a fork until smooth. Blend in lemon rind, olive oil, lemon juice, salt and pepper to taste, and Tabasco. Fill egg halves with the mixture and top each with 3 capers. Cover with a plate and chill before serving.

Prosciutto-Stuffed Eggs

6 servings

Uova Farcite al Prosciutto

All-Italian

6 hard-cooked eggs, peeled
⅓ cup minced prosciutto
2 tablespoons minced sour pickles
2 tablespoons minced green pepper or drained pimiento

⅓ cup mayonnaise
¼ teaspoon dry mustard
freshly ground pepper
parsley sprigs without stems

Cut eggs lengthwise into halves. Lift out the yolks and mash with a fork until smooth. Add all other ingredients except black pepper and parsley; taste before adding pepper. Fill egg halves with the mixture and top each with a parsley sprig. Cover with a plate and chill before serving.

Carpaccio

6 servings

from Lombardy, Veneto

A raw meat appetizer that has become very popular during the last few years in both Italy and New York. *Carpaccio* may be served with embellishments to taste, such as capers and chopped onion, or with a mustardy mayonnaise or as here, the way I had it at a private home in Milan.

1 pound lean boneless
  shell steaks
  salt
  freshly ground pepper
6 flat anchovies, drained
  and minced

¾ cup olive oil
  juice of 1 large lemon
12 very small sour pickles,
  such as French
  cornichons

Trim any fat off the meat and cut it into 6 equal slices. Lay the meat slices on a chilled platter, sprinkle lightly with salt and pepper, and top each slice with a little minced anchovy. Combine olive oil and lemon juice and spoon over the meat. Garnish the platter with the pickles. Serve immediately.

NOTE: The meat is best sliced by the butcher. If it is to be sliced at home, freeze the meat partially to make slicing easier; use a very sharp knife.

Stuffed Artichokes
6 servings

Carciofi Ripieni
from Sicily

6 medium-size artichokes	2 tablespoons drained
1 quart cold water	capers
3 tablespoons lemon juice	salt
2 cups minced parsley	freshly ground pepper
2 tablespoons minced	dash of Tabasco
fresh basil, or 2	1 lemon, sliced
teaspoons dried basil	3 tablespoons olive oil
¼ cup minced salami	boiling water
6 flat anchovies, drained	3 cups French dressing
and minced	made with lemon

Cut off artichoke stems at the base and pull off the tough outer leaves. Trim the artichoke base, cutting off all scaly leaf bases. Cut off the top third of each artichoke to remove the spiny tips. Put artichokes upside down on a chopping board and press the stem ends to open them. Drop the artichokes, as you finish with them, into the cold water mixed with lemon juice to prevent discoloring. Taking out 1 artichoke at a time, dig out the fuzzy chokes with the point of a knife, a grapefruit knife or a spoon. Drop artichokes back into the water. Combine parsley, basil, salami, anchovies and capers and mix well. Taste, and if necessary add a little salt. Season with pepper to taste and the Tabasco. Drain 1 artichoke at a time. Pull the leaves slightly open and stuff them with a little of the stuffing. Put some of the stuffing into the middle of each artichoke. Tie each artichoke with a string to prevent it opening during cooking. Place artichokes side by side in a deep frying pan or a saucepan just large enough to hold them tightly. Top each with 1 lemon slice. Pour olive oil into the frying pan and add about 1 inch of boiling water. Cook without a cover for 3 minutes. Turn the heat to low, cover, and simmer for 20 to 30 minutes, or until artichokes are tender when pierced at the stem with a skewer. Check for moisture; if necessary, add a little more water and a tablespoon of oil to keep the liquid at the 1-inch level. When cooked, transfer to a serving dish and cool. Serve with French dressing as a dunk for the artichokes.

Stuffed Mushroom Caps

6 to 8 servings

Funghi Imbottiti All-Italian

¼ cup fresh lemon juice
½ cup water
24 large mushroom caps (save stems for soups, stews and sauces)
3 tablespoons butter
3 tablespoons olive oil
1 pound sweet Italian sausages, skinned and crumbled
1 cup fresh white bread crumbs

6 flat anchovies, drained and chopped, or 2 tablespoons anchovy paste
grated rind of 1 lemon
salt
freshly ground pepper
1 egg, beaten
⅓ cup minced parsley
dry red or white wine (optional)

Combine lemon juice and water in a bowl. Wash mushroom caps in the mixture. Dry them carefully inside and out with kitchen paper. Combine butter and olive oil in a frying pan. Heat the mixture, but do not cook it; the butter should just be melted. With a pastry brush, brush the outside of the mushroom caps with some of the butter-oil mixture. Place the caps side by side in a buttered shallow baking dish. Add sausage to the frying pan, and cook over medium heat, stirring constantly, for about 5 minutes, or until sausage has yielded most of its fat. Pour off the fat. Add bread crumbs, anchovies, lemon rind, a little salt and pepper, the egg and parsley to the sausage. Cook over low heat, stirring frequently, for 5 to 8 minutes, or until mixture is well blended. If too dry, add a little wine, 2 tablespoons at a time. Cool the mixture a little. Pile lightly into the mushroom caps. Bake in a preheated moderate oven (350°F.) for about 15 minutes. Serve hot.

Stuffed Sweet Peppers   6 servings

Peperoni Imbottiti Piccanti   from Puglia

6 large sweet green, red or yellow peppers
⅓ cup olive oil
½ cup fresh white bread crumbs
6 drained flat anchovies, mashed
¼ cup drained capers (chop if large)

¼ cup currants, plumped in warm water and drained
⅓ cup pine nuts (pignoli)
salt
freshly ground pepper
¼ cup minced parsley
⅓ cup chopped pitted black or green olives

Place peppers over high direct heat; turning them frequently, char them on all sides; the skin should be black and ashy. Under running cold water, rub off the charred skin with your hands and with a kitchen knife. Cut peppers lengthwise into halves, removing seeds and membranes. Dry the peppers carefully. Place pepper halves side by side in an oiled shallow baking dish. Heat half of the olive oil in a frying pan. Add all other ingredients except olives. Cook over medium heat, stirring constantly, for about 3 minutes, or until the mixture somewhat clings together. Stuff a little of this mixture into each pepper half and top with some chopped olives. Sprinkle with remaining olive oil. Cook in a preheated moderate oven (350°F.) for 20 to 30 minutes. Serve hot or cold.

Puglia

Stuffed Tomatoes

4 to 6 servings

Pomodori al Forno

from Rome

It is impossible to give exact amounts for the rice used since the size of the tomatoes varies. If the tomatoes are very large, about 2 tablespoons of raw rice are needed for each tomato. If any rice stuffing is left over, cook it alongside the tomatoes. The saffron in the rice gives a pretty color effect.

8	large ripe but firm tomatoes	2	cups hot chicken consommé
½	cup olive oil		salt
⅓	cup minced parsley		pepper
2	garlic cloves, minced	⅛	teaspoon ground cinnamon
1	cup raw long-grain rice		
1	teaspoon saffron (optional)		

Cut a slice from the top of each tomato, under the stem, and scoop out the pulp with a teaspoon. Be careful not to break the shells. Strain the pulp through a sieve and reserve. Place tomatoes side by side in a shallow baking dish. Sprinkle each tomato with a few drops of olive oil. Heat remaining oil in a saucepan, and cook parsley and garlic in it for 2 minutes. Add rice and cook, stirring constantly, for 3 more minutes. Stir saffron into the consommé. Add hot consommé to rice and cover the saucepan. Cook over low heat, stirring frequently, for about 10 minutes, or until rice is three-quarters done. Remove from heat and season rice with salt and pepper to taste and the cinnamon. Fill tomato shells with the rice mixture. Pour the strained tomato pulp over the tomatoes to the depth of ½ inch; if there is not enough strained pulp, add a little water. Bake in a preheated moderate oven (350°F.) for about 30 minutes, or until rice is tender and liquid has been absorbed. Check for scorching; if necessary, add a little more hot water. Baste occasionally with the pan juices. Serve hot or lukewarm or cool but not chilled.

Bresaola with Lemon Juice   4 servings

Bresaola al Limone   from Lombardy

Bresaola is beef which has been very lightly salted and dried. It is a specialty of the Valtellina valley of Lombardy, and a cousin to *Bündnerfleisch,* the dried meat of the Swiss Grisons. *Bresaola* can occasionally be found in Italian groceries and some American gourmet shops.

24 very thin slices of   olive oil
    bresaola   freshly ground pepper
    fresh lemon juice

Place the meat on a large serving platter. Sprinkle it with plenty of fresh lemon juice, making sure that all the slices are coated. Sprinkle olive oil over the lemon juice, and once more, lemon juice over the oil. Sprinkle with plenty of freshly ground pepper. Let stand at room temperature from 15 to 30 minutes to allow the meat to soften and to absorb the lemon and oil flavors.

Chicken Liver Toasts   8 servings

I Crostini del Marchese   from Tuscany

Tuscans like toast appetizers and make many different kinds, piled with cheese mixtures or meat mixtures and different seasonings. Basically, *crostini* are the kind of dish you make with what you have at hand, adapting ingredients and cooking times.

¼ cup olive oil
2 tablespoons minced onion
2 tablespoons minced celery
2 tablespoons minced carrot
½ pound chicken meat, approximately, cut from legs or breast, and cut into ¼-inch cubes
salt
freshly ground pepper
¼ to ⅓ cup dry white wine
½ pound chicken livers, trimmed and chopped

¼ cup drained capers
4 flat anchovies, drained
2 tablespoons brandy
⅛ teaspoon grated nutmeg
2 tablespoons butter, at room temperature and cut into small pieces
⅓ cup hot chicken bouillon, approximately
1 long loaf of French or Italian bread, cut into ½- to ¾-inch slices
olive oil

Heat ¼ cup olive oil in a large, deep frying pan. Add onion, celery and carrot. Cook, stirring constantly, for about 5 minutes, until onion is soft and golden but not brown. Add chicken, season with salt and pepper, and cook for 3 to 4 minutes. Stir in ¼ cup of the wine. Cook over low heat, without a cover, for about 10 minutes, or until chicken is cooked. Add chicken livers and mix well. Cook over low heat, stirring frequently, for about 10 minutes. If the mixture looks too dry, add remaining wine. Add capers and anchovies and cook for 5 minutes longer. Stir in brandy and nutmeg, and cook for 2 or

3 more minutes. Stir in the butter. The mixture should be very thick. Spoon half of it into the container of a blender with 2 or 3 tablespoons of the bouillon, and purée. Repeat. Return all of the mixture to the frying pan. Over low heat and stirring constantly, cook for about 2 minutes to dry out. Remove from heat and keep warm. Lay the bread slices on a baking sheet. Brush each with about 1 teaspoon of olive oil. Bake in a preheated hot oven (400°F.) for 5 to 10 minutes, or until toasted golden brown. Spread each slice with some of the chicken mixture and serve immediately, very hot.

Chicken Liver and Prosciutto Toasts 6 to 10 servings

Crostini coi Fegatini di Pollo e Prosciutto All-Italian

The number of helpings depends on the size of the bread slices.

2 ounces butter
1 pound chicken livers, chopped into coarse pieces
6 slices of prosciutto, chopped into coarse pieces
  salt
  freshly ground pepper
1 teaspoon ground sage or crumbled dried sage

juice of 1 lemon
2 tablespoons minced parsley
6 slices of crustless firm white bread, toasted, or 10 slices of a long thin Italian or French loaf

Heat butter in a heavy frying pan. Add chicken livers and prosciutto. Cook over high heat, stirring constantly, for 3 minutes. Add salt and pepper to taste and the sage, and cook for 1 minute longer. Remove from heat and stir in the lemon juice. Spread the mixture over the bread slices and sprinkle a little parsley on each. Serve immediately, very hot.

Antipasto Chick-Pea Salad   6 servings

Insalata di Ceci   from Rome

2 to 3 cups cooked or
        canned chick-peas,
        drained
1 garlic clove, minced
¼ cup minced scallions
1 large ripe tomato, cut
        into bite-size pieces

½ cup olive oil
2 tablespoons wine
        vinegar
salt
freshly ground pepper

Combine first 6 ingredients in a salad bowl and toss well. Add salt and pepper to taste and toss again.

Fennel Salad

Insalata di Finocchi   from Rome

An outstanding and easy dish.

Remove the green fingers and tough outer leaves from fennel heads. Slice the tender white hearts into wafer-thin slices. Sprinkle with a little salt and pepper, olive oil and lemon juice. Let stand for 1 to 2 hours before serving.

Lentil Salad

6 servings

Insalata di Lenticchie   All-Italian

2 cups dried brown
   lentils
4 cups chicken bouillon
   or water
½ cup olive oil
3 tablespoons wine
   vinegar
⅓ cup minced shallots or
   onions

1 small garlic clove,
   mashed
salt
freshly ground pepper
¾ cup minced curly
   parsley, or ⅓ cup
   minced Italian
   parsley
lettuce leaves

Pick over lentils; wash and drain them. Cook lentils in the chicken bouillon over low heat for about 30 minutes, or until lentils are tender; they should keep their shape. Combine olive oil, wine vinegar, shallots and garlic, and mix well. Add salt (the bouillon may be salty) and pepper to taste, and mix. Pour dressing over the lentils. Chill. At serving time, add the parsley and toss. Serve on lettuce leaves.

Cauliflower Salad
4 to 6 servings

Insalata di Cavolfiore   from Naples

1 large head of
  cauliflower
  boiling salted water
⅓ cup olive oil
⅔ cup vinegar, preferably
  white vinegar
1 teaspoon salt
¼ teaspoon freshly
  ground pepper

½ teaspoon dried basil
6 anchovy fillets, drained
  and chopped
¼ cup chopped pitted
  black olives
¼ cup drained capers
  curly endive leaves

Wash cauliflower and break it into flowerets, cutting off the tough part of the stems. Place in a saucepan with 1 inch of boiling salted water. Bring to the boiling point, then cover and cook for 3 to 5 minutes, or until cauliflower is tender but still crisp. Drain well and place in a salad bowl. Combine oil, vinegar, salt, pepper, basil, anchovies, half of the olives and half of the capers; mix well. Pour over cauliflower and toss gently. Garnish the edges of the salad bowl with leaves of curly endive and sprinkle remaining olives and capers over the cauliflower.

Rice Salad

6 servings

Insalata di Riso

All-Italian

The cook's fancy may add other goodies to this salad, such as tuna, sliced salami, cooked shrimps, cooked lobster or sliced hard-cooked eggs. It is a favorite summer dish.

1 cup raw rice
6 tablespoons olive oil
3 tablespoons white
   vinegar
   salt
   freshly ground pepper
1 tablespoon minced
   fresh tarragon, or 1
   teaspoon dried
   tarragon
¼ cup minced onion or
   shallots

⅓ cup chopped pimiento
   or green pepper
½ cup minced parsley
1 cup drained cooked
   green peas
1 cup cooked asparagus
   tips
1 tablespoon drained
   capers
   tomato wedges
   green and/or black
   olives

Cook rice in plenty of boiling salted water until just tender; do not overcook. Drain and place in a bowl (not aluminum). While rice is still hot, toss it with olive oil, vinegar, salt and pepper to taste, the tarragon and onion. Cool. Add pimiento or green pepper, parsley, peas, asparagus tips and capers. Chill. At serving time, pile the rice on a serving platter in the shape of a mound and decorate with tomato wedges and olives.

Soups

Minestre

The word *soup* is translated as *minestra*, but the two words do not have the exact same meaning. Our soups are invariably liquid dishes whereas Italian *minestre* can be either *minestre in brodo*, broth soups, or *minestre asciutte*, dry soups. Either way, a *minestra*, to use the singular, is the first course of a meal or the course that comes after the antipasto. Since *minestre asciutte* consist of pasta, rice, polenta and dumplings, recipes for these dishes are found in other chapters of this book; what follows now is soup in our meaning, namely liquid soup.

Italians are great soup eaters. Soup starts a meal or, especially in the evening, *is* the meal. If you have soup at a meal, with the possible exception of an elegant consommé in *tazza*, consommé served in a cup, you do not have pasta and other *minestre asciutte*.

There are three kinds of basic soups. First, those made with or consisting of *il brodo*, broth or stock made from meat, fowl, fish or vegetables. Once, the aroma of beef or chicken *brodo* simmering for hours on the kitchen stove was common to all Italian kitchens; it remains an unforgettable memory to those who knew it. A *brodo* may be served plain, clarified into consommé, or it may contain tiny pasta, rice, bits of meat, eggs or other ingredients. *Brodo* is also the base for other thicker soups, as well as the liquid used for cooking other dishes such as rice. Italian home cooking constantly specifies a ladleful of *brodo* in this or that meat, vegetable or pasta dish. Thick, substantial soups are called *minestrone*, or big soups; they are composed of vegetables and usually include either pasta or rice, but never both in the same soup. There are other soup classifications, such as the *zuppe*, which also contain vegetables, and are usually served over toasted bread. Fish soups are also called *zuppe*. Finally, there are cream soups, which resemble French soups and are not as typical of Italian regional cooking as the other soups in this book.

As in most Italian home cooking, soups are made from whatever is available in the kitchen, and local or seasonal ingredients are put together according to the way the cook wants the soup to taste. Here too, times are changing as more and more Italian women go out to work and/or are less disposed to spend time in the kitchen. Nowadays *brodo* is made from scratch mainly as a treat, and the *brodo di dadi*, the stock made from bouillon cubes, has triumphed in the Italian kitchen. Even quite elegant recipes allow it as an ingredient; and I've never met an Italian cook who felt guilty about using bouillon cubes in daily cooking, for they are quick and economical, especially when only a little *brodo* is needed to flavor a dish. In all fairness it must be said, however, that Italian bouillon cubes are much more flavorful than ours.

With the exception of consommé in *tazza*, consommé in a cup which is served for formal occasions, Italians eat soup from soup plates rather than from bowls and do not use the American rounded medium-size soup spoon but what we would call serving spoons. Almost always, a bowl of grated Parmesan or Pecorino cheese is served along with the soup at the table, to be sprinkled at the diner's discretion over his soup.

Beef Bouillon or Stock

8 to 10 cups

Il Brodo

All-Italian

2 pounds lean soup meat
   (brisket, plate, shank,
   or flank)
1 veal shank, cracked
1 beef marrowbone,
   cracked
4 quarts water
1 medium-size onion,
   stuck with 3 cloves
1 large carrot, scraped
   and cut into pieces
1 celery stalk, white and
   green leaves, cut into
   pieces

2 leeks, cut into pieces
1 garlic clove
3 bay leaves
½ cup parsley, with stems
2 sprigs of fresh thyme,
   or ½ teaspoon dried
   thyme
1 tablespoon salt
8 peppercorns

In a large deep soup kettle, combine the soup meat, veal shank, marrowbone and 4 quarts water. Bring to the boiling point and skim. Cook for 5 minutes, skimming as needed. Add all the other ingredients. Bring again to the boiling point and skim. Reduce heat to low, cover, and simmer for 3 to 5 hours, skimming as needed. If necessary, add more hot water to keep the original level of the liquid in the soup kettle. Skim off any fat. Strain the soup through a triple layer of cheesecloth, moistened and wrung dry, into a clean soup kettle. Over high heat, boil without a cover until the stock is reduced to 2½ to 3 quarts. Taste for seasoning and, if necessary, add some salt and pepper. Cool and chill. When chilled, remove the layer of fat that has risen to the top. Refrigerate or freeze; in the refrigerator, covered, the stock will keep for about 6 days. At room temperature, it quickly sours.

NOTE: This stock can be clarified in any standard manner.

Chicken Bouillon or Stock   8 to 10 cups

Il Brodo di Pollo   All-Italian

1   chicken, 2 to 3 pounds
½   pound lean beef
    stewing meat (chuck,
    shank, or plate)
1   beef marrowbone,
    cracked
3   quarts water
1   small onion
2   carrots, scraped and cut
    into pieces

1   celery stalk, cut into
    pieces
1   leek, cut into pieces
½   cup parsley, with stems
1   tablespoon salt
6   peppercorns
1   egg white, lightly
    beaten

Combine chicken, meat, marrowbone and 3 quarts water in a large deep soup kettle. Bring to the boiling point and skim. Reduce heat to very low and add all the other ingredients except the egg white. Simmer covered for about 2 hours, stirring occasionally, and skimming as needed. With one or two slotted spoons, remove the chicken, meat, bone and as many of the vegetables as you can. Reserve the chicken for other uses calling for cooked chicken, such as fricassee, croquettes or soufflés; the chicken is overcooked for salad use. Add the egg white, beating constantly and energetically with a wire whip. Strain the soup through a triple layer of cheesecloth, moistened and wrung dry. Cool and chill. When chilled, remove the layer of fat that has risen to the top.

NOTE: This, like all bouillons, may be concentrated by reducing it over high heat as desired. It can be clarified in any standard manner.

Vegetable Bouillon or Stock   8 to 10 cups

Il Brodo Vegetale   All-Italian

2 large carrots, scraped
   and chopped
2 large potatoes, peeled
   and diced
2 small onions, peeled
   and cut into halves
1 leek, white and green
   parts, chopped
2 celery stalks with
   leaves, chopped
2 medium-size zucchini,
   chopped
3 large ripe tomatoes,
   peeled and chopped

1 cup chopped cabbage
   leaves
1 cup chopped green
   beans
⅓ cup parsley, with stems
2 tablespoons fresh basil
   leaves, or 1 teaspoon
   dried basil
½ teaspoon dried thyme
1 tablespoon salt
1 teaspoon freshly
   ground pepper
3 quarts water

Combine all the ingredients in a large deep soup kettle. Bring
to the boiling point. Reduce heat to very low, and simmer
covered, skimming when necessary, for about 3 hours. Stir
occasionally. Strain the soup through a triple layer of cheesecloth, moistened and wrung dry. Use the strained stock for
soup, adding a little rice or small pasta. Or purée the vegetables
and add them to the strained soup to make a vegetable purée
soup. In this case, add to each serving 1 tablespoon of heavy
sweet cream or sour cream.

Consommé Mille Fanti

4 to 6 servings

All-Italian

Soups consisting of consommé with an egg mixture that shreds in the cooking are found throughout Italy. In Rome the soup is called *stracciatella* (the ragged one). Easy to make and nourishing, these soups are elegant enough for a dinner party or as food for children and invalids. The bread crumbs should be fresh and very fine; they can be made by pushing crustless fresh white bread through a strainer.

3 eggs	6 to 7 cups clear beef or
¼ cup fresh white bread	chicken consommé,
crumbs	at boiling point
3 tablespoons freshly	salt
grated Parmesan	freshly ground pepper
cheese	freshly grated
⅛ teaspoon grated	Parmesan cheese
nutmeg	

In a bowl, beat the eggs, bread crumbs, 3 tablespoons Parmesan and the nutmeg together until very well mixed. Using a wire whisk or a fork, stir the mixture into the boiling consommé. Reduce heat and check the seasoning; add a little more salt and pepper if consommé is not sufficiently seasoned. Simmer covered over lowest possible heat for about 5 minutes. Turn into a heated soup tureen and serve with extra Parmesan on the side.

Cream of Celery

4 to 6 servings

Crema di Sedani

from Lombardy

2 ounces butter
4 to 5 cups ½-inch slices
   of celery
2 medium-size carrots,
   cut into thin slices
1 large leek, white and
   green parts, sliced, or
   2 bunches of
   scallions, white and
   green parts, sliced
6 cups water

salt
freshly ground pepper
1 egg yolk
½ cup heavy cream
⅓ cup freshly grated
   Parmesan cheese
1 celery heart with no
   leaves, cut into thin
   slices (optional)
   toast fingers

Heat the butter in a large saucepan. Add celery, carrots and leek. Simmer covered over low heat, stirring frequently, for about 3 minutes. Add 1 cup of the water. Simmer covered, stirring frequently, for 10 minutes longer, or until vegetables are tender. Purée in a blender or food processor or strain through a food mill. There should be 2 to 2½ cups puréed vegetables. Return to pan, add remaining water, and bring to the boiling point. Reduce heat and simmer for about 5 minutes, or until the soup is thoroughly hot. Season lightly with salt (the Parmesan will be salty) and pepper to taste. Beat together the egg yolk, heavy cream and Parmesan. Remove soup from the heat, and stir a spoonful of hot soup into the egg mixture. Stir this into the soup and blend thoroughly. Sprinkle the soup in the tureen or in each soup plate with a few slices of celery heart for crispness. Serve hot, with toast fingers.

Cream of Vegetables   4 to 6 servings

Crema di Verdure   from Venice

This soup may be made with any combination of leaf vegetables; they determine the flavor.

6 to 8 cups shredded
romaine lettuce
3 bunches of watercress,
with stems
1 large leek, green and
white parts, sliced, or
2 bunches of
scallions, green and
white parts, sliced
2 cups peeled diced
potatoes

6 cups hot chicken
bouillon
salt
freshly ground pepper
1 to 2 tablespoons
butter, or ½ cup
heavy cream
½ cup very thin slices of
zucchini or cucumber
(optional)

Combine romaine, watercress, leek, potatoes and bouillon in a large saucepan. Bring to the boiling point, reduce heat, and simmer covered for 10 to 15 minutes, or until potatoes are tender. (Cooking the soup for too long will make it taste less fresh.) Purée soup in a blender, or strain through a food mill. Taste—the bouillon may be salty—and season with salt and pepper to taste. Stir in the butter or cream. Sprinkle zucchini or cucumber slices over the top for a touch of crispness.

Greens and Rice Soup with Pesto   5 or 6 servings

Preboggion col Pesto   from Genoa

2 cups fine shreds of
   green cabbage,
   preferably Savoy
   cabbage
2 cups fine shreds of beet
   greens or Swiss
   chard
½ cup minced Italian
   parsley

7 cups chicken or beef
   bouillon or water
⅓ cup raw Italian or long-
   grain rice
1 cup (1 recipe) Pesto
   (p. 143)
   salt
   freshly ground pepper

Put cabbage, greens and parsley into a soup kettle. Add bouillon and bring to the boiling point. Reduce heat and simmer covered for 15 to 30 minutes. Bring again to the boiling point and stir in the rice. Reduce heat and cook covered for 8 to 10 minutes, or until rice is half tender. Stir in ½ cup of Pesto and mix well. Continue to cook, covered, until rice is tender. Check seasoning and add some salt and pepper if needed. Turn remaining ½ cup Pesto into a heated soup tureen. Add the soup and mix well. Serve very hot.

Minestrone   6 to 8 servings

Minestrone alla Milanese   from Milan

One of the many versions of Italy's most famous soup. Contrary to common American belief, a minestrone is not a catch-all for every available vegetable but a mixture of judiciously balanced ones. What makes it "Milanese" is the addition of rice; minestroni from other cities may use a pasta as a thickener.

4 tablespoons butter	1 carrot, cubed
2 tablespoons minced blanched salt pork	5 tablespoons minced parsley
½ medium-size onion, minced	½ teaspoon ground sage, or 4 leaves of dried sage, crumbled
1 garlic clove	
1 veal shank bone	½ teaspoon crumbled dried rosemary
3 tomatoes, peeled and chopped	¼ teaspoon dried oregano
4 medium-size potatoes, peeled	¼ teaspoon dried basil
	2 cups hot consommé
1 cup shelled fresh kidney or other beans, or dried beans that have been soaked in water overnight	2½ quarts boiling water
	1 cup shredded beet greens or Swiss chard
	2 cups shelled or frozen peas
1 leek, white and green parts, sliced	½ cup raw rice
2 celery stalks, sliced	½ cup freshly grated Parmesan cheese

In a deep soup kettle, cook together 2 tablespoons butter, the salt pork, onion and garlic clove until onion is soft. Remove garlic clove and discard it. Add veal shank bone and tomatoes. Cook over medium heat for 3 to 4 minutes, or until the bone is golden on all sides. Cut 2 potatoes into small dice. Add diced potatoes, beans, leek, celery and carrot to the kettle. Combine 4 tablespoons of the parsley, the sage, rosemary, oregano and basil and divide the mixture into 2 parts. Add 1 part to the

vegetables. Simmer over lowest possible heat, stirring frequently, for 5 minutes. Add the consommé and the 2 whole
potatoes. Simmer covered over low heat, stirring occasionally,
for 15 minutes. Add the boiling water and simmer covered for
about 1 hour. Mash the whole potatoes with a fork against the
side of the kettle and stir into the soup. Add remaining parsley
and herb mixture, beet greens and peas. When the soup has
come to the boiling point, add the rice. Cook over medium
heat, stirring occasionally, until rice is tender. Remove the veal
shank bone. Cream together remaining butter, the Parmesan
and remaining parsley. Remove the soup from heat, and stir
the butter and cheese mixture into it before serving. Serve with
additional grated Parmesan cheese.

NOTE: During the hot season, this minestrone is eaten cooled,
but not chilled.

Rice and Escarole Soup   6 servings

Minestra di Riso e Scarola   All-Italian

---

3   tablespoons olive oil   8   cups chicken bouillon
1   small onion, minced   ¼   cup raw rice
1   garlic clove, minced   salt
1½ pounds escarole,   freshly ground pepper
    washed and chopped   grated Parmesan cheese
    into coarse pieces

Heat the olive oil in a 4-quart saucepan over moderate heat.
Add onion and garlic. Cook, stirring constantly, for about 3
minutes. Add escarole and cook, stirring frequently, for about
3 more minutes. Add 1 cup of the bouillon, bring to the boiling
point, reduce heat to low, and simmer covered for about 5
minutes, or until escarole is limp. Add remaining chicken
bouillon and bring to the boiling point. Add the rice. Check
the seasoning and, if necessary, add some salt and pepper.
Simmer covered for about 10 minutes, or until rice is tender.
Top with grated Parmesan and serve with more Parmesan on
the side.

Summer Minestrone

6 servings

Minestrone Estivo   All-Italian

Vegetable soup-stews of this kind are found frequently in central and southern Italy. This Tuscan version was made by our cook Isolina. Since there is no water in this minestrone, the flavor of the vegetables is intense.

2 large tomatoes (about 1 pound), peeled and sliced

2 medium-size onions (about ½ pound), cut into thin slices

2 garlic cloves, minced

2 large or 4 small zucchini, sliced

1 medium-size head of romaine lettuce, shredded

2 pounds fresh peas, shelled, or 10 ounces frozen peas

1 cup parsley sprigs, minced

2 tablespoons fresh basil leaves, minced, or 1 teaspoon dried basil (optional)

2 pounds fresh fava (broad) beans, shelled, or 10 ounces frozen lima beans

⅓ to ½ cup olive oil

salt

freshly ground pepper

freshly grated Parmesan cheese

Use a deep 3-quart casserole that can go to the table. Put sliced tomatoes on the bottom, then sliced onions and garlic. Top onions with zucchini and shredded lettuce. Put peas on top of lettuce. Sprinkle half of the parsley and the basil over the peas. Top peas with beans. Sprinkle remaining parsley and the olive oil over the vegetables. Be sure to follow this order. Do not stir or mix the vegetables. Cook over moderate heat for 10 minutes, or until the vegetables release their liquid. Season with salt and pepper to taste. Now stir and mix the vegetables thoroughly. Simmer covered over low heat, stirring frequently, for about 30 minutes, or until beans are tender. Do not overcook; do not add water; the vegetables have enough moisture of their own. Serve hot or lukewarm with plenty of freshly grated Parmesan cheese.

Mushroom and Tomato Soup

4 to 6 servings

Acqua Cotta

from Tuscany

The literal translation of *acqua cotta* is "cooked water," but this tasty soup is anything but that. An ancient peasant soup from Tuscany, it is quickly and easily made. The wild mushrooms used there enhance the soup's flavor.

4 tablespoons olive oil	freshly ground pepper
2 garlic cloves	½ teaspoon dried
1 pound mushrooms, cut	marjoram
into thin slices	5 to 6 cups hot water
1 pound fresh tomatoes,	2 eggs
peeled and chopped,	½ cup freshly grated
or 2 to 3 cups	Parmesan cheese
drained canned plum	6 slices of Italian bread,
tomatoes	toasted
salt	

Heat the olive oil in a large saucepan. Cook garlic until browned; then discard garlic. Add mushrooms to the oil and cook over medium heat, stirring constantly, for about 5 minutes. Add tomatoes and mix well. Season with salt and pepper to taste and the marjoram. Simmer covered over low heat for about 15 minutes. Add the water and simmer covered for 15 more minutes. In a soup tureen, beat the eggs with the Parmesan. Pour the soup over the mixture, stirring to amalgamate soup and eggs. Serve hot.

NOTE: This soup can be made in half the time given above, but the taste is better when it is cooked longer since the ingredients will have the time to blend properly.

Spinach Soup   4 to 6 servings

Paparot   from Trieste

1 pound fresh spinach, or
  20 ounces frozen
  chopped spinach
4 tablespoons butter
2 tablespoons flour
1 garlic clove, mashed

6 to 7 cups hot chicken
  or beef bouillon
3 tablespoons yellow
  cornmeal
salt
freshly ground pepper

Trim and wash the spinach, using several changes of water. Drain. With the water clinging to the leaves, place the spinach in a large saucepan. Cook covered over high heat for 3 to 4 minutes; drain well. Chop spinach fine. If frozen spinach is used, cook according to package directions and drain well. Heat the butter in a large saucepan. Stir in flour and the garlic clove. Cook, stirring constantly, for 2 minutes. Add spinach and 1 cup of the bouillon. Simmer covered over low heat for 5 minutes, stirring occasionally. Stir in remaining bouillon and simmer covered for 10 minutes. Slowly stir in the cornmeal, taking care not to make any lumps. Cook, stirring frequently, for 5 more minutes. Check the seasoning (the bouillon may be salty) and, if necessary, add a little salt and pepper. Serve hot.

Summer Soup

4 or 5 servings

Minestra Estiva

from Lombardy

6 cups well-flavored beef
bouillon
1 large potato, peeled
and cut into ½-inch
pieces
1 cup green beans, each
broken into 2 or 3
small pieces
1 zucchini, peeled if skin
is damaged, and cut
into ½-inch pieces
1 cup shelled peas

1 cup shelled fava beans
or lima beans
2 tablespoons olive oil
salt
freshly ground pepper
¼ cup minced fresh basil,
or 1 tablespoon dried
basil
¼ cup minced parsley
freshly grated
Parmesan cheese

Bring the beef bouillon in a large kettle to the boiling point.
Add potatoes and beans. Reduce heat and simmer covered for
5 minutes. Add remaining ingredients except the cheese. Simmer covered for 10 to 15 minutes, or until vegetables are tender
but still crisp. Serve warm or lukewarm, but not chilled, with
grated Parmesan on the side.

Chick-Pea Soup   4 to 6 servings

Caciucco di Ceci   from Tuscany

One half cup dried chick-peas will yield approximately 1¼ cups cooked and drained.

2 to 3 tablespoons olive oil
1 small onion, minced
1 garlic clove, minced
2 or 3 flat anchovy fillets, drained and minced
2 to 2½ cups drained cooked chick-peas, or 1 pound canned chick-peas, *not* drained
1 pound Swiss chard, trimmed, washed and cut into ¼-inch strips

6 cups water
¼ cup tomato sauce, or 1 large ripe tomato, peeled and chopped
salt
freshly ground pepper
¼ cup minced fresh sage or basil leaves, or 1 teaspoon dried sage or 2 teaspoons dried basil
slices of Italian bread, toasted
freshly grated Parmesan or Romano cheese

Heat the olive oil in a soup kettle. Add onion, garlic and anchovies. Cook over medium heat, stirring constantly, for 3 to 4 minutes, or until onion is soft and anchovies have melted into onion and garlic. Add chick-peas; if canned chick-peas are used, add them with their liquid. Add Swiss chard, 6 cups water, the tomato sauce, salt and pepper to taste and the basil. Stir well to mix. Simmer covered over low heat for up to 1 hour, or until ingredients are well blended but not mushy. Serve hot or lukewarm over slices of toast with plenty of freshly grated Parmesan or Romano cheese.

Tuscany (Cortona)

Rice and Bean Soup   6 servings

Minestra di Riso e Fagioli   from Tuscany

1 cup dry white
cannellini or Great
Northern beans,
soaked in cold water
overnight
6 cups boiling water
1 small onion, chopped
fine
1 large garlic clove,
chopped fine
1 medium-size carrot,
chopped fine
2 celery stalks, white part
only, chopped fine
½ cup parsley sprigs,
chopped fine
½ to 1 teaspoon minced
dried hot red pepper,
without seeds and
membranes

2 ounces pancetta,
chopped fine, or ⅓
cup minced
prosciutto
4 tablespoons olive oil
2 cups undrained canned
plum tomatoes
salt
freshly ground pepper
1 teaspoon dried basil, or
2 tablespoons minced
fresh basil
⅓ cup raw Italian or long-
grain rice

Combine beans and 6 cups boiling water in a large kettle and
bring to the boiling point. Reduce heat to low, cover, and simmer for about 1 hour, or until beans are almost tender. Meanwhile, combine the chopped onion, garlic, carrot, celery, parsley, red pepper and pancetta or prosciutto; either chop them
together once more to make almost a paste, or mix thoroughly.
Heat the olive oil in a medium-size saucepan and add the vegetable mixture. Cook over medium heat, stirring frequently,
for about 10 minutes, or until vegetables are soft; do not brown.
Add tomatoes and mix well. Cook over low heat for about 15
minutes, stirring frequently. Add this mixture to the beans and
mix well. Season with salt and pepper to taste and stir in the
basil. Simmer covered for 10 more minutes. Add the rice in a
stream to avoid lumping. Cook covered, stirring frequently,

until rice is tender. Serve hot or lukewarm, or cool but not chilled in the summer.

NOTE: The thickness of this soup depends upon individual taste. For a more liquid soup add more water, ¼ cup at a time, to the soup before the addition of the rice. For a thicker soup, increase the rice up to ¾ cup.

Thick Bean Soup

4 to 6 servings

Minestra di Fagioli

from Rome

This kind of bean soup is found all over Italy.

2 tablespoons olive oil
⅓ cup minced pancetta or blanched salt pork
1 large onion, minced
2 garlic cloves, minced
2 celery stalks, diced fine
3 large ripe tomatoes, peeled and chopped
salt
freshly ground pepper
¼ teaspoon ground sage
⅛ teaspoon hot red pepper, or to taste

4 to 6 cups hot beef bouillon or water
1 cup uncooked elbow macaroni
1 to 1½ cups cooked white beans (if canned, drained)
freshly grated Parmesan or Romano cheese

Heat the oil in a large soup kettle. Add pancetta, onion, garlic and celery. Cook over medium heat, stirring constantly, for 5 to 7 minutes, or until vegetables are soft. Add tomatoes, salt and pepper to taste, sage, hot pepper and bouillon, and mix well. Bring to the boiling point. Add the macaroni and cook until barely *al dente*. Stir frequently. Add beans and cook for 5 minutes longer. If a thinner soup is wanted, add a little more hot water, ¼ cup at a time. Serve hot or lukewarm, with plenty of grated Parmesan on the side.

Bean and Red Cabbage Soup   6 to 8 servings

Incavolata   from Tuscany

A substantial, tasty, inexpensive country soup; quantities and
cooking times do not have to be strictly observed. For a thinner
soup, add more bouillon. For a main-dish soup, add ½ pound
sweet or hot Italian sausage, cooked and cut into 1-inch slices,
to the soup for the last 10 minutes of cooking time.

1 pound dried white (navy) cannellini beans	1 cup chopped fresh tomatoes or drained canned tomatoes
5 cups boiling water	salt
4 large bacon slices, minced	freshly ground pepper
2 tablespoons minced fresh sage, or 2 teaspoons dried sage	4 to 6 cups shredded red cabbage
	⅓ cup cornmeal (optional)
2 garlic cloves	freshly grated Parmesan cheese
6 cups hot beef bouillon	

Put the beans into a 3-quart soup kettle or saucepan. Add 4
cups of the boiling water and boil for 2 minutes. Remove from
heat, cover tightly, and let stand for 1 hour. Add remaining 1
cup boiling water, the bacon, sage and garlic. Bring the beans
slowly to the boiling point, reduce heat, and cook covered over
low heat for 1 to 1½ hours, or until beans are tender but not
mushy. If necessary to prevent scorching, add a little hot water, ¼ cup at a time. Put a strainer or a food mill over a large
soup kettle or Dutch oven. Strain half of the cooked beans
into the kettle. (Or purée half of the beans in a blender or food
processor and put them into the kettle.) Reserve the remaining beans. Add hot beef bouillon and tomatoes to the puréed
beans. Stir to blend and season with salt and pepper to taste.
Bring to the boiling point and add cabbage. Simmer covered
over very low heat until cabbage is tender; this takes at least
1 hour, and it does not matter if the cabbage cooks for 2 hours.
Stir frequently. When cabbage is soft, add reserved whole
beans. Cook covered, stirring frequently, for 10 more minutes,

or until whole beans are heated through. For a very thick soup, bring to the boiling point. Stir in the cornmeal in a slow, steady stream, stirring all the while to prevent lumping. Cook, stirring constantly, for 10 more minutes. Serve in bowls, with plenty of Parmesan cheese.

Lentil Soup with Chard

6 servings

Minestra di Lenticchie e Bieta

from Umbria

1½ to 2 pounds Swiss chard	2 garlic cloves, minced
8 cups beef bouillon	1 sweet pepper, cut into strips
1½ cups dried lentils, washed and picked over	salt
	freshly ground pepper
6 tablespoons olive oil	¼ cup minced parsley
1 large onion, minced	freshly grated Parmesan

Wash and drain the chard. Cut off the white stems and save for further use (see below). Cut the leaves into ½-inch strips. Combine bouillon and lentils in a large, heavy kettle. Bring to the boiling point, reduce heat to very low, and simmer covered for about 20 minutes. Add the green leaves of Swiss chard, and cook covered for 20 more minutes, or until lentils are tender. While lentils are cooking, heat the olive oil in a frying pan. Add onion, garlic and pepper strips. Cook over low heat, stirring constantly, for 5 to 10 minutes, or until vegetables are soft. Stir the mixture into the soup and season with salt and pepper to taste. Cook for 5 more minutes. At serving time, sprinkle with the parsley and serve with grated Parmesan on the side.

NOTE: Trim and wash the white stems of Swiss chard. Cook them in boiling water to cover for 3 to 5 minutes, or until tender. Drain. Serve hot with a cheese or tomato sauce, or cold with a lemony French dressing.

Tripe Soup   6 servings

La Busecca   from Milan

A traditional dish, consisting of a thick vegetable soup made more nourishing by the addition of tripe. Buy partially precooked tripe for this dish and cook it over very low heat to a finish in the soup, or it will be stringy rather than soft. Forget about the American prejudice against tripe: it is virtually tasteless and adds protein to soups and sauces.

3 pounds partially precooked tripe
boiling water
2 small onions
4 whole cloves
2 celery stalks
4 bacon slices, minced
3 tablespoons butter
2 medium-size carrots, diced
4 medium-size potatoes, diced
½ small cabbage (preferably Savoy cabbage), shredded

4 medium-size tomatoes, peeled, seeded and chopped, or 3 tablespoons tomato sauce
salt
freshly ground pepper
1 cup cooked navy or pinto beans
slices of Italian bread, toasted
freshly grated Parmesan cheese

Wash the tripe, drain it, and cut it into narrow strips. Put it into a deep soup kettle. Add boiling water to cover, one of the onions stuck with cloves, and one of the celery stalks. Simmer covered over lowest possible heat until almost tender. (Cooking time varies with the kind of tripe and the length of time it has been precooked.) Mince remaining onion and celery stalk. In another deep kettle, heat together the minced bacon and butter. Add minced onion and celery, and cook over medium heat, stirring constantly, until onion is soft. Add carrots, potatoes, cabbage, tomatoes, and salt and pepper to taste. Cook, stirring constantly, for about 2 minutes. Remove the whole onion and celery stalk from the tripe. Add tripe and its cooking liquid to the vegetable mixture. Simmer covered over lowest possible heat for about 45 minutes, or until tripe and vegetables are tender. Add beans and cook for 10 more minutes. If the soup is too thick during cooking time, add hot water to achieve the desired consistency. Serve over toasted Italian bread with plenty of freshly grated Parmesan cheese.

Clam Soup
4 servings

Zuppa di Vongole
from Rome

You can make this dish with mussels as well.

⅓ cup olive oil
2 large garlic cloves
4 dozen well-scrubbed clams (Little Necks or Cherrystones)
1 cup tomato sauce
1 cup dry white wine
¼ cup minced parsley
2 teaspoons dried hot red pepper flakes without seeds, or Tabasco to taste

1½ teaspoons dried oregano
salt
4 to 8 slices of Italian bread, toasted

Heat the oil in a deep kettle. Add garlic and cook until garlic is browned; discard garlic. Add clams, tomato sauce, wine, parsley, hot pepper, oregano and a little salt. Bring to the boiling point over high heat and cook for about 5 minutes, or until clams have opened. With a slotted spoon distribute the clams among 4 large bowls or soup plates. Taste the broth for saltiness; if no hot pepper was used, add Tabasco to taste. Pour some of the broth over each serving of clams. Serve immediately, with toasted Italian bread on the side.

Creamy Fish Soup with Shrimps and Saffron

6 servings

Zuppa di Pesce con i Gamberi   from Sicily

1 pound medium-size or
  large shrimps
2 quarts water
1 small onion
1 garlic clove
2 bay leaves
1 sprig of fresh thyme, or
  ½ teaspoon dried
  thyme
1 tablespoon salt
6 peppercorns

1 teaspoon saffron
3 pounds mixed fish, as
  varied as possible
  (mackerel, porgy,
  croaker, whiting or
  other; see below)
1 cup dry white wine
½ cup heavy cream
6 to 8 slices of Italian
  bread, toasted

Divide the shrimps into two parts and reserve. In a large saucepan combine 2 quarts water, the onion, garlic, bay leaves, thyme, salt, peppercorns and saffron. Bring to the boiling point, reduce heat, and simmer without a cover for 15 minutes. Add half of the shrimps and all the fish. Again bring to the boiling point, reduce heat to very low, and simmer covered for 15 to 20 minutes. Meantime, shell and devein remaining raw shrimps. Strain the soup and reserve the broth; there should be 5 to 5½ cups. Skin and bone the fish and shell the cooked shrimps. Using a food processor, a blender or a food mill, purée the skinned and boned fish and shelled cooked shrimps. Put the mixture into a clean saucepan or, better, the top part of a double boiler. Measure 5 cups of the reserved broth and stir it into the puréed fish. Stir in the wine and mix well with a wooden spoon. Bring very slowly to the boiling point, stirring constantly with the wooden spoon; if using a double boiler, do this over, not in, boiling water. Remove from heat and keep hot. Measure another ½ cup of the reserved broth into a saucepan. Add shelled raw shrimps and simmer for 3 to 5 minutes, or until they turn pink. Add shrimps and their broth to the soup. Stir in the cream. Put back over lowest possible heat and heat through. Be careful not to boil. Serve immediately, with toasted Italian bread.

NOTE: When using whole fish, keep heads and tails on the fish; this gives a more flavorful broth. On the other hand, it is easier to have the fish market fillet the fish, keeping heads, tails and bones separate and cooking them together, than it is to skin and bone cooked whole fish.

Use ½ cup of mayonnaise instead of heavy cream if you like.

Pasta

Pasta

Not so very long ago, pasta, meaning spaghetti and macaroni, were food that Neapolitans ate in a picturesque manner under the indulgent eyes of foreign tourists. Now foreign tourists, in their German, English and American home countries, have become pasta eaters themselves. Pasta is the international food success of our age, respectable and beloved. And why not? What other foods are so inexpensive and versatile, so quick and cheap to cook (when fuel costs are high), and so adaptable?

In Italy, too, pasta enjoys a universal position rather than being the food of the southern, poor parts of the country. In restaurants and even in homes, pasta has replaced rice and polenta dishes, which take longer to prepare and are not quite as satisfying. There has also been a change in the kind of pasta which is most frequently eaten. At one time, peasant women and those of the lower-income groups made fresh pasta every day, sometimes twice daily, because it was much less expensive than buying it. During my childhood in Rome we used to get young women from the nearby mountain villages to help in the kitchen. Some of them had never worn shoes except to church on Sundays; invariably they made excellent homemade noodles, ravioli and other fancies. Today, when most Italian working-class women hold jobs outside the home and their higher-placed sisters keep themselves busy with work or play, *la pasta fatta in casa*, homemade pasta, has become a treat. Commercial pasta has triumphed; it comes in dozens of shapes and sizes: minute to be put into soup, enormous to be stuffed, and always, in the favorite spaghetti shape.

Homemade pasta is almost always made with eggs, as is some commercial pasta. The first is eaten fresh and the second is dried, which means a longer cooking time. On the whole, I find most commercial fettuccini far superior to most homemade ones, which tend to be heavy if not properly made. As for spaghetti, macaroni and the dozens of hard pastas in their marvelous odd shapes—nobody could make all the varieties at home. Dr. Mario Pei, a distinguished Columbia Professor of Romance languages, once figured out that there are over a hundred names for the various members of the pasta family: snails, sparrows' tongues, angels' hair, big butterflies and similarly picturesque names. To add to the confusion is the fact that each Italian province has different names for almost identical kinds of pasta.

Italians cannot do without their pasta, even though Italy has to import wheat for it. Mussolini tried an all-out campaign to have Italian-grown rice take the place of spaghetti, without success. It is cheering to think that centuries of civilized eating could not be wiped out.

How to Cook Pasta

To cook any pasta properly, it is essential to cook it in a great deal of rapidly boiling salted water and not to overcook it.

For 1 pound of pasta, use at least 6 quarts of water. Bring the water to a rapid boil in a large pot. Add 2 tablespoons salt for each 6 quarts of water only *after* the water is boiling and just *before* adding the pasta. (This keeps the pasta fresher-tasting.) You may also add 1 tablespoon olive oil to the boiling salted water to keep the pasta strands or pieces from sticking together. This is a good procedure but not absolutely necessary. When the water is boiling and you have added salt and olive oil, turn up the heat. This keeps the water at boiling temperature while you are adding the pasta. Add the pasta by handfuls and submerge all of it in the water, pushing it down with a wooden fork and stirring it at the same time. When cooking spaghetti or similar pasta, separate the strands; with other pieces, separate the pieces.

Cover the pot (but not entirely or the contents will run over) to return to the boiling point. Once the water is rapidly boiling again, take off the cover. Stir frequently to keep the pasta evenly distributed and moving in the boiling water.

TESTING FOR DONENESS:
Regardless of package directions and charts there is only one way to know if pasta is done—by testing it. Cooking time varies with the size and thickness of pasta; imported pasta, which is harder than our varieties because of its exclusive use of hard wheat (at least the majority of it), needs to cook longer than American pasta. Angels' hair, the very fine noodles, cook in a minute or two, while large thick pasta can take 10 minutes and more. The smaller the pasta, the sooner and more often you will have to test it. The only way to do this is to fish out a strand or a piece and bite into it.

All pasta should be cooked *al dente*, tender but still firm to the bite. If pasta is to be cooked further in a casserole, it should not be more than three-quarters done or the end result will be mushy.

TO DRAIN COOKED PASTA:
One way is to dump the cooked pasta into a colander or a strainer, shake it free of water, and put it into a heated serving

dish, spooning the sauce over it. Some aficionados prefer to put in the sauce first and top it with the pasta, for better tossing. Or it may be put into heated individual soup plates, as is done in Italian restaurants, with some of the sauce on top. The other way, practiced by Italian chefs, when the pasta is spaghetti or other long strands, is to take a long-handled fork or tongs and dip out the pasta, shaking it over the pot to drain off the water. This method keeps the pasta hot and moist so that the strands don't stick together. It is then dropped into heated individual soup plates or a large heated bowl, and the sauce is spooned over it. Each diner mixes his own, or it is mixed at the table. When cooking small or cut pieces of pasta, such as rigatoni, elbow macaroni and shells, they can be drained in a colander or strainer as described above, or removed with a slotted spoon or a big perforated skimmer. The main thing to remember is to rush the pasta to the table piping hot; it is no good when it starts cooling. Pasta can be cooked only when people are ready to eat it (unless it is to be cooked further). Pasta *cannot* be cooked ahead of time nor can it be reheated and still be worth eating. Pasta should never be rinsed after cooking.

HOW MUCH PASTA TO COOK:
The amounts depend on whether the pasta is to be a first course or the main dish. I find ¼ pound an ample single serving. Often, depending on what is to be served as the main course, 1 pound of pasta can make 5 or 6 servings. Pasta swells in cooking, and pasta imported from Italy increases more in cooking than American pasta. A general rule is that 8 ounces of spaghetti will yield around 5 cups cooked; 8 ounces of macaroni such as elbows, 4½ cups cooked; 8 ounces of egg noodles, 4 cups cooked.

PASTA SAUCES:
Small, thin pasta, like little shells or fine noodles, call for lighter and more delicate sauces than the larger and heavier pastas. Pastas without holes absorb their sauce from the outside and do not need as substantial a sauce as pastas with holes, crevices and fluting, which absorb sauce on the inside as well as on the outside.

I think it improves pasta to add a little butter (or olive oil, depending on the sauce) before adding the sauce, especially when it is a tomato sauce. Use 1 teaspoon for each serving, or 1 or 2 tablespoons when the pasta is served in a bowl. When adding larger amounts of butter cut the butter into small pieces or shave it into the pasta for easier amalgamation. Another way of lubricating the pasta is to melt a little butter or heat some olive oil (1 or 2 tablespoons) before adding the pasta to it, then toss the pasta and spoon the sauce over the top.

PASTA CHEESES:
In Italy, pasta is always served with grated cheese with few exceptions such as fish and seafood sauces, or very simple dishes such as pasta with olive oil and garlic. The standard cheeses are Parmesan and Pecorino, described on pages 145-146. Both keep well when wrapped tightly in foil or plastic, making it worthwhile keeping a chunk in the refrigerator. There is no comparison between freshly grated and packaged grated Parmesan or Romano. Since the cheese is now expensive, ask to taste a little before buying. It should be yellow and grainy; don't buy it if it is whitish and dry.

I strongly urge that you grate the Parmesan or Romano cheese just before using. Italian gourmets grate their cheese into the pasta or rice right at the table, using a little round grater; a good restaurant will do the same.

HOW TO SERVE PASTA:
The main thing is to serve it very hot, from heated serving dishes onto heated plates. Large, old-fashioned soup plates (not soup bowls) rather than plates are used for serving pasta, as frequenters of Italian restaurants know. This is also recommended for the home table since soup plates keep the pasta hot and make it easy to toss it with its sauce.

Penne with Red Hot Sauce, à la "Furious"

6 servings

Penne all'Arrabiata   from Rome

Penne are a short, thick pasta, about 2 inches long, cut diagonally at both ends. This dish should be highly seasoned.

1 tablespoon olive oil
½ pound pancetta or lean salt pork, blanched and diced
1 medium-size onion, minced
2 garlic cloves, mashed
4 anchovies, drained and minced, or 1 tablespoon anchovy paste
2 pounds ripe tomatoes, peeled, seeded and chopped

1 to 2 teaspoons hot red pepper flakes, or to taste, or 2 red chili peppers, membranes and seeds removed, chopped, or to taste
salt
1 to 1½ pounds penne
1 cup freshly grated Parmesan cheese

Combine olive oil, diced pancetta or salt pork, onion and garlic in a large deep frying pan. Cook, stirring constantly, for 5 to 10 minutes, or until pieces are golden. Add anchovies and cook, stirring constantly, until they are blended into the first mixture. Add tomatoes and hot pepper flakes or chili peppers and mix well. Season with salt. Cook over high heat, stirring constantly, for about 3 minutes. Reduce heat to low and simmer for about 15 minutes, or until the sauce thickens to usual tomato sauce consistency, but on the thick side. As the sauce is cooking, cook the penne in plenty of rapidly boiling salted water until *al dente*. Drain the pasta and return to the cooking pot. Pour the sauce and half of the cheese over pasta and toss thoroughly. Turn into a heated serving dish and cover with remaining cheese. Serve immediately, on heated plates.

Spaghetti with Amatriciana Sauce   4 to 6 servings

Spaghetti all'Amatriciana   from Lazio

To be authentic this Roman specialty must be made with pancetta, lard and plenty of pepper.

¼ pound pancetta or
   streaky salt pork,
   blanched
2 tablespoons lard
1 medium-size onion,
   sliced thin
3 pounds fresh plum
   tomatoes, seeded and
   chopped
   salt

¾ teaspoon freshly
   ground pepper
½ teaspoon hot pepper
   flakes, or to taste
1½ pounds spaghetti
⅔ cup freshly grated
   Romano cheese
⅔ cup freshly grated
   Parmesan cheese

Cut pancetta into tiny dice. Put it into a saucepan and add lard and onion. Cook over low heat, stirring constantly, until onion is soft. Add tomatoes, salt to taste, pepper and hot pepper flakes. Cook over high heat, stirring constantly, for 5 to 7 minutes, or until tomatoes are soft and just cooked; they must retain their shape. Cook spaghetti in plenty of rapidly boiling salted water until *al dente;* drain. Turn pasta into a heated serving dish, spoon the sauce over the pasta, and toss. Sprinkle Romano and Parmesan over the pasta. Serve hot.

Spaghetti with Carbonara Sauce   4 to 6 servings

Spaghetti alla Carbonara   from Lazio

A famous Roman dish. Speed is of the essence in preparing it, since it must be eaten very hot and as soon as it is served; lukewarm, it loses its character.

1½ to 2 pounds spaghetti
       or linguine
  6 slices of very lean
       bacon, minced
  2 tablespoons butter
  1 small onion, minced
  ⅔ cup dry white wine
  3 eggs

¼ teaspoon salt
4 tablespoons minced
     parsley
⅔ cup freshly grated
     Parmesan cheese
   freshly ground pepper
   grated Parmesan cheese

Start cooking the spaghetti in plenty of rapidly boiling salted water so that it is ready by the time you finish the sauce. Combine bacon and butter in a saucepan and heat. Add onion, and cook, stirring constantly, until onion is soft. Stir in the wine, and cook over high heat, stirring constantly, until wine has evaporated. Remove from direct heat and keep as hot as possible over a flame guard, or cover and keep hot in a slow oven (275°F.). In a very hot, deep serving dish, beat together the eggs with the salt, parsley, Parmesan and plenty of pepper. Drain the spaghetti and turn immediately into the dish with the egg mixture; toss. Add the bacon and toss again thoroughly so that the sauce coats all the spaghetti. Serve immediately with additional Parmesan cheese.

Greened Thin Spaghetti   4 to 6 servings

Spaghettini Verdi   from Tuscany

1 to 1½ pounds thin
   spaghetti (thinnest
   kind)
1½ cups butter (¾ pound)
   cut into small pieces
1 garlic clove, mashed
2 cups freshly grated
   Parmesan cheese

2 cups tightly packed
   minced Italian
   parsley
salt
freshly ground pepper

Cook the spaghetti in plenty of rapidly boiling salted water. Drain and return to pot. Add butter, garlic, Parmesan and parsley. Cover the pot and shake it vigorously to mix. Check the seasoning and add pepper; if necessary, add a little salt. Cover the pot again and toss some more. Turn into a very hot deep serving dish and serve immediately, on heated plates. The spaghetti should be in a sort of creamy green sauce.

NOTE: If desired, add chopped fresh basil leaves or fresh thyme to taste to the parsley, or any other preferred herb.

Thin Spaghetti Syracuse Style   6 servings

Spaghettini alla Siracusana   from Sicily

This dish must be piquant. Since anchovies, capers and olives vary in pungency, you may have to adjust the seasoning.

2 eggplants, each 1 pound
salt
½ cup olive oil
2 garlic cloves
6 large ripe tomatoes, 2 to 3 pounds, peeled, seeded and chopped
¼ cup minced parsley
2 large sweet peppers, preferably red and yellow
1 2-ounce can flat anchovy fillets, drained and mashed
½ cup pitted Italian or Greek olives, cut into halves or chopped

¼ cup drained small capers or chopped large capers
2 tablespoons minced fresh basil, or 1 teaspoon dried basil
freshly ground pepper
dash of Tabasco (optional)
1½ pounds thin spaghetti or vermicelli
½ cup freshly grated Romano or Parmesan cheese

Wash eggplants and cut off both ends. Without peeling them, cut them into thin slices; halve the slices. Place slices in a colander and sprinkle with salt, mixing the salt into the eggplant with your hands. Set the colander in the sink or on a plate, to drain off the bitter juices. Stand at room temperature for 30 minutes to 1 hour. Then squeeze the eggplant slices with your hands to extract any remaining juices; the drier the eggplant, the better the dish. Heat the oil in a heavy saucepan large enough to take all the ingredients. Add the garlic and cook over medium heat until garlic is browned. Discard garlic. Add eggplant slices and cook, stirring constantly, for 3 to 4 minutes, or until eggplant begins to turn golden. Add tomatoes and parsley and simmer covered over low heat, stirring frequently, for about 20 minutes. Meantime, place peppers over direct high heat until they are black and charred, turning them to achieve even charring. Under running cold water, peel off the charred outer skin with your fingers and with a paring knife. Cut peppers into halves, trim off seeds and membranes, then cut them into strips. Stir pepper strips into the tomato sauce. Simmer covered for 5 minutes. Stir in anchovies, olives, capers and basil. Check the seasoning and, if necessary, add a little salt. Add pepper to taste and the Tabasco. Simmer covered, stirring frequently, for 10 to 15 minutes. The sauce must be very hot.

While the sauce is simmering, cook the spaghetti in plenty of rapidly boiling salted water. Drain thoroughly and turn into a heated deep serving dish. Sprinkle with the cheese and spoon the sauce over the spaghetti. Serve immediately, tossing spaghetti and sauce at the table.

Egg Noodles or Spaghetti with Peas 4 to 6 servings

Pasta con i Piselli   from Tuscany

¼ pound prosciutto, lean
   and fat parts, or
   Canadian bacon
1 medium-size onion
1 garlic clove
3 inches of celery stalk
1 cup parsley sprigs
¼ cup olive oil
5 tablespoons butter
1 to 2 pounds fresh
   peas, shelled, or 10
   ounces frozen peas,
   or 2 cups peas

⅓ cup beef bouillon
1 large tomato, peeled,
   seeded and chopped
3 tablespoons minced
   fresh basil, or 2
   teaspoons dried basil
   salt
   pepper
1½ pounds egg noodles
   freshly grated
   Parmesan cheese

On a chopping board, mince together prosciutto, onion, garlic, celery and parsley until they are almost a paste. Heat together olive oil and 3 tablespoons of the butter. Add the minced mixture and cook over low heat, stirring frequently, for about 5 minutes. Add peas and bouillon. Cover and simmer for 10 minutes, or until peas are almost tender. Toward the end of the cooking period, add chopped tomato and basil. Season with salt and pepper to taste; the mixture should be like a thick stew; if it is too thin, cook without a cover. While peas are cooking, cook the pasta in plenty of rapidly boiling salted water until *al dente*. Drain and place in a heated serving dish. Add remaining 2 tablespoons butter cut into small pieces and the sauce. Toss to mix well, and serve with grated Parmesan cheese.

White or Green Noodles with Four Cheeses

4 to 6 servings

Tagliatelle ai Quattro Formaggi   from Emilia

6 tablespoons butter
¼ pound Fontina cheese, cut into ¼-inch cubes
¼ pound Gorgonzola cheese, cut into ¼-inch cubes
¼ pound fresh mozzarella cheese, cut into ¼-inch cubes

1½ pounds medium or fine green or white noodles
1 cup freshly grated Parmesan cheese
1 cup heavy cream
salt
freshly ground pepper

In a large casserole that can go to the table, heat the butter. Add Fontina, Gorgonzola and mozzarella cheeses. Cook over low heat, stirring constantly, until cheeses have melted. Keep warm over lowest possible heat. Cook the noodles in plenty of rapidly boiling salted water, stirring frequently, for 5 to 10 minutes, or until barely tender. Cooking time depends on the kind and quality of the noodles; imported Italian noodles take longer in cooking; do not overcook. While noodles are cooking, stir the Parmesan into the sauce, stirring until it is melted. Stir in the cream and heat through thoroughly, but do not boil. Check the seasoning; if necessary, add salt and pepper to taste. Drain noodles thoroughly and put them into the casserole with the sauce. Toss thoroughly and serve very hot.

Thin Noodles with Ricotta   6 servings

Fettuccine con la Ricotta   from Umbria and points South

A refined version of a popular dish, best made with thin egg noodles or vermicelli.

1 pound homemade or commercial thin, narrow egg noodles	salt freshly ground white or black pepper
¾ cup heavy cream	2 or 3 drops of Tabasco, or to taste (optional)
2 cups (1 pound) fresh ricotta, whole or skim milk, or 1 15-ounce container	1 cup freshly grated Parmesan cheese
1 tablespoon olive oil	

Cook the noodles in 6 quarts rapidly boiling salted water until barely *al dente*; cooking time depends on the kind of noodles, but is usually 5 to 8 minutes. While noodles are cooking, heat cream in a heavy saucepan but do not boil it. Stir in ricotta. Stir with a wooden spoon or wire whip until ricotta and cream are blended into a creamy mixture. Stir in olive oil, salt and pepper to taste, Tabasco and ½ cup of the Parmesan. Mix well. Keep very hot (over a flame guard) without boiling. Drain pasta and turn it into a heated deep serving dish. Add the sauce and remaining Parmesan, and toss well. Serve immediately on hot plates.

Umbria (Assisi)

Straw and Hay Pasta Fantasia   4 to 6 servings

Paglia e Fieno Fantasia   from Genoa

This dish combines yellow and green egg noodles; they are cooked and served together rather than separately. It can be made from homemade pasta dough or from noodles bought in Italian groceries which carry good brands of this pretty fantasy. *Paglia e Fieno* has become a new, rather chic way of eating pasta, and it can be served with any pasta sauce. Fresh basil leaves are essential in the following recipe.

1 tablespoon olive oil	1 cup heavy cream
8 tablespoons butter	½ cup freshly grated
2 garlic cloves	Parmesan cheese
12 cherry tomatoes,	⅓ cup minced fresh basil
stemmed and cut into	leaves, or more to
halves	taste
salt	1 pound Paglia e Fieno
freshly ground pepper	noodles, freshly
2 tablespoons minced	cooked *al dente* and
parsley	drained, hot

Heat olive oil and 2 tablespoons of the butter in a frying pan. Add garlic and cook until garlic is browned; discard garlic. Add cherry tomatoes, and sprinkle them with salt and pepper to taste, and the parsley. Cook over medium heat, stirring with a spoon, for 3 to 5 minutes, or until tomatoes are just cooked through but retain their shape. Reserve and keep hot. In a saucepan large enough to hold the cooked pasta, heat together remaining butter, the cream and Parmesan; stir until blended. Add cooked noodles and toss to coat. Cook, stirring with a fork, for 2 to 3 minutes, or until pasta and sauce are thoroughly heated through. Add tomatoes and their pan juices and the basil. Toss again and turn into a heated serving dish. Serve immediately, very hot.

Fettucine with Creamy Ham and Mushroom Sauce
4 servings

Fettucine alla Golosa   from Milan

2 tablespoons butter
2 tablespoons olive oil
½ pound mushrooms, cut into thin slices
½ pound prosciutto or smoked ham, cut into julienne strips
½ cup tomato juice, or 1 large tomato, peeled and minced
 salt
 freshly ground pepper
½ teaspoon rubbed leaf sage

⅛ teaspoon grated nutmeg
½ cup heavy cream, lightly whipped
½ pound fettuccine, preferably homemade, cooked *al dente* and kept hot
¼ cup minced parsley
½ cup freshly grated Parmesan cheese

Heat butter and olive oil in a large, deep frying pan. Add the mushrooms and cook over medium heat, stirring constantly, for 5 to 8 minutes, or until mushrooms have yielded their liquid and are golden brown. Add prosciutto and tomato juice and season lightly with salt and pepper. Stir in sage, nutmeg and cream. Over high heat cook, without a cover and stirring constantly, for about 3 minutes, or until the sauce has somewhat thickened. Turn fettuccine into a heated deep serving dish. Sprinkle with the Parmesan. Pour sauce over the pasta and sprinkle with parsley. Serve immediately, tossing at the table.

Pasta with Artichokes   4 to 6 servings

Maccheroni con Carciofi   from Calabria

This dish requires a sturdy kind of short pasta, such as mostaccioli, rigatoni, or large elbows.

6 medium-size artichokes, cut into slices (p. 248), about 4 cups
1 quart water
3 tablespoons lemon juice
⅓ cup olive oil
3 slices of lean bacon, minced
1 medium-size onion, minced
1 large ripe tomato, peeled and chopped

½ cup minced parsley
3 tablespoons chopped fresh basil, or 2 teaspoons dried basil
½ cup dry white wine
salt
freshly ground pepper
1 to 1½ pounds mostaccioli
1 cup freshly grated Romano cheese

Keep the sliced artichokes in the water and lemon juice until ready to use. Combine olive oil, minced bacon and minced onion in a heavy saucepan. Cook over low heat, stirring frequently, for 7 to 10 minutes, or until onion is soft. Dry artichokes between sheets of kitchen paper. Add artichokes, tomato, parsley, basil and wine to the saucepan, and mix well. Season with salt and pepper to taste; the dish requires a fair amount of pepper. Bring to the boiling point, reduce heat, and simmer covered for about 20 minutes, or until artichokes are tender; cooking time depends on their age and the thickness of the slices. Stir frequently and check the moisture; if necessary add a little more wine; if too soupy, cook without a cover. Cook the mostaccioli in plenty of rapidly boiling salted water. Drain and turn into a heated serving dish. Sprinkle with the cheese and top with the artichokes. Toss to mix and serve immediately.

Linguine with Broccoli

4 to 6 servings

Pasta con i Broccoli   from Central and Southern Italy

1½ pounds broccoli
½ cup olive oil
4 garlic cloves, peeled
   and mashed
1 pound (2 cups) canned
   plum tomatoes
   salt
   freshly ground pepper
½ cup pine nuts (pignoli)
⅓ cup seedless golden
   raisins or currants,
   plumped in warm
   water and drained

2 tablespoons lemon juice
½ pound linguini or other
   pasta
⅔ cup freshly grated
   Parmesan cheese
2 tablespoons butter

Trim and wash broccoli: remove tough peel of the stalks; keep small flowerets whole, and cut stalks and large flowerets into ¼-inch slices. Heat olive oil in a large, deep frying pan or saucepan. Add garlic, and cook over medium heat until garlic is browned; remove it with a slotted spoon and discard. Add broccoli slices and cook, stirring constantly, for about 3 minutes. Add tomatoes and season with salt and pepper to taste. Reduce heat and simmer covered, stirring occasionally, for about 15 minutes. Add pine nuts and raisins and stir in lemon juice; mix well. Simmer covered for 5 more minutes. Meantime, cook linguini in plenty of rapidly boiling salted water until *al dente*. Drain and place in a heated deep serving dish. Add the butter and toss lightly. Sprinkle pasta with Parmesan, and pour broccoli sauce over. Serve very hot and toss at the table.

Tony's Linguine with Zucchini and Sausage

4 servings

Linguine Ghiotte   from Northern Italy

2 tablespoons olive oil
2 links of sweet Italian sausage, skinned and crumbled
2 garlic cloves, minced
1 tablespoon butter
2 tablespoons minced onion
2 tablespoons minced celery
2 tablespoons minced carrot
2 tablespoons dry Italian vermouth
1 pound zucchini (3 5- to 6-inch zucchini), cut lengthwise into strips, then chopped across into ½-inch pieces

1 teaspoon salt
¼ teaspoon freshly ground pepper
1 cup heavy cream
½ teaspoon dried tarragon
½ teaspoon dried basil
½ pound linguine
⅓ cup freshly grated Parmesan cheese
3 tablespoons minced parsley

Heat 1 tablespoon of the olive oil in a frying pan. Add sausage and cook, stirring constantly, for 5 minutes. Add garlic and cook for 1 minute longer. With a slotted spoon, transfer sausage to a bowl and reserve. Add butter to the juices in the frying pan. Add onion, celery and carrot, and cook over medium heat, stirring constantly, until vegetables are just beginning to soften but are still crisp. Stir in the vermouth and cook until it evaporates. Again with a slotted spoon, transfer vegetables to the bowl with the sausage. Add remaining tablespoon of oil to the frying pan. Add zucchini pieces and cook, stirring constantly, until they are barely tender; do not let the zucchini brown. Season with salt and pepper. Return sausage and vegetables to the frying pan with the zucchini. Stir in cream, tarragon and basil and mix well. Simmer without a cover over very low heat for about 7 minutes, or until heated through. Cook the linguine in plenty of rapidly boiling salted water until *al dente*. Drain and turn into a heated deep serving dish. Sprinkle with Parmesan and spoon sauce over the pasta. Sprinkle with the parsley and toss at the table.

Audrey's Noodle Timbale
6 servings

Il Timballo di Tagliatelle di Audrey
from Naples

¼ ounce imported dried mushrooms
water
12 thin slices of Italian prosciutto (no substitutes)
8 ounces medium-size noodles or homemade tagliatelle

10 ounces frozen tiny peas
½ cup water
4 tablespoons butter
1½ cups heavy cream
1 cup freshly grated Parmesan cheese
salt
freshly ground pepper

Soak the mushrooms in water to cover for 30 minutes. Drain and cut into small pieces. Generously butter a 1-quart soufflé or baking dish with straight sides. Line it with 8 or 9 slices of the prosciutto, letting the prosciutto edges hang over the dish. Cut remaining prosciutto into small pieces. Put peas into a saucepan with ½ cup water; add mushrooms and prosciutto pieces. Cook until peas are just tender; don't overcook. Cook the noodles in plenty of rapidly boiling salted water until *al dente*, or just tender. Drain. In the same saucepan, heat the butter and stir in 1 cup of the cream. Bring almost to the boiling point. Add peas, mushrooms and ham and mix well. Stir in the Parmesan cheese and remaining ½ cup of cream. Stir in the cooked noodles and season with salt and pepper to taste. Mix well. Turn the mixture into the baking dish lined with prosciutto. Cover the top with the overlapping prosciutto slices. Bake in a preheated moderate oven (375°F.) for 10 minutes. Turn off the oven heat and leave the oven door open. Let dish stand for 5 minutes before unmolding on a heated serving dish.

Baked Pasta and Zucchini   4 to 6 servings

Pasta al Forno   from Naples

½   pound rigatoni
     boiling salted water
1½ pounds zucchini (four
     6-inch zucchini or
     three 7½- to 8-inch
     zucchini)
     salt
  1 large onion, sliced
½   pound potatoes (2
     medium-size), peeled
     and cut into thin
     slices
  8 tablespoons butter
  4 ounces prosciutto or
     smoked ham, cut into
     julienne strips (about
     1 cup)

  1 pound tomatoes (3
     medium-size), peeled
     and chopped, or 2
     cups drained canned
     plum tomatoes
⅔   cup minced Italian
     parsley
⅓   cup minced fresh basil,
     or 1 to 2 tablespoons
     dried basil
  1 teaspoon salt
     freshly ground pepper
¾   cup freshly grated
     Parmesan cheese

Cook the rigatoni in plenty of rapidly boiling salted water until they are almost but not quite tender. Drain and reserve. Trim zucchini but do not peel. Cut zucchini lengthwise into thin strips, place strips in a colander in the sink, and sprinkle with salt. Let stand at room temperature for 30 minutes to drain off excess moisture. Put zucchini between sheets of kitchen paper and squeeze dry with hands. Place zucchini in a generously buttered 3-quart baking dish. Top with onion slices, then with potato slices. Dot with 2 tablespoons of the butter and sprinkle with the prosciutto. Dot with 2 more tablespoons of butter. Distribute drained rigatoni over the vegetables in the baking dish. Top them with the tomatoes and sprinkle with parsley and basil. Season lightly with salt (zucchini are somewhat salty) and plenty of pepper. Dot with remaining butter and sprinkle with Parmesan. Cook in a preheated moderate oven (350°F.) for 45 minutes to 1 hour. Turn off the oven, open the oven door, and let the dish stand for about 10 minutes before serving.

Pasta with Sweet Peppers and Tomato Sauce

6 servings

Rigatoni con i Peperoni   from Southern Italy

6 large sweet peppers,
   red, yellow and
   green
½ cup olive oil
2 garlic cloves
2 pounds ripe tomatoes,
   peeled, seeded and
   chopped
   salt
   freshly ground pepper

2 tablespoons minced
   fresh basil, or 1
   teaspoon dried basil
1 to 1½ pounds rigatoni
   or ziti or farfalle or
   conchiglie
¼ cup minced parsley
   freshly grated
   Parmesan cheese

Char and peel the peppers as on page 32. Remove seeds and
membranes and cut peppers into strips. Put 2 tablespoons of
the oil in a heavy frying pan and add pepper strips. Cook,
stirring constantly, for 3 to 4 minutes, or until peppers are
cooked through. Transfer peppers to a hot plate and keep hot.
Add remaining oil to the frying pan and cook garlic in it until
it is browned. Take it out with a slotted spoon and discard it.
Add tomatoes, salt and pepper to taste and the basil. Simmer
covered for 15 to 20 minutes, or until tomatoes are soft. Add
peppers and cook for 5 minutes longer. As the tomatoes are
cooking, cook the pasta in plenty of rapidly boiling salted water
until *al dente*. Drain and place in a heated serving dish. Pour
the pepper-tomato sauce over the pasta and sprinkle with the
parsley. Serve immediately on hot plates, with plenty of Parmesan cheese.

Timbale of Tortellini
6 servings as main dish, 8 servings as first course

Sformato di Tortellini   from Emilia

Frozen tortellini are found in Italian groceries. This is an impressive and easy party dish.

butter	salt
fine dry bread crumbs	freshly ground pepper
3 packages of frozen tortellini, each 15 ounces	⅛ teaspoon grated nutmeg
	grated Parmesan cheese
1 cup (½ pound) butter, cut into pieces	1 recipe Tomato Sauce (p. 135)
2 cups freshly grated Parmesan cheese	

Generously butter a straight-sided 12-cup mold such as a soufflé dish. Coat the bottom and the sides with bread crumbs, taking care that all the surfaces are well coated. Cook the tortellini in plenty of rapidly boiling water until they are almost but not quite done. Drain thoroughly. (The cooking time indicated on the packages is usually too long; taste as you go along.) Heat ½ pound butter in a large saucepan, but do not let it brown. Add the tortellini. With a wooden spoon, stir carefully to coat all tortellini with butter. Stir in 2 cups cheese, and again mix well. Season with salt if necessary, pepper to taste, and the nutmeg. Turn the tortellini into the crumb-coated buttered mold. With the wooden spoon, press down the tortellini to fill the mold evenly. The mixture should be close, but not squashed; the tortellini are to retain their shape. Bake in a preheated hot oven (400°F.) for 15 minutes. Turn off the oven and open the door. Let the tortellini stand in the oven for 5 minutes; this will settle them and make unmolding easier. Unmold on a heated platter, and sprinkle the top with a little additional grated Parmesan cheese. Dribble a little Tomato Sauce in a star pattern over the tortellini. Serve remaining Tomato Sauce on the side. Serve immediately and very hot.

Tortellini with Cream

4 to 6 servings

Tortellini alla Crema

from Venice

2 quarts chicken bouillon made from bouillon cubes	1 teaspoon salt freshly ground pepper
2 pounds fresh or frozen tortellini	¼ teaspoon Tabasco, or to taste
2 cups heavy cream	⅔ cup freshly grated Parmesan cheese

Bring chicken bouillon to the boiling point in a large saucepan. Add the tortellini and cook until they are three-quarters done, 5 to 7 minutes; they must be undercooked since they will be cooked again later. Drain and keep warm. While tortellini are cooking, pour the cream into a large frying pan and stir in salt, pepper to taste and Tabasco. Cook over medium heat for 1 minute, or until cream boils. Reduce heat and add tortellini. Mix well. Cook for 3 to 5 minutes, or until tortellini are tender. Turn into a heated serving dish and sprinkle with the Parmesan. Serve immediately, with more Parmesan on the side.

Homemade Pasta

La Pasta Fatta in Casa

Homemade pasta is generally made with eggs and cut into noodle shapes. The noodles are of various widths, which give them their Italian names. The thinnest are *capellini,* angels' hair, which are rather difficult to cut by hand because they are so thin. Next are *tagliolini* or *tagliarini* and, in ascending order of width, *fettuccine* or *tagliatelle* (about ¼ inch wide), *lasagne* (1½ to 2 inches wide). These measures are approximate and there is no rule that homemade egg noodles cannot be made in other widths. Depending on their place of origin in Italy, there may be slight variations; for example, Roman fettuccine tend to be a little thicker and so do Sicilian lasagne.

Making pasta at home is no more difficult than making pastry; it is a matter of practice and there is no way around this basic truth. There are variables in the ingredients: certain flours absorb more moisture than others, eggs vary in size, and even the humidity of a kitchen can make a difference. Only experience, and I hasten to say, it comes very quickly, tells when the dough is right.

To make pasta at home, you need a clean, hard, flat surface about 24 by 30 inches in size, a thick hardwood rolling pin measuring approximately 1½ to 2 inches in diameter, and a sharp knife. The ideal length for the rolling pin is 24 inches or longer, but these long rolling pins are hard to find even in stores which import Italian equipment. You may ask an obliging carpenter to make you one, or in a pinch, cut up an unpainted, unvarnished broom handle. The rolling pin must be very smoothly sanded down and kept very clean: scrape off any bits of dough that cling to it. Occasionally, and certainly when it is new, the rolling pin should be very lightly massaged with olive oil, then floured and given a good rubdown to remove excess oil and flour. Ordinary American rolling pins are no good for pasta making because their rolling surface is too short; but it is possible to use a smooth French 20-inch rolling pin with tapered ends which can be found in a well-stocked kitchen equipment store.

Semolina flour is the best pasta flour because it is made from hard wheat; flour from hard wheat holds the pasta together while it is cooking. Semolina flour can be found in many Italian groceries, but not in all. Therefore I advocate making pasta from regular American flour, preferably unbleached flour. Self-raising, instant or cake flours *cannot* be used for making pasta at home.

In Italy, using semolina flour, the ratio between flour and eggs is 1 cup flour to 1 egg. American flour works better by starting with ¾ cup flour for each large egg. The eggier the pasta, the tenderer it will be; it will also be harder to handle and roll out, because it is more fragile.

The use of olive oil in very small quantities in pasta making is optional. I find it easier to work by adding a little oil, but then that is the way my mother made her pasta. Pasta without oil is just as good, however.

Homemade egg pasta cooks much faster than commercial pasta. General cooking times for homemade egg pasta are short: a few seconds for angels' hair, and 1 to 2 or 3 minutes for tagliarini and fettuccine, depending on their size. These times apply after water has returned to the rapidly boiling point after adding the pasta.

Pasta machines, which knead and roll out the dough, are now readily available; they are not too expensive and they are a great convenience for people who make pasta often. If these cooks also make large quantities of pasta, the new electric pasta machines will be a great convenience and worth the investment. Although machines are built on generally similar principles, they vary slightly; the manufacturer's instruction manual should serve as a guide on how to use a particular machine. As to the results, purists say that pasta well made by hand is better than good machine pasta. Personally, I don't detect any difference between the two when they are properly made.

Egg Noodles

about 1½ pounds

Pasta all'Uovo

All-Italian

For all types of noodles

3½ to 4 cups flour (plus
    extra flour for rolling
    out)
1 teaspoon salt

4 eggs
1 tablespoon olive oil
2 tablespoons lukewarm
    water

Pour 3½ cups of the flour onto the baking board and stir in the salt. Shape the flour into a mound. Make a deep well in the middle of the mound. Add eggs, olive oil and 1 tablespoon of the water. Beat the mixture lightly and quickly with a fork, or mix the liquid ingredients with your fingers. With a fork or your fingers, and with a circular motion, start mixing the flour into the egg mixture, drawing it from the inside of the well. When eggs and flour make a wet dough, spread ¼ cup of the remaining flour over the wet dough and mix it with your hands. If the dough is still too wet and sticky to knead, mix in remaining ¼ cup of flour. Flour the baking board. Gather the dough into a ball and knead with your hands for 8 to 10 minutes, or until dough is smooth and elastic. Cover the dough with a kitchen cloth and let it rest for 30 minutes. Divide dough into 2 or 4 parts; work on one part at a time and keep the other parts covered. Shape each dough ball with your hand into an oblong about 1 inch thick. Lightly flour the rolling pin. Roll the dough away from you, without pressing it down on the baking board. Turn the dough crosswise and again roll it away from you. Repeat until the dough is no more than ⅛ inch thick and preferably thin enough to be almost transparent. If at any time the dough begins to stick, lift it carefully and sprinkle a little flour under it, and also flour the rolling pin. Roll up your sheet of rolled-out pasta on the rolling pin. The pasta roll should be loose and about 3 inches wide. With a heavy sharp knife, cut the pasta roll crosswise into noodles of the desired width— about ⅛ inch wide for tagliarini, ¼ inch wide for fettuccine or tagliatelle, and 1½ to 2 inches wide for lasagne. Spread a clean cloth on the kitchen table or counter, or over both sides of a kitchen chair back. Separate the cut noodles and spread them on the cloth or drape them over the chair back. Dry the noodles at room temperature for 30 minutes to 1 hour.

In this same manner, roll out and shape remaining dough. Cook the noodles in plenty of boiling salted water, bearing in mind that homemade noodles, like all homemade pasta, cook faster than commercial noodles.

For *making noodles with a pasta machine*, follow manufacturer's instructions.

Dough for Stuffed Pasta   about 110 small agnolotti

Agnolotti alla Piemontese   from Piedmont

A variation on the dough for Egg Noodles, but somewhat firmer in texture to hold in the stuffing. Agnolotti are similar to ravioli.

3 to 3⅓ cups flour (plus extra flour for rolling out)
3 eggs
¼ to ½ cup lukewarm water

1 teaspoon olive oil
2 eggs, lightly beaten with 2 tablespoons water (for brushing dough)
Filling (recipe follows)

Pour 3 cups of the flour onto a baking board or kitchen counter and shape it into a mound. Make a deep well in the middle of the flour mound. Add 3 eggs, ¼ cup of the water and the olive oil. Beat the mixture lightly and quickly with a fork or mix the liquid ingredients with your fingers. With a fork or your fingers, and with a circular motion, start mixing the flour into the egg mixture, drawing it from the inside of the well. When the eggs and flour make a wet dough, spread the rest of the flour over the wet dough and mix with your hands. Flour the baking board. Gather the dough into a ball and knead with your hands for 8 to 10 minutes, or until dough is smooth and elastic. You may have to knead in the remaining ⅓ cup flour, a little at a time; this depends on the way the liquid absorbs the flour. Cover the kneaded dough with a clean kitchen towel and let it rest for 15 minutes. If the day is hot, refrigerate it. Flour the baking board. Divide the dough into two parts and shape each into a ball. Keep one ball covered and put the other on the baking board. Flatten it with your hand into an oblong about 1 inch thick. Lightly flour the rolling pin. Roll the dough *away* from you into an oblong, without pressing it on the baking board. Turn the dough crosswise and again roll it away from you. Repeat, lightly flouring the rolling pin as needed, until the dough is about ⅛ inch thick or even thinner. Cut the rolled-out dough into matching 1½- to 2-inch-wide strips. Brush one strip lightly and to the edges, with the egg-water mixture. Place about 2 teaspoons of the filling in mounds on the dough brushed with the egg-water mixture, leaving 2 inches between mounds. Place a matching strip over the first, pressing firmly around the filling. With a sharp knife or a pastry wheel, cut the dough into squares; each square contains a mound of filling. (If you are making pasta with the machine, make a finished set of agnolotti with two strips of dough before rolling out more dough.) Let the agnolotti dry for 30 to 60 minutes. Then cook in plenty of rapidly boiling salted water for 4 to 5 minutes, or until tender, gently stirring them from time to time with a wooden spoon to prevent sticking. Drain thoroughly and serve immediately with a sauce, or with plenty of butter and freshly grated Parmesan cheese.

Agnolotti Filling with Meat

about 4 cups, for about 110 agnolotti

Agnolotti di Carne   from Piedmont

¾ pound top or bottom
   round of beef, in one
   piece
½ cup olive oil
8 tablespoons butter
1 cup full-bodied dry red
   wine such as Barolo
   salt
3 tablespoons raw natural
   rice
1 cup milk
2 bacon slices
3 thin slices of prosciutto
2 sweet Italian sausages,
   skinned
¼ of a small head of
   escarole, minced (1
   cup tightly packed)

1 garlic clove
1 parsley sprig
6 teaspoons grated
   Parmesan cheese
   freshly ground pepper
¼ teaspoon grated
   nutmeg
2 eggs, beaten
1 white truffle, scrubbed,
   washed and grated
   (optional)
⅛ teaspoon ground sage
1 recipe Agnolotti dough
   (preceding recipe)

Put meat, oil and 2 tablespoons of the butter into a heavy
saucepan. Over high heat brown the meat, turning it over several times, for about 3 minutes. Reduce heat to very low. Add
wine, season lightly with salt, and simmer covered for about
2 hours.

Cook rice in milk until rice is tender and milk has been absorbed; stir frequently and beware of scorching. Mince together
bacon, prosciutto and sausages. Over medium heat, and stirring constantly, cook them for about 3 minutes. Pour off excess
fat. Add minced escarole, mix well and cook, stirring frequently, until escarole is tender. Check for scorching; if too
dry, add a little water, 1 tablespoon at a time. Add cooked rice
to this mixture and mix well. Remove from heat. Drain the
meat, reserving the pan juices. Push the meat through the
finest blade of a meat grinder and mince, or use a food processor, taking care that meat does not become pasty because

of overprocessing. Add the meat to the first mixture and mix thoroughly.

Heat remaining 2 tablespoons of butter in a heavy saucepan. Add garlic and parsley; cook until garlic turns golden; then discard garlic and parsley. Stir ground meat mixture into the saucepan, and add 3 tablespoons of the grated Parmesan, a little pepper and the nutmeg. Stir in the beaten eggs, the truffle and sage, and mix well. Cook, stirring constantly, for 2 to 3 minutes. Remove from heat and cool before using. Check the seasoning and, if necessary, season with a little salt.

Make and cook the agnolotti as described on pages 98-99. Drain carefully and place in a heated serving dish. While the agnolotti are cooking, heat reserved meat juices and stir in remaining butter. Pour over the agnolotti and sprinkle with remaining Parmesan. Toss gently and serve very hot, with additional Parmesan.

Lasagne with Bolognese and Béchamel Sauces

8 servings

Lasagne Pasticciate   All-Italian

Similar versions of this dish are found in most parts of Italy. Make the sauces first.

FOR THE BOLOGNESE SAUCE:
- 4 tablespoons butter
- 1 cup minced onion
- ½ cup minced celery
- ¼ cup minced carrot
- ¼ pound prosciutto or smoked ham, minced
- 2 tablespoons olive oil
- ¾ pound lean beef round, ground twice
- ¼ pound lean pork, ground twice
- 1 cup dry white wine
- 1½ cups beef bouillon
- 2 tablespoons tomato paste
- ½ pound chicken livers, cut into pieces
- grated rind of 1 lemon

FOR THE BÉCHAMEL SAUCE:
- 8 tablespoons butter
- ½ cup flour
- 4 cups milk
- 1½ teaspoons salt
- freshly ground pepper
- ⅛ teaspoon grated nutmeg

TO ASSEMBLE THE DISH:
- 1 pound curly-edge lasagne
- 1½ cups freshly grated Parmesan cheese

TO MAKE BOLOGNESE SAUCE:

Heat 2 tablespoons of the butter in a large, deep drying pan. Add onion, celery, carrot and prosciutto. Cook over medium· heat, stirring constantly, for 3 to 4 minutes, or until vegetables are tender. Transfer vegetables to a 3- to 4-quart saucepan. Add the oil to the same frying pan, then beef and pork. Cook over medium heat, stirring frequently, until meat is browned. Use 2 forks to prevent the meat lumping. Stir in the wine, and cook until pan juices have been reduced to one fourth, or have almost evaporated. Stir in beef bouillon and tomato paste and mix well. Add meat to the vegetables in the saucepan. Bring to the boiling point, then reduce heat to very low and simmer covered for 20 minutes. Uncover and cook for 15 more minutes, or until the mixture is on the thick side. Meanwhile, in the same frying pan, heat remaining 2 tablespoons butter and add chicken livers. Cook over medium heat, stirring constantly, for about 4 minutes. Stir chicken livers and lemon rind into the meat for the last 10 minutes of cooking the meat. Set aside and reserve.

TO MAKE THE BÉCHAMEL SAUCE:
Heat butter in a heavy saucepan. Stir in flour, salt, pepper to taste and nutmeg. Cook over medium heat, stirring constantly, until mixture is bubbly; do not brown. Gradually stir in the milk. Reduce heat to low and cook, stirring constantly, until sauce thickens, is smooth, and is beginning to boil. Remove from heat and set aside.

TO ASSEMBLE THE LASAGNE:
Fill a 6- to 8-quart cooking pot with water and add 2 table-spoons salt. Bring to a rapid boil. Gradually add lasagne, taking care that the water does not stop boiling rapidly. Cook without a cover, stirring frequently with a long fork, until lasagne are tender but still on the firm side. Snip off a piece of a lasagna to test doneness. Drain in a colander. Separate the cooked lasagne and lay them on kitchen paper to dry.

Using a buttered baking dish, 13 × 9 × 2 inches, spoon about 1 cup Béchamel sauce over the bottom of the dish. Add a layer of lasagne and enough Bolognese sauce to cover the pasta. Sprinkle with 2 tablespoons of the Parmesan cheese. Layer more lasagne, cover them with Béchamel sauce, and sprinkle with more Parmesan. Spread more Bolognese sauce over lasagne and Parmesan and sprinkle with more cheese. Another layer of lasagne is now covered with Béchamel sauce and sprinkled with cheese. Repeat layering, ending with Béchamel sauce to cover the whole surface. Sprinkle remaining cheese on top. Bake without a cover in a preheated moderate oven (350°F.) for 30 minutes, or until mixture is bubbly and golden brown. If necessary, broil for 1 minute to brown the top.

Cheese-Stuffed Manicotti   6 servings

Manicotti Imbottiti   from Campania

The manicotti used in this recipe are commercial pasta, 3 to 4 inches long and about 1½ inches in diameter. The filling stuffs about 14 of these manicotti shells.

FOR THE CHEESE FILLING:

½ pound fresh mozzarella cheese, cut into ½-inch dice

2 pounds ricotta cheese, or 2 15-ounce containers

¼ pound prosciutto, cut into ¼-inch dice

2 eggs

½ cup freshly grated Parmesan cheese

salt

freshly ground pepper

¼ cup minced parsley

14 manicotti shells

1 recipe Tomato Sauce (p. 135)

½ cup freshly grated Parmesan cheese

freshly grated Parmesan cheese

TO MAKE THE FILLING:
Combine all the ingredients and mix very thoroughly.

Add 2 tablespoons oil to 4 to 6 quarts rapidly boiling salted water; this will help prevent sticking of the pasta during cooking. Add half of the manicotti and cook for 6 to 8 minutes, or until almost but not quite *al dente;* cooking time depends on the different kinds of pasta. Occasionally stir gently with a long-handled fork. Spread a clean kitchen towel on the kitchen counter. Holding a strainer over the manicotti pot, use a slotted spoon to remove 1 or 2 manicotti at a time from the boiling water, placing them in the strainer. Shake manicotti free of water over the pot, and place them side by side on the kitchen towel, which will absorb all remaining moisture. (The shells must be completely dry before stuffing.) Repeat until all the shells are cooked. Cool. Generously butter a baking dish, 13 × 10 inches. Fill each shell with some of the stuffing, letting a little of the stuffing come out on either side of the shell. This is best done with a pastry tube with a big nozzle; otherwise use a regular teaspoon. Lay stuffed manicotti shells side by side in the buttered dish and surround them with any shells that may not have found space. Pour half of the Tomato Sauce over the shells and sprinkle with ½ cup Parmesan. Bake in a preheated moderate oven for 15 to 20 minutes. Heat remaining Tomato Sauce and serve separately. Also serve additional Parmesan cheese.

Rice

Il Riso

Rice is the typical starch of Lombardy, the Piedmont and the Veneto. It grows in the *risaie,* the rice fields of the Po plain of northern Italy, which is as flat as a pancake. Its watery rice fields are divided by Lombardy poplars and mulberry trees, which feed the silkworms of Milan's and Como's world-famous silk mills.

Italian rice dishes are creamy rather than fluffy like pilafs, with a very slight resistant heart to each grain. Also, these dishes are cooked in a special way, in a small amount of liquid at a time; more hot liquid is added slowly and only when the rice has absorbed the first amount. The cook stands over the stove, stirring the pot all the time, watching for the right moment to add the next ladleful of liquid. The result is a dish with a special texture.

The texture of an Italian risotto, which is both creamy and chewy at the same time, can be perfectly achieved only with the Italian Arborio rice, which can be found in all Italian groceries. If it is not available, long-grain rice will do, although the results are less perfect. The specially treated or precooked rice is not suitable, the former because it does not absorb liquid properly and the latter because it is apt to disintegrate.

Any risotto must be eaten as soon as it is ready. It cannot be kept warm or warmed up; at best, leftover risotto can be made into croquettes. The reason that so few Italian restaurants here, and even in Italy, feature risotto is that it must be made to order and takes much longer (about 25 minutes) than cooking pasta to order.

In Italy rice is always served as a first course, and never as a side dish except with *ossobuco*, veal shank. Risotto should be rushed to the table and served immediately in warmed, wide soup plates or bowls. Many Italians eat it with a spoon.

Risotto and Peas   4 to 6 servings

Risi e Bisi   from Venice

One of Venice's most famous dishes.

¼ pound butter	3½ to 4 cups hot chicken
1 medium-size onion,	bouillon
minced	4 cups shelled or thawed
¼ cup minced prosciutto	frozen peas
or smoked ham	salt
1½ cups raw Arborio or	freshly ground pepper
Carolina long-grain	⅔ cup freshly grated
rice	Parmesan cheese

Heat butter in a heavy saucepan. Add onion and prosciutto, and cook over medium heat, stirring constantly, until onion is soft but still white. Add rice and cook over medium heat, stirring all the time, until rice is translucent. Add chicken bouillon, ½ cup at a time, stirring all the time from the bottom up, until the rice is drying out. Then repeat the process. When the rice is three-quarters done, stir in the peas. Season lightly with salt and pepper (bouillon may be salty). Stir in Parmesan cheese before serving.

Green Rice

Mignestris di Ris Vert

4 to 6 servings

from Friuli

1 pound fresh spinach, or
   10 ounces frozen
   whole leaf spinach,
   not thawed
5 tablespoons butter
1 small onion, minced
1 medium-size carrot,
   minced
1 celery stalk, minced
2 small leeks, white and
   green parts, or 2
   bunches of scallions,
   white and green
   parts, cut into thin
   slices

1¾ cups raw Arborio or
   Carolina long-grain
   rice
4½ cups beef bouillon, hot
   salt
   freshly ground pepper
¼ cup minced parsley
½ cup freshly grated
   Parmesan cheese

Trim fresh spinach and wash in several changes of water. Cook fresh or frozen spinach in the water that clings to the leaves for 3 to 4 minutes, or until barely tender. Drain thoroughly and chop fine. Heat 3 tablespoons of the butter in a heavy saucepan. Add spinach, onion, carrot, celery and leeks. Cook over low heat, stirring frequently, for about 15 minutes. Add the rice. Cook over medium heat, stirring constantly, for 3 to 4 minutes, or until rice is opaque. Make sure the beef bouillon is kept hot. Add it ½ cup at a time to the rice, stirring constantly until rice has absorbed the bouillon before adding more. The finished rice should be creamy, but not soupy or dry. Since different kinds of rice absorb liquids differently, a little more bouillon may have to be added to the rice. Season with salt and pepper to taste. When the rice is just tender, or *al dente,* remove it from the heat and stir in remaining butter and the parsley. Turn into a heated serving dish and sprinkle with the Parmesan. Serve very hot, on heated plates.

Rice with Eggs and Lemon

4 to 6 servings

Riso al Limone

from Venice

A delicate first course.

2 cups raw long-grain
  rice or Italian Arborio
  rice
  boiling salted water
3 eggs
  juice of 1 large lemon
1 cup freshly grated
  Parmesan cheese

salt
freshly ground pepper
2 tablespoons butter

Cook the rice in about 3 quarts rapidly boiling salted water for 10 to 15 minutes, or until rice is tender but still firm; cooking time depends on the kind of rice. Drain rice thoroughly and return it to the pot. While rice is cooking, beat together eggs, lemon juice and Parmesan. Place the pot with the rice over lowest possible heat. Stir the egg mixture into the hot rice. Check the seasoning; if necessary, add a little salt. Season with pepper. Turn rice into a heated serving dish and stir in the butter. Serve immediately.

Risotto alla Milanese   4 to 6 servings

from Lombardy

What makes this splendid risotto different from others is saffron. Risotto alla Milanese may be served plain or with chicken
livers, mushrooms and any savory sauce, provided the sauce
is not too robust, or it would overwhelm the delicate flavor of
the rice. As with any risotto, it is impossible to give the exact
amount of liquid needed; you have to judge for yourself when
the rice is both creamy and chewy.

7 tablespoons butter (it
  must be butter)
¼ cup chopped beef
  marrow (if not
  available, use 2 more
  tablespoons butter in
  its place)
¼ cup minced onion
2 cups raw Arborio rice
  or Carolina long-
  grain rice
½ cup dry Marsala or dry
  white wine

about 5 cups very hot
  (simmering) chicken
  bouillon, in a
  separate saucepan
½ to ¾ teaspoon ground
  or chopped whole
  saffron, steeped in 1
  cup of the bouillon
⅔ cup freshly grated
  Parmesan cheese

In a heavy saucepan, heat together 4 tablespoons butter and
the beef marrow. Add onion and cook over medium heat, stirring constantly, until onion is golden but not browned. Add
rice. Cook, stirring constantly, for about 3 minutes, or until
rice is translucent; the rice must not brown. Reduce heat a
little and stir in the Marsala. Cook, stirring all the time, until
Marsala has evaporated. Then add about ½ cup of the hot
chicken bouillon, about a ladleful, kept hot over low heat. Stirring rice constantly from the bottom up to prevent sticking,
cook until rice is drying out. Then add another ½ cup bouillon,
and cook, stirring all the time from the bottom up, until rice
is drying out; repeat. After about 15 minutes of cooking, or
before the rice is tender, stir in the saffron bouillon. When
saffron liquid has been absorbed, finish cooking the rice with

remaining bouillon. When rice is cooked, stir in remaining 3 tablespoons butter and the grated Parmesan. Rush to the table and serve with additional Parmesan.

NOTE: A lighter risotto can be made by substituting the Marsala with 1 cup dry white wine and using about 4½ cups chicken bouillon.

Rice Croquettes with Mozzarella   12 to 16 croquettes

Suppli al Telefono   from Rome

The *telefono* refers to the mozzarella which gets stringy in cooking. This is a Roman specialty, and a good way of using leftover rice.

2 cups cooked rice	¼ teaspoon freshly
½ cup freshly grated	ground pepper
Parmesan or Romano	12 to 16 cubes of
cheese	mozzarella, ½-inch
1 egg, well beaten	size
2 tablespoons melted	fine dry bread crumbs
butter	olive oil for deep-frying
1 teaspoon salt	

Combine rice and grated cheese and mix well. Stir in egg, butter, salt and pepper, and mix thoroughly. Shape the rice with your hands into 2- to 3-inch balls or croquettes. Make a hole in the middle of each and fill it with 1 mozzarella cube. Cover cheese with rice, making sure it is well covered so that it will not ooze out during frying. Coat croquettes or balls with bread crumbs. Fry in deep hot fat (365°F. on a frying thermometer) until golden brown on all sides. Remove with a slotted spoon and drain on kitchen paper. Serve hot or cool, but not chilled.

Rice and Sausage   4 to 6 servings

Riso e Luganega   from Venice

½ pound Italian sausage
6 tablespoons butter
1 medium-size onion,
   minced
1 cup dry white wine
1½ cups raw Carolina long-
   grain or Italian
   arborio rice
4 cups beef bouillon, hot
   salt

freshly ground pepper
2 tablespoons minced
   fresh sage, or ½
   teaspoon dried sage
½ cup heavy cream
   (optional)
2 tablespoons minced
   parsley
   freshly grated
   Parmesan cheese

Remove sausage casings and chop sausages into coarse pieces.
Heat 4 tablespoons of the butter in a heavy saucepan. Add
onion and sausage bits. Cook over medium heat, stirring constantly, for about 5 minutes, or until sausage bits are cooked.
If sausages were very fat (fat content varies) and there is too
much fat in the saucepan, pour off half of it. Stir in the wine
and bring to the boiling point. Stir in rice and cook over medium heat, stirring constantly, for about 3 minutes, or until
rice is opaque. Stir in bouillon and mix well. Taste (bouillon
may be salty) and season with salt and pepper to taste; stir in
the sage. Simmer covered over low heat for about 15 minutes,
or until rice is cooked *al dente,* tender but still firm. Check the
liquid and stir frequently since different kinds of rice absorb
liquids differently. If necessary, add a little more bouillon or
cook without a cover for the last 5 minutes. This dish, like
many risottos, should be moist and a little soupy. Stir in remaining 2 tablespoons butter and the cream, and heat through.
Sprinkle with parsley and serve immediately, with plenty of
freshly grated Parmesan cheese.

Veneto (Venice)

Rice Timbale   6 to 8 servings

Timballo di Riso   from Lombardy

This is a good buffet supper dish.

2⅔ cups Carolina long-
    grain or Italian
    Arborio rice
½ cup (¼ pound) butter,
    cut into pieces, at
    room temperature

⅓ cup freshly grated
    Parmesan cheese
4 egg yolks
    fine dry bread crumbs
    Filling (recipe follows)
    Tomato Sauce (p. 135)

Cook rice in plenty of boiling salted water until almost but not quite tender. Drain, and place in a bowl. Mix in butter, Parmesan cheese and egg yolks. Generously butter a 3-quart casserole or baking dish and coat the bottom and sides thoroughly with bread crumbs; there must not be any uncovered spots or the timbale will not unmold. Spoon two thirds of the rice mixture into the casserole. Press the rice against the bottom and sides, leaving a well in the middle. Spoon the filling into the well. Spoon remaining rice over the filling and over the entire top of the casserole, taking care that the meat is well covered. Bake without a cover in a preheated moderate oven (350°F.) for about 1 hour, or until rice is thoroughly set. Unmold carefully onto a heated platter. Cut into wedges and serve immediately, with Tomato Sauce on the side.

FILLING:

2 tablespoons butter
¼ cup minced onion
1 garlic clove, minced
½ pound boneless veal,
    trimmed free of fat
    and gristle, ground
    twice
½ pound boneless lean
    pork, trimmed free of
    fat, ground twice

½ pound chicken livers,
    trimmed and
    chopped
⅓ cup drained chopped
    pimiento
1 cup cooked peas
4 tablespoons tomato
    paste flavored with
    basil

2 tablespoons dry white   ½ teaspoon dried oregano
     wine   ¼ teaspoon freshly
1 teaspoon salt   ground pepper
½ teaspoon sugar   dash of Tabasco

Heat the butter in a deep frying pan. Add onion and garlic and
cook, stirring constantly, until onion is soft and golden. Add
veal and pork; stir well to mix meats and blend them together.
Stir in chicken livers. Cook over low heat, stirring frequently
for about 15 minutes, or until meats are cooked through. (The
pork must be well cooked.) Add all remaining ingredients and
mix well. Cook over low heat, stirring frequently, for about 15
minutes. The filling must be very thick or it will ooze out of
the rice during baking. But check for sticking and, if necessary,
add a little wine, 1 tablespoon at a time.

Sicilian Rice Balls
about 25 balls, 1- to 1½-inch size

Arancine alla Siciliana   from Sicily

These bring nostalgia to all who came from Sicily.

1   cup raw rice
2   tablespoons olive oil
¼   pound lean beef,
      ground
2   chicken livers, chopped
      to coarse pieces
½   small onion, minced
2   garlic cloves, mashed
¼   pound mushrooms, cut
      into thin slices
2   tablespoons tomato
      paste

¾   cup hot water or
      tomato sauce
½   teaspoon salt
¼   teaspoon freshly
      ground pepper
3   tablespoons butter
¼   cup freshly grated
      Parmesan cheese
2   eggs, lightly beaten

FOR FRYING:
1½   cups fine dry bread
      crumbs
1   egg, lightly beaten
1½   cups olive oil,
      approximately

Cook the rice in plenty of boiling salted water until tender.
Drain and reserve; keep rice warm. (If leftover rice is used,
heat it up with 1 to 2 tablespoons water to prevent burning.)
Heat 2 tablespoons olive oil in a large frying pan. Add beef,
chicken livers, onion and garlic. Cook over medium heat, stirring constantly, for 3 to 4 minutes, or until meats are browned.
Add mushrooms, tomato paste, hot water (or tomato sauce),
salt and pepper; mix well. Simmer covered over low heat for
about 15 minutes. Uncover and simmer for 15 minutes longer,
stirring frequently. Meantime, stir butter and Parmesan into
the hot rice, then the beaten eggs; mix carefully with a fork in
order not to mash the rice. Drain the tomato sauce, reserving
the meat and mushrooms. Stir drained tomato sauce into the
rice. Take a rounded tablespoon of rice in the palm of your

hand and make a well in the middle. Put 1 tablespoon of meat and mushroom mixture into the well. Place 1 teaspoon more rice over the meat and form a ball, covering the meat completely with rice so that it won't ooze out during frying. Roll each rice ball *lightly* in bread crumbs first, then in the beaten egg, and again in bread crumbs. Heat enough olive oil in a deep-frying pan to reach just over half the depth of rice balls. Fry rice balls, a few at a time, until golden brown on all sides. Drain on kitchen paper and serve hot or cool, but not chilled.

NOTE: The rice balls can be fried at once, or refrigerated and fried later. They make good cocktail party fare.

Risotto with Chicken   4 to 6 servings

Risotto alla Sbirraglia   from Veneto

1   frying chicken, 2½ to 3
   pounds
7   cups water
2   small onions
1   medium-size carrot,
   sliced
½   celery stalk, sliced
1   medium-size leek,
   white and green part,
   sliced
   salt
6   peppercorns

2   tablespoons minced
   pancetta or minced
   blanched salt pork or
   blanched bacon
4   tablespoons butter
½   cup dry white wine
1   tablespoon tomato
   paste
2   cups Carolina long-
   grain rice
   freshly grated
   Parmesan cheese

Cut all the meat from the chicken. Remove all fat, gristle and
skin from the meat, and cut meat into thin strips. Mince
chicken liver and gizzard. In a deep kettle, put 7 cups water,
the chicken bones and neck, 1 onion, the carrot, celery and
leek. Season with salt to taste and add peppercorns. Bring to
the boiling point, skim, and reduce heat. Simmer covered over
low heat for about 45 minutes, skimming as needed. Strain the
broth and remove all the fat. On a chopping board, mince
together into a paste the remaining onion and the pancetta or
salt pork. Put the mixture into a heavy saucepan and add the
butter. Cook over medium heat, stirring constantly, for about
3 minutes, or until slightly golden. Add chicken, chicken liver
and gizzard. Cook, stirring constantly, for about 3 minutes.
Mix together wine and tomato paste and add it to the chicken;
mix well. Simmer covered over low heat, stirring frequently,
for about 10 minutes. Measure 6 cups of the chicken bouillon
and heat it. Stir the rice into the chicken mixture and cook for
2 minutes. Stir in the hot chicken bouillon. Simmer covered,
stirring frequently, for about 15 minutes, or until rice is tender
and has absorbed almost all the liquid. If too dry, add a little
hot water, 1 tablespoon at a time; if too liquid, cook without
a cover to allow for evaporation. Serve hot, with grated Parmesan on the side.

Polenta and Dumplings

Polenta e Gnocchi

Polenta is yellow cornmeal mush. It was once the staple starch of much of northern Italy, notably Piedmont, Lombardy and some parts of the Veneto, the mountainous regions where wheat could not be grown profitably. Now that northern Italy is no longer poor, white bread and pasta are displacing polenta. And as women spend less time in the kitchen, gnocchi, or dumplings, are also passing into oblivion since it takes a certain amount of time to make them.

Farina gialla, yellow flour, as polenta is also known (specifically, polenta is the cooked mush), comes in different degrees of fineness; our own cornmeal resembles the fine polenta. Coarse polenta is far tastier, but since it is hard to find even in our Italian grocery stores, I have adapted the recipes to American cornmeal, which is not that different from the Italian. White cornmeal, to my knowledge, is used in Venice and the Veneto only. The word "polenta" is used for other porridges and mushes as well. The word comes from Latin *pulmentum,* and the Romans used it for both a mush and a cake made from simple flours. Later, polenta was also made from ground barley and chestnut flour, as it still is in some parts of Sardinia. Corn reached Italy only in the seventeenth century, and since it came via Turkey, it was (and still is) called *granturco,* Turkish grain.

To make good polenta takes time and elbow grease.

First, it must be boiled in plenty of water, and stirred constantly, preferably for 45 minutes, as the old cookbooks say. Actually, the longer you stir polenta, the better it is. The proper cooking utensil is a *paiuolo*, a copper pan that is not tin-lined. It has either a long handle on the side, or a rounded handle from which the pot hangs on an iron arm over the fire in the kitchen fireplace. How well I remember the kitchen of the farmer who looked after our house on Lake Maggiore! It was a large room, and the fireplace took the greater part of a wall; we would sit at either side of the fire on two built-in benches, warming ourselves and watching the cornmeal stream into the boiling pan. The *paiuolo* hung over the fire, stirred by the women with a long wooden paddle. (Polenta must always be stirred with wood; a wooden spoon will do.) When a delicious crust had formed on the bottom and sides of the pot, it was turned out on a wooden board and cut with a piece of string attached to two wooden clothespins. We ate it in place of bread, with a meat or cheese sauce, or with boiled chestnuts and milk, or sliced cold and fried to a delicious crisp. Ours was a mild way of eating polenta. The dish for which it is most famous is *polenta e osei*, a bed of polenta on which repose those pitiful little song birds that Italians shoot with such glee. (After each hunting season, the air of Italy is quiet as the grave.)

Polenta can be made in any heavy cooking pot or a double boiler with excellent results. Now there is an instant prepackaged polenta on the market, very popular in Italy, which takes 5 minutes to cook; it is also available in this country. It is surprisingly acceptable, and a way of keeping the polenta habit alive.

Italian gnocchi, or dumplings, are wonders of ingenuity, albeit time-consuming to make. Basically, they are made from whatever ingredients will hold together when poached in soup, or in simmering salted water, until cooked, when they rise to the surface. They are drained, and served with butter and cheese or a sauce. Their character varies; potato gnocchi are robust and spinach and ricotta gnocchi delicate. They all make excellent entrées instead of pasta or rice.

Polenta with Three Cheeses
6 servings

Polenta d'Oropa
from Piedmont

Serve as a main luncheon dish with a salad and dessert, or as a side dish to ham, roasted meats and stews.

8 cups water
2 teaspoons salt
1¾ cups polenta or yellow cornmeal
1 cup finely diced Fontina or Swiss cheese
1 cup finely diced mozzarella cheese
½ cup grated Parmesan cheese
½ cup (¼ pound) butter, melted and hot, but not browned

Bring the water and salt to a full rolling boil in a heavy 4-quart saucepan. Gradually sprinkle in the polenta in a thin steady stream, stirring constantly with a wooden spoon to prevent lumping. Cook over low heat, stirring constantly, for 4 to 5 minutes. Continue cooking over low heat, without a cover, for 15 minutes. Stir in Fontina and mozzarella cheeses, mixing well. Continue cooking for another 15 minutes, stirring frequently. Turn the polenta out on a heated serving dish. Sprinkle polenta with Parmesan and drizzle with melted butter; serve immediately.

NOTE: The classic cooking time for polenta is 1 hour; in order to produce a soft, homogenized dish, polenta must be cooked for a long time.

Polenta   about 4 cups, 4 to 6 servings

La Polenta   from Northern Italy

1   cup yellow cornmeal   1   teaspoon salt
4   cups water

Mix the cornmeal with 1½ cups of the water to a smooth paste.
Pour remaining water and the salt into the top part of a double
boiler. Bring to the boiling point over direct heat. Stir the cornmeal paste gradually into the boiling water. Cook over medium
heat, stirring constantly, until mixture has reached the boiling
point. Then set the double-boiler top over the bottom pan filled
with boiling water. Cook covered, stirring frequently, for 30 to
45 minutes.

Polenta and Sausages   4 to 6 servings

Polenta e Salsiccie   from Northern Italy

1   recipe Polenta (p. 124)   salt
4   tablespoons butter   freshly ground pepper
1½   pounds sweet or hot   ½   cup freshly grated
     Italian sausages   Parmesan cheese
1   recipe Pizzaiola Sauce
     (p. 136)

While polenta is cooking, heat the butter in a large deep frying
pan. Prick sausages with a fork, and cook, turning them over
constantly, until they are browned on all sides. Pour off the fat
in the frying pan. Add the Pizzaiola Sauce and check seasoning, adding salt and pepper if necessary. Simmer covered over
low heat, stirring frequently, for 30 minutes. Turn the polenta
out on a heated shallow serving dish and flatten it out with a
spatula dipped into water. Place the sausages on top of the
polenta. Pour the sauce over sausages and polenta and sprinkle
with the grated Parmesan. Serve hot.

Baked Polenta with Mushrooms
6 servings

La Polenta Pasticciata con Funghi
from Veneto

¼ cup olive oil
1 medium-size onion, minced
1 garlic clove, minced
2 tablespoons minced parsley
¾ pound mushrooms, cut into thin slices
⅔ cup drained canned tomatoes

salt
freshly ground pepper
8 cups cooked hot polenta (2 recipes Polenta, p. 124)
½ cup (¼ pound) butter
1 cup freshly grated Parmesan cheese

Heat the olive oil in a deep frying pan. Add onion, garlic and parsley, and cook, stirring constantly, until onion is soft. Add mushrooms and tomatoes. Cook over medium heat for 7 to 10 minutes, or until mushrooms have given up almost all of their liquid but are still firm. Season with salt and pepper to taste. While polenta is still hot, beat in half of the butter and the Parmesan cheese. Spoon polenta into a loaf pan, 9 × 5 × 3 inches, and cool. Unmold polenta and cut it into two parts. Return one part to the loaf pan and top with the mushroom sauce. Top mushroom sauce with remaining polenta and dot with remaining butter. Bake in a preheated moderate oven (350°F.) for 30 minutes, or until the top is golden brown and crusty. Unmold on a warm platter and serve with a tossed green salad.

Cornmeal Croquettes

4 to 6 servings, about 18 croquettes, 2½- to 3-inch size

Polpettini di Polenta   from Piedmont

1 recipe Polenta (p. 124)	2 egg yolks
1½ cups grated Swiss cheese	1 small white truffle, minced (optional)
½ cup freshly grated Parmesan cheese	fine dry bread crumbs
1 tablespoon flour	1 egg, beaten with 1 teaspoon olive oil
1 cup milk	6 tablespoons butter
salt	2 tablespoons olive oil
freshly ground pepper	
⅛ teaspoon grated nutmeg	

Spoon the hot polenta onto a baking sheet in a layer ½ inch thick. Smooth the top with a spatula, and cool. Cut cooled polenta into ¼-inch dice. Combine Swiss cheese, Parmesan, flour and milk in a large saucepan. Mix well and season with salt (if necessary—the cheeses are salty) and pepper to taste and the nutmeg. Beat in egg yolks. Over low heat, stirring constantly, bring the mixture to the boiling point. Cook over lowest possible heat, stirring all the time, for 3 to 4 minutes. Remove from heat. Stir in polenta dice and the truffle, and mix thoroughly. Spoon the mixture onto a baking sheet in a layer ½ inch thick. Smooth the top, and cool. With a small round cookie cutter or glass, 2½ to 3 inches in diameter, dipped repeatedly into cold water, cut out small rounds. Dip each round first into bread crumbs, then into beaten egg and again into bread crumbs; shake off excess crumbs, but make sure that the rounds are evenly coated. Heat butter and olive oil in a large frying pan. Fry the rounds, a few at a time, until they are crisp and golden. Drain on kitchen paper. Arrange the cooked rounds in overlapping rows on a heated serving dish lined with a napkin and keep hot in a low oven. Serve as soon as ready, as an accompaniment to meats.

Roman Dumplings

4 to 6 servings

Gnocchi alla Romana

from Rome

The word *gnocco* means a dumpling when applied to food and a dope when applied to a human. In Italy, these gnocchi are made with semolina, which can be found here in Italian groceries. I have adapted the recipe to farina or Cream of Wheat; both give similar results.

1½ cups water	½ cup (¼ pound) butter
1½ cups milk	2 cups freshly grated
1½ teaspoons salt	Parmesan cheese
1 cup farina or Cream of Wheat	3 eggs, well beaten

Combine water and milk in a saucepan. Add the salt and bring to the boiling point. Gradually stir in the farina or Cream of Wheat, taking care to avoid lumping. Cook over medium heat, stirring constantly, for 5 to 7 minutes, or until very thick; remove from the heat. Stir in half of the butter, mix well, and stir in ½ cup of the Parmesan, mixing well. Stir in the eggs and mix well. Spread the mixture on a shallow platter or a baking sheet in a layer ¼ inch thick, smoothing the top with a spatula dipped into water. Cool. With the rim of a glass or a cookie cutter measuring 1½ to 2 inches, cut the mixture into circles. Arrange in a buttered shallow baking dish in overlapping circles, making several layers. Sprinkle each layer with bits of the remaining butter and remaining 1½ cups cheese Bake in a preheated moderate oven (350°F.) for about 20 minutes, or until gnocchi are golden and crisp.

NOTE: This dish can be prepared in advance and refrigerated until needed.

Spinach and Ricotta Dumplings   4 servings

Gnocchi Verdi   from Tuscany

These delicious green dumplings make an excellent first course. They should be very light. The trick is to use spinach squeezed very dry, whole milk, dry ricotta and as little flour as possible. If the ricotta looks at all watery, drain it thoroughly through a sieve before using.

20 ounces (2 10-ounce packages) frozen chopped spinach	⅛ teaspoon freshly ground pepper
½ cup water	¼ teaspoon grated nutmeg
1 tablespoon butter plus ½ cup (¼ pound) butter, melted	2 eggs
	3 tablespoons flour
1 cup whole-milk ricotta	1½ cups freshly grated Parmesan cheese
1 teaspoon salt	flour

Cook frozen chopped spinach without a cover in the water, breaking the block apart with a fork, for 3 to 4 minutes, or until spinach is soft and most of the cooking liquid has evaporated. Drain spinach in a strainer and with the back of a wooden spoon press it against the sides of the strainer to extract as much liquid as possible. Squeeze the spinach with your hands to make it as dry as possible; there should be about 1 cup cooked spinach. The spinach may be chopped further into smaller parts but this is not necessary if it has been thoroughly squeezed; the squeezing breaks it down. Return spinach to the saucepan, and add 1 tablespoon butter, the ricotta, salt, pepper and nutmeg. Cook over very low heat, stirring all the time, for 4 to 5 minutes, or until the mixture turns somewhat gooey; remove from heat. Beat in the eggs, one at a time, beating well after each addition. Beat in the flour and ¾ cup of the Parmesan. Blend thoroughly into a homogenous mass; there should be about 3 cups of the spinach-ricotta mixture. Turn it into a bowl and cover tightly, or wrap in wax paper or plastic wrap. Refrigerate for about 2 hours.

At cooking time, have ready a shallow baking dish and the

¼ pound butter, melted and hot; take care that the butter does not brown. Put some flour on a dinner plate or a piece of wax paper. Fill a large, deep frying pan or large shallow saucepan with water. Bring it to the boiling point, then reduce heat so that the water barely simmers. Dust your hands lightly with a little flour. Shape the gnocchi mixture into small 1½-inch-long loaves or gnocchi. Dip each gnocco into the flour, shaking off excess. Carefully lower the gnocchi, one at a time, into the simmering water. Cook a few at a time since they must not touch each other while cooking. The gnocchi will be cooked when they rise to the surface; this should take 2 to 3 minutes, depending on the gnocchi. Remove them with a slotted spoon, shake off the moisture, and place them in the baking dish. Sprinkle a little butter over the gnocchi. Keep the cooked gnocchi warm in a preheated moderate oven (350°F.). Continue cooking until all the gnocchi are cooked. Drizzle with any remaining butter and sprinkle with remaining ¾ cup Parmesan. Turn the oven to hot (400°F.) and cook the gnocchi for 3 to 4 minutes, or until the Parmesan has melted. Serve very hot.

NOTE: The gnocchi may also be served with a light tomato sauce, but I think any saucing takes away from their delicate flavor.

Potato Dumplings   4 to 6 servings

Gnocchi di Patate   All-Italian

To make light little dumplings, add as little flour as possible, just enough to hold the potato dough together; some potatoes absorb more flour than others. As in pie making, gnocchi making succeeds with experience; one gets a feeling for the consistency of the dough. Cooked gnocchi can be dressed in any way, like pasta, and served as a first course.

> 2   pounds mealy potatoes   salt
>   (not new potatoes)   flour
> 1½   cups flour,
>   approximately

Do not peel the potatoes. Wash them and boil them in salted water until tender. Drain, return to the pot, and dry out for a minute or two over medium heat, shaking the pot to prevent sticking. Peel potatoes while still hot. Mash them or force them through a ricer as in making mashed potatoes. Gradually stir in enough flour to make a soft, smooth, somewhat sticky dough. Dipping your hands into more flour, and shaking off the excess, roll the dough into 1-inch round strips of approximately the thickness of your thumb. Cut the strips into approximately ¾-inch slices. With your thumb, gently press each dumpling into a concave, or shell, shape, all the while keeping your hands lightly floured. Or press each dumpling against the inner side of a fork and then press your thumb into the dumpling to make a shell shape ridged at the side where it touched the fork. Lay the finished gnocchi on a lightly floured kitchen towel, in a single layer and not touching one another or they will stick together. Have ready a saucepan full of gently boiling salted water; a low, wide saucepan is best. Have ready a clean kitchen towel. Also have ready a heated serving dish and the sauce you will be using, or simply some melted butter and freshly grated Parmesan cheese. Drop a few gnocchi at a time into the water. They should cook without touching each other. As they cook, they will rise to the surface. Fish the gnocchi out with a slotted spoon and lay them on the cloth to dry, in a single layer and not touching each other. When all the gnocchi are cooked, spoon a little of the sauce or butter into the serving dish. Top with a layer of gnocchi, more sauce, and a little grated Parmesan cheese; repeat until all gnocchi and sauce are used. Sprinkle with some more Parmesan and serve immediately, very hot.

Potato Dumplings with Cheese 30-35 1½-inch gnocchi

Gnocchi alla Bava   from Piedmont

---

1 recipe Potato
   Dumplings (p. 130)
½ pound Fontina, Swiss
   or Munster cheese,
   cut into thin slices

4 tablespoons butter, cut
   into small pieces

Layer potato dumplings in a buttered baking dish, topping each layer with slices of cheese. Dot the last layer with butter. Cover the baking dish with a lid or with aluminum foil, tying it with a string. Bake in a preheated hot oven (425°F.) for about 5 minutes. Turn off the heat. Remove cover and return baking dish to the oven for a few minutes, or until golden on top. Serve immediately.

Parmesan Dumplings   4 to 6 servings

Gnocchi alla Parmigiana   from Emilia

Serve as a first course, or as a luncheon main dish, with a tossed salad.

½ cup milk
½ cup water
½ cup (¼ pound) butter,
   cut into pieces
¼ teaspoon salt
1½ cups flour

4 eggs
Cheese Sauce (p. 134)
½ cup freshly grated
   Parmesan cheese
paprika

Combine milk, water and butter in a saucepan. Bring to the boiling point over medium heat. Add salt and flour all at once. Stir vigorously until the mixture is smooth, leaves the sides of the saucepan, and forms into a ball. Remove from heat. Beat in the eggs, one at a time, beating well after each addition. Have ready a wide saucepan or a deep frying pan with simmering, not boiling, water. Drop the mixture by ½ teaspoon into the water. Do this in batches, so as not to crowd the dumplings. Dip the teaspoon frequently into cold water to prevent the dumpling mixture sticking. There should be 70 to 80 little dumplings. Have ready a bowl of cold water. When dumplings rise to the surface, remove them from the hot water with a slotted spoon. Drop them quickly into the cold water, remove them immediately, and drain well first in a strainer, then on kitchen paper. The dumplings will be irregular in shape. Place them in a buttered round 9-inch baking dish. Add the Cheese Sauce and mix gently with a fork. Sprinkle with the Parmesan and a little paprika. Bake dumplings in a preheated moderate oven (350°F.) for 20 to 30 minutes, or until golden brown on the top.

Sauces for Pasta, Rice, Polenta and Dumplings

Sughi e Salse per le Minestre Asciutte

Pasta, rice, polenta and dumplings are marvelous vehicles for practically every kind of sauce: vegetable, meat, fish, alone or in combinations, all taste good; and the only limit to saucing up these dishes is the cook's imagination. When this fails, there is always the simplest way, the classic *all'inglese*, that is, plenty of fresh, preferably sweet butter, plenty of freshly grated Parmesan or Romano cheese, and plenty of freshly ground pepper on a piping hot dish of pasta, rice, polenta or dumplings; tossed right at the table. The serving dish and the plates should be heated.

As with all Italian cooking, you make do with the ingredients you have at hand. Northern Italy favors lighter, more delicate dressings, often containing cream. From Rome on down, the tomato becomes plentiful in most sauces, as do the larger vegetables such as eggplant and broccoli. Along the coast, where fish and seafood are plentiful, sauces are composed of these. Sauces can be made more interesting by adding anchovies, pine nuts, currants, olives, capers, put together in a way that pleases your taste.

Cheese Sauce
about 1¾ cup

Salsa col Formaggio
from Emilia

2 tablespoons butter
2 tablespoons minced
   onion
1½ tablespoons flour
½ teaspoon salt
¼ teaspoon freshly
   ground pepper

⅛ teaspoon grated
   nutmeg
1½ cups milk
½ cup freshly grated
   Parmesan cheese

Heat the butter in a saucepan and stir in the onion. Cook, stirring constantly, for about 3 minutes, or until onion is soft; do not brown it. Stir in flour, salt, pepper and nutmeg. Cook over low heat, stirring constantly, for about 1 minute. Gradually stir in the milk, stirring well after each addition to prevent lumping, until the sauce is smooth and thickened. Remove from the heat and stir in the Parmesan.

Tomato Sauce　　　　　　　　　　　　　　6 servings

La Pomerola　　　　　　　　　　　　　　from Tuscany

For pasta or any other dish needing a tomato sauce. This is a quick-cooking meatless tomato sauce, which preserves the fresh tomato taste. It is different from the long-simmered tomato sauces of the Italian South, which are made with tomato paste.

3　pounds fresh, ripe plum tomatoes, cut into halves and seeded, or 3 cups canned plum tomatoes, drained, plus 1 cup of their juice
1　medium-size to large onion, cut into halves
1　medium-size carrot, minced
1　celery stalk, minced
salt
freshly ground pepper
2　to 3　tablespoons minced fresh basil, or 1 teaspoon dried basil
⅓　cup olive oil

Into a heavy saucepan put the tomatoes, one half of the onion, the carrot, celery, salt and pepper to taste and the basil. Bring to the boiling point quickly. Cook over high heat, stirring constantly, for about 5 minutes, or until tomatoes are soft. Purée through a food mill. Mince remaining ½ onion. Heat the olive oil and cook onion in it until soft. Add puréed tomatoes. Check seasoning; if necessary, add a little more salt and pepper. Cook over medium heat, stirring frequently, for 10 to 15 minutes, no longer. Quickness of cooking preserves the flavor of the tomatoes.

Pizzaiola Sauce   for ½ to 1 pound pasta

La Pizzaiola   from Naples

The tomatoes are cooked just long enough to soften, but no longer, so as not to lose their fresh taste. The sauce is also served on steaks.

¼ cup olive oil
2 pounds tomatoes (6 to 8), peeled, seeded and chopped
2 garlic cloves, minced
   salt

¼ teaspoon hot red pepper flakes, or to taste
1 teaspoon dried oregano
2 tablespoons minced parsley

Heat the olive oil in a saucepan and add all the other ingredients. Cook over high heat, stirring frequently, for 5 to 10 minutes, or until tomatoes are soft.

Campania (Naples)

Zucchini Sauce

for ½ to 1 pound pasta

Salsa di Zucchine alla Friulana

from Friuli

1 tablespoon olive oil
4 tablespoons butter
½ cup minced onion
1 garlic clove, minced
⅓ cup minced sweet
   pepper
2 pounds zucchini, sliced

3 cups peeled, seeded
   and chopped
   tomatoes
½ teaspoon dried thyme
   salt
   freshly ground pepper

Heat olive oil and butter. Over medium heat, stirring constantly, cook onion and garlic until onion is soft and golden. Add all the other ingredients. Cook covered over low heat for about 20 minutes, stirring frequently. The zucchini should be tender but not mushy, and slices should preserve their shape.

NOTE: This may also be served as a side dish. If desired, sauté ½ pound sliced mushrooms in 2 tablespoons butter and add to the sauce for last 5 minutes of cooking.

Pirate Sauce for Pasta   for ½ to 1 pound pasta

La Salsa del Pirata   from Genoa

This sauce tastes best with fettuccine, but may be served with a heavier pasta such as linguine, rigatoni, or elbows. The olives give the sauce a deep purple-red color.

1 pound ripe plum tomatoes, chopped
4 tablespoons minced fresh basil, or 2 teaspoons dried basil
2 tablespoons butter
2 tablespoons olive oil
1 large garlic clove, mashed
4 anchovy fillets, drained and chopped, or 2 tablespoons anchovy paste
1 tablespoon drained capers

½ cup chopped pitted black Italian or Greek olives
¼ teaspoon dried oregano
1 to 2 teaspoons minced hot red pepper, or ½ teaspoon dried hot pepper flakes
salt
freshly ground pepper
1 pound freshly cooked fettuccine, *al dente*
freshly grated Parmesan cheese

Put the tomatoes into a saucepan with 2 tablespoons of the basil. Bring to the boiling point, reduce heat to low, and cook without a cover for 7 to 10 minutes, or until tomatoes are soft. Push them through a strainer or a food mill, or purée them in a blender or food processor. Reserve the tomato purée. Heat butter and olive oil in a heavy saucepan. Stir in garlic and anchovies or anchovy paste. Over medium heat, using a wooden spoon, blend garlic and anchovies into the butter and oil to make a thin paste; this takes about 3 minutes. Stir reserved tomato purée into the anchovy mixture and blend. Stir in capers, olives, oregano and hot pepper. Cook covered over low heat, stirring frequently, for about 20 minutes. Season with salt and black pepper to taste. Meantime, cook the fettuccine, drain, and place in a heated serving bowl. Spoon the sauce over the pasta and sprinkle with Parmesan. Serve immediately and very hot, with more Parmesan on the side.

Anchovy Sauce   about ¾ cup, for 1 to 1½ pounds pasta

Salsa di Alici   All-Italian

For pasta, fish, seafood and boiled meats.

¼ cup olive oil
4 tablespoons butter
2 to 4 garlic cloves, minced
1 or 2 cans (2 ounces each) anchovies, drained and chopped

¼ cup dry white wine
⅓ cup minced parsley

Heat together olive oil and butter. Add garlic and cook over low heat, stirring constantly, until garlic is soft but not browned. Add anchovies and wine and mix well. Cook over low heat, stirring frequently, until anchovies have dissolved into the sauce. Stir in the parsley.

Stracotto Meat Sauce

for 1 to 1½ pounds pasta

Lo Stracotto

from Rome

Stracotto means overcooked in Italian, and overcooking is the secret of this sauce, one of the best in Italian cookery. The sauce must be absolutely free of fat; the only way of achieving this is to choose lean, top-quality beef, and then trim off any fat. The mushrooms should be an imported dried species. Dry red wine may be used instead of Marsala, but Marsala gives the best flavor by far to the sauce.

2	ounces imported dried mushrooms	½	celery stalk, minced
1	pound boneless top-quality beef	½	cup minced parsley
		⅔ to 1	cup dry Marsala
8	tablespoons butter	1	cup beef bouillon
1	medium-size onion, minced		salt
			freshly ground pepper
1	medium-size carrot, minced	2	teaspoons grated lemon rind

Crumble the mushrooms into a bowl and soak them in lukewarm water to cover for 30 minutes. Cut the meat into the smallest possible dice but do *not* grind it; ground meat gives a different flavor and texture to the sauce. Heat the butter in a heavy saucepan. Add the onion, carrot, celery and parsley. Cook over medium heat, stirring constantly, for about 3 minutes. Add the meat. Cook, stirring all the time, until meat is lightly browned. Add mushrooms and their liquid, Marsala and bouillon. Season with salt and pepper to taste and add the lemon rind. Cover tightly. Simmer over lowest possible heat, preferably on an asbestos fireguard, for about 3 hours, or until the meat has almost dissolved. Stir frequently. The length of cooking time is necessary for the flavors to blend. The sauce should be thick; if too liquid, cook without a cover to allow for evaporation.

Chicken-Liver Sauce for Risotto, Polenta and Pasta
for ½ to 1 pound pasta

Salsa di Fegatini di Pollo   from Lombardy

¼ pound pancetta or
   blanched lean bacon,
   minced
1 small onion, minced
¼ cup minced parsley
1 tablespoon butter
1 pound chicken livers,
   trimmed and cut into
   halves or quarters

½ pound mushrooms, cut
   into thin slices
½ cup dry Marsala
½ teaspoon ground sage
   salt
   freshly ground pepper

On a chopping board, mince together to a paste the pancetta, onion and parsley. Or use a food processor. Put the butter and the pancetta mixture into a deep frying pan. Cook over medium heat, stirring constantly, for about 3 minutes. Add chicken livers and mushrooms. Cook over medium heat, stirring all the time, for 3 more minutes, or until the livers have browned. Stir in Marsala, sage, and salt and pepper to taste. Cook over low heat for 10 more minutes, stirring occasionally.

Pesto (Basil Sauce)

about 1 cup

Pesto alla Genovese

from Genoa

This famous sauce has now become popular in the United States. It is used as a pasta dressing or, by the spoonful, as an addition to soups and vegetables. Basil gives the Pesto its basic flavor. As with all classic recipes, there are individual interpretations. The recipe below is the standard one. Traditionally Pesto is made in a mortar with a pestle, by first grinding the dry ingredients together and then adding the olive oil. I think it is as good made in a blender or a food processor. It must be made with fresh basil which is chopped fine rather than puréed, and the texture should have the consistency of thick pancake batter.

2 cups loosely packed fresh basil leaves, no stems
2 garlic cloves, or to taste, chopped
¼ cup pine nuts (pignoli)
2 tablespoons grated Romano cheese and 2 tablespoons grated Parmesan cheese, or 4 tablespoons either Romano or Parmesan cheese

4 to 6 tablespoons olive oil
salt
freshly ground pepper

Put the basil, garlic and pine nuts into a blender container. Blend at low speed for a few seconds, until the ingredients are chopped. Add cheese and half of the olive oil, and blend again. Scrape the mixture down from the sides of the blender. Turn speed to low and trickle in remaining olive oil while blending. By hand, stir in salt and pepper to taste.

NOTE: Pesto keeps well refrigerated, in a jar, with a thin film of olive oil on the top. It also freezes well.

Professor Pezzo's Pesto

about ⅔ cup

Il Pesto del Professor Pezzo

from Genoa

The professor is a distinguished antiquarian who likes to cook. His Pesto is milder than the preceding one.

40 large basil leaves (1 to 1½ loosely packed cups)
boiling water
2 tablespoons pine nuts (pignoli)
2 tablespoons grated Pecorino cheese
2 tablespoons grated Parmesan cheese
2 tablespoons olive oil
2 tablespoons butter, softened
milk

Put the basil into a small bowl and cover with boiling water. Let stand for 3 minutes, drain, and put into a blender container. Put the pine nuts into a small bowl and cover with boiling water. Let stand for 3 minutes, drain, and add to the basil. Add cheeses, olive oil and butter. Add ¼ cup milk and blend at low speed. If the mixture is too thick, add a little more milk, 1 tablespoon at a time, and blend again at low speed.

NOTE: This Pesto does not keep and should be used when freshly made.

VARIATION: PARSLEY SAUCE
Substitute the basil by Italian parsley sprigs (no stems) and proceed as above.

Eggs and Cheese
Uova e Formaggi

Italian cooks treat eggs as ordinary food rather than as culinary works of art as French cooks do. Eggs are not eaten at breakfast, but as the first or main course of a meal, quite often as a frittata. This solid omelet always tastes good hot or cold. A frittata can be varied in scores of ways with ingredients apt to be always at hand, such as onions, bits of vegetables or leftover pasta. Another popular dish is *due uova al tegamino*, eggs fried in individual little baking dishes or frying pans, and eaten out of them; transferring the eggs even to a heated plate would cool them off too much for Italian tastes.

Italian cheese cookery is also uncomplicated. While there is not a great deal of it, cheese is a very important part of the diet, serving as the meat substitute when meat is a rare luxury. A few cheeses find their way into cooked foods; but most are table cheeses that are eaten with bread (not crackers) at the end of a meal, or out of hand for a simple lunch. Italian cheeses are few compared to the number of French cheeses and not nearly as fancy. Basically, they can be divided into three categories: grating cheeses, cooking cheeses, table cheeses; sometimes their uses overlap.

Parmesan, or Parmigiano-Reggiano, the full name of the king of grating cheeses, is one of the world's finest cheeses. In cooking, it does not toughen, or melt prematurely, or become stringy, and best of all, it enhances the flavors of every food it is combined with. Parmesan is golden yellow, compact and grainy. Deliciously sharp, but not biting when eaten fresh, it improves with age for grating, and also gets increasingly expensive. Parmesan has two ages: *vecchio* (old) and *stravecchio* (very old) as sold in the shops; the latter cheese is over two years old, costs more, and is better. Proper Parmesan has never been duplicated anywhere else in the world. I have tried all the American, Argentine and other so-called Parmesans, and had no use for them. Parmesan is made only in several officially designated areas around Parma in northern Italy, from mid-April to November. It belongs to the *grana* (grainy) family of cheeses, which resemble Parmesan in texture, flavor and usage; in Italy, they are specified by name, such as Grana Lodi, the grainy cheese from Lodi in Lombardy.

Pecorino is the generic Italian name for the other grating cheese, the one made from sheep's milk. In this country, and in others, it is known as Romano, from the Roman variety, though there are many other kinds of Pecorino, made throughout the country and qualified by their origin, such as Pecorino Sardo, the cheese from Sardinia. Most Italians have their favorite kind.

Pecorino is a much sharper and coarser cheese than Parmesan, with varied flavors, some milder, some stronger, depending on where it is made. Parmesan is the cheese of northern Italy, where lush pastures fatten the cows and enrich their milk, whereas Pecorino is the cheese of the south of Rome, where pastures will do only for sheep. Fresh Pecorino, made also in Tuscany and Umbria and wherever there are sheep, is a soft but not creamy white cheese, and very good to eat. Age hardens and sharpens Pecorino. It is less expensive than Parmesan.

Although some of the table cheeses, such as Fontina (p. 150) are used for cooking, the two main Italian cooking cheeses are Mozzarella and Ricotta. Mozzarella and its kin, Provatura, are soft, somewhat rubbery very white cheeses made originally around Naples from buffalo's milk. They are still made from buffalo's milk throughout the South, but since there are fewer buffaloes and more Mozzarella lovers, the cheese is also made from cow's milk, as it is in the United States. The buffalo's milk variety is more delicately but definitely flavored. Real Mozzarella must be eaten fresh. It is usually kept fresh in a bowl of water, dripping with its own whey, both in the shops and at home. This is very different in taste and texture from the solid, bland mass wrapped in plastic sold as Mozzarella in supermarkets. Fresh Mozzarella is worth seeking out in Italian groceries; for that matter, so are the imported originals of all the cheeses from Italy imitated in the United States. There is also a smoked, tan-colored Mozzarella, which is better for eating than for cooking.

Ricotta means "twice cooked," as it is, from the whey of other cheeses such as Mozzarella or Pecorino. The genuine Ricotta is made particularly in southern Italy, and very often from sheep's milk. It is a white, soft, unsalted curd cheese; more solid, salted Ricottas are also made in some parts of Italy. Italian Ricotta is more flavorful than the American version, which is usually sold in 15-ounce cartons. However, dishes calling for 1 pound (16 ounces) ricotta can be made with a 15-ounce container. (Cottage cheese, though of a similar consistency, is never a substitute for Ricotta.) In southern Italian cooking, Ricotta frequently fills the role of cream, or of dessert, eaten with sugar and fruit, or sprinkled with brandy or powdered (not instant) coffee.

Among the table cheeses, the best known are semisoft cheeses like Fontina (the best one of all), Bel Paese, Taleggio, Stracchino, Gruviera (the Italian Swiss-type cheese) and Gorgonzola, the rich and luscious "blue" cheese of Italy. There are many variations of these throughout Italy, often with local names or simply called "little cheeses," *caciotelle*. Most should be eaten fresh. Be sure to try Provolone, which is now made from cow's rather than buffalo's milk. It is the cheese in amusing shapes, tied with string, that hangs from the ceilings of Italian grocery stores.

Fried Eggs with Mozzarella

Uova Fritte alla Mozzarella   All-Italian

This dish should be cooked in individual little baking or frying pans, called *tegamino* in Italy.

butter	salt
eggs	freshly ground pepper
mozzarella cheese, cut into ¼-inch slices	

Generously butter as many individual baking dishes as needed. Line the bottom with mozzarella slices. Break 1 or 2 eggs over the mozzarella in each dish. Sprinkle with salt and pepper. Cook covered over low heat until cheese is melted and eggs are set. Serve hot.

Scrambled Eggs with Peppers   3 servings

Uova Strapazzate con i Peperoni   from Tuscany

2 large green, red or yellow sweet peppers	6 eggs, slightly beaten
3 tablespoons olive oil	salt
1 garlic clove	freshly ground pepper
½ teaspoon crumbled dried oregano	6 slices of Italian bread, freshly toasted

Trim the peppers, remove seeds and membranes, and cut peppers lengthwise into ¼-inch strips. Wash and dry them between sheets of kitchen paper. Heat the oil in a large deep skillet. Add garlic and cook until garlic is browned; discard. Add peppers and oregano. Cook over medium heat, stirring constantly, for 3 to 4 minutes. Stir in the eggs and season with salt and pepper to taste. Cook over low heat, stirring gently, until the eggs are set to the desired consistency. Serve hot, with toasted Italian bread.

Fried Mozzarella

8 appetizer or 4 luncheon servings

Mozzarella Fritta · All-Italian

As a luncheon dish, serve with a well-flavored tomato or mushroom sauce, and with a green salad.

1 pound mozzarella
   cheese
salt
freshly ground pepper
flour
2 eggs, slightly beaten

1 cup fine dry bread
   crumbs,
   approximately
olive oil for frying
lemon wedges

If mozzarella is the fresh Italian kind that is kept moist in water, dry it carefully between sheets of kitchen paper. Cut the mozzarella into ½-inch slices, then cut the slices into fingers; there should be about 20 of them. Lay the cheese fingers on wax paper side by side and sprinkle lightly with salt and pepper. Coat the fingers on all sides with flour and shake off excess flour. Dip fingers first into beaten eggs, then into bread crumbs, shaking off excess bread crumbs. Place on a plate lined with wax paper and chill for 1 to 2 hours. Heat about 2 inches of olive oil in a large, deep frying pan or shallow saucepan. The oil should be heated to 375°F. on a frying thermometer. Fry the cheese fingers, a few at a time, until they are pale golden, turning them over to ensure even frying. Drain on kitchen paper. Place on a serving dish lined with a napkin and serve immediately, very hot. Garnish with lemon wedges.

Fondue

6 servings

La Fondua Piemontese   from Piedmont

This is one of the most famous and most delicious of Piedmontese dishes. It must be made with Fontina, a soft buttery cheese from Piedmont which can be bought in all good cheese shops. Do not substitute Swiss or Gruyère cheese because they make a different-tasting dish. An aromatic white truffle from Alba enhances the *fondua* but is not as essential as the Fontina cheese. White Alba truffles reach the United States in the fall and good Italian groceries sell them, worth their weight in gold.

1 pound Fontina cheese, cut into small dice	freshly ground pepper
milk	1 white truffle, sliced thin (optional)
2 tablespoons butter	hot buttered toast fingers
4 egg yolks, well beaten	
salt	

Put the Fontina into a deep narrow bowl and add milk to cover. Steep for at least 4 hours or overnight. Melt but do not brown the butter in the top part of a double boiler over, not in, hot water. Add egg yolks, cheese, the milk in which it was steeped and a little salt and pepper. Cook over low heat, stirring constantly with a wooden spoon, until eggs, cheese and milk have combined into a thick, smooth cream. There must not be any stringiness in this dish, and it must not be put over direct heat for this reason. Pour the *fondua* into heated soup plates, scatter the truffle slices over each serving, and serve with hot toast fingers. Or pour it over the toast fingers. Eat hot.

Piedmont (Turin)

Mozzarella Skewers   6 servings

Crostini alla Mozzarella   from Rome

In Rome, these are made with the Provatura, a mozzarella-like small soft cheese, the size of an egg.

1 pound mozzarella cheese salt freshly ground pepper Italian bread or stale firm white bread	½ cup (¼ pound) butter, melted in a small saucepan 6 to 8 anchovy fillets, drained and chopped

Cut mozzarella into ½-inch slices and sprinkle each slice lightly with salt and pepper. Cut as many slices of bread as there are of mozzarella, plus 6 extra, all of the same thickness and size as the cheese. Beginning and ending with a slice of bread, thread the mozzarella and bread slices on 6 skewers. Preheat a baking dish deep and wide enough to let the skewers rest on its sides without touching the bottom of the dish. Bake in a preheated hot oven (400°F.) for 10 to 15 minutes, or until bread is toasted and mozzarella beginning to melt. Baste occasionally with a little melted butter. While the skewers are cooking, stir anchovies into the melted butter and place over low heat. Cook, stirring constantly, until the anchovies have dissolved into the butter. Place each skewer on a heated dining plate and pour a little anchovy butter over it. Serve very hot.

Mozzarella Tart

4 servings

Tortino di Mozzarella

from Naples

4 to 6 thick slices of
      stale firm white bread
      or white or whole-
      wheat Italian bread
1 cup milk,
      approximately
½ pound mozzarella
      cheese, or more to
      taste, sliced

4 eggs
½ cup freshly grated
      Parmesan cheese
salt
freshly ground pepper

Butter an 8- or 9-inch deep pie pan or baking dish generously.
Cut the crusts off bread slices and line the bottom and about
½ inch of the sides of the pie pan with the bread. Sprinkle the
milk over the bread. Depending on the kind of bread, you may
need a little less or a little more milk; the bread should be soft
and moist but still retain its shape. Place mozzarella slices over
the bread, covering it. Beat together eggs and Parmesan
cheese. Taste for saltiness; if necessary add a little more salt
and season with plenty of pepper. Pour the mixture over the
bread and mozzarella. Bake in a preheated hot oven (400°F.)
for about 10 minutes, or until the egg mixture is puffed up and
golden and the mozzarella melted. Serve hot.

NOTE: For a richer dish, place slices of prosciutto or other ham
over the mozzarella before adding the egg mixture.

Potato and Cheese Tart   4 servings

Tortino di Patate   from Puglia

3 medium-size potatoes,
   boiled, peeled and
   mashed
1 cup flour
   salt
   freshly ground pepper
½ cup olive oil
1 cup drained canned
   tomatoes

½ pound mozzarella
   cheese, cut into ½-
   inch dice
¼ cup freshly grated
   Parmesan cheese
1 tablespoon crumbled
   dried rosemary

Mix together to a smooth paste mashed potatoes, flour, and salt and pepper to taste. Using your hands is the easiest way. Generously oil a 9-inch flat baking dish. Line the bottom with the potato mixture, making a layer ¼ to ½ inch thick. Sprinkle with half of the olive oil. Top with tomatoes, mozzarella and Parmesan, and sprinkle with rosemary and remaining oil. Bake in a preheated hot oven (400°F.) for 20 minutes, or until browned. Serve hot as a first course or as a side dish with cold meats.

Spinach and Ricotta Soufflé

4 to 6 servings

Souffle di Spinaci e Ricotta

from Naples

2 pounds fresh spinach, or 2 10-ounce packages frozen whole-leaf spinach	salt
	freshly ground pepper
	⅛ teaspoon grated nutmeg
½ cup olive oil	1 tablespoon butter
1 pound ricotta cheese	3 tablespoons fine dry bread crumbs
3 eggs, separated	
⅓ cup freshly grated Parmesan cheese	

Trim the spinach and wash it in several changes of cold water; drain. Put spinach with the water that clings to its leaves into a big pot. Cook covered over high heat for 3 to 4 minutes, or until spinach is wilted. Do not overcook or spinach will lose flavor. Drain spinach thoroughly, pressing it with a wooden spoon against the sides of the strainer. Finally, squeeze dry with your hands. Chop the spinach. Heat the olive oil in a frying pan and cook the spinach in it, stirring constantly, for about 3 minutes. Combine ricotta, egg yolks, Parmesan, salt and pepper to taste and nutmeg, and mix well. Beat until light. Add spinach and mix well. Butter a 6-cup baking dish and coat it with the bread crumbs. Beat egg whites until stiff and carefully fold them into the spinach mixture. Turn into the baking dish. Cook in a preheated moderate oven (350°F.) for about 30 minutes, or until the top is golden. Serve hot.

NOTE: A lighter soufflé will result if 4 egg whites are used. However, if they are not handy, it is not worthwhile breaking up 1 egg for this purpose since the soufflé is perfectly good as it is.

Frittata   All-Italian

Frittata, the Italian equivalent of an omelet, is flat, rather like a pancake, and well cooked on the outside yet still moist inside. A frittata can be made of eggs only, or with cheese or herbs or vegetables. A frittata is a splendid way of using up the dabs of cooked vegetables that linger in refrigerators.

A proper frittata is made only with eggs and enrichments, but if you are short of eggs, you can cheat a little, the way it is done in Italy. For each missing egg, and for not more than 2 eggs, blend together 2 teaspoons flour with 3 tablespoons water or milk. The result is not perfect, but it will do in an emergency.

To cook a frittata, heat a frying or omelet pan over medium heat and add just enough oil or butter to coat the bottom and sides lightly. Add the egg mixture and reduce the heat. Cook until the bottom is golden brown and well set, lifting the edges with a fork to allow the uncooked egg on top to trickle into the pan. Put a plate or a lid slightly larger than the frying pan over the frittata. Hold the plate down with one hand. With the other hand hold the frying pan handle and turn the frying pan and plate upside down, so that the frittata, cooked side up, will be on the plate or lid. Slide it, uncooked side down, back into the frying pan and cook until golden brown and set. Then slide it onto a serving plate, cut into wedges, and serve hot or cold as a first or main course.

If you are making little frittate, you can turn them over with a pancake turner, just as you would a pancake. It is impractical to make a very large frittata and better to make two when needed. The thickness of a frittata should be around ¾ to 1 inch.

Pepper and Potato Frittata

6 servings

Frittata di Peperoni e Patate

from Rome

¼ cup olive oil
2 medium-size green, red or yellow sweet peppers, seeded and cut into thin strips
1 medium-size onion, cut into very thin slices
2 medium-size potatoes, cooked, peeled and cut into thin slices

2 tablespoons water
6 to 8 eggs, slightly beaten
salt
freshly ground pepper

Heat the olive oil in a large, deep frying pan. Add the peppers and cook over medium heat, stirring constantly, for 3 to 4 minutes, or until peppers are soft. Add onion and potatoes and mix with a fork. Reduce heat and cook, stirring frequently, until onion is soft. Beat the water into the eggs and season with salt and pepper. Pour eggs over the vegetables and stir with a fork to distribute vegetables. Cook over low heat until golden brown and set on one side as described on page 156; turn and cook until golden brown and set.

Mozzarella and Bread Cubes Frittata   4 servings

Frittata con la Mozzarella e Crostini   from Naples

6 eggs, beaten
  salt
  freshly ground pepper
4 ounces mozzarella, cut
  into ¼-inch cubes

4 slices of firm white
  bread
5 tablespoons butter

Combine eggs, salt and pepper to taste and the mozzarella; mix well. Trim crusts from the bread and cut slices into ¼-inch cubes. Heat the butter in a frying pan large enough to hold the frittata. Add bread cubes and sauté over medium heat until golden and crisp. Pour the egg mixture over the bread cubes and distribute bread and mozzarella cubes. Cook over low heat until golden brown and set on one side as described on page 156; turn and cook until golden brown and set.

Zucchini Frittata   3 or 4 servings

Frittata di Zucchine   from Tuscany

6 eggs
¼ cup minced parsley
½ teaspoon dried sage
  salt
  freshly ground pepper

3 tablespoons olive oil
3 small zucchini, trimmed
  and cut into thin
  slices (do not peel if
  young)

Beat together the eggs, parsley, sage, and salt and pepper to taste. Heat the olive oil in a deep frying pan. Add zucchini and cook over high heat, stirring with a fork, until zucchini is soft and golden but still firm. Reduce heat. Add the eggs and stir with a fork to distribute zucchini. Cook over low heat until frittata is golden brown and set on one side as described on page 156; turn and cook until golden brown and set.

Spaghetti Frittata   4 to 6 servings

Frittata di Pasta   All-Italian

Leftover pasta either plain or sauced can be used in this dish.

6 eggs	¾ cup freshly grated
2 teaspoons salt	Parmesan cheese
freshly ground pepper	6 tablespoons butter
1 cup chopped	½ to 1 pound cooked
mozzarella cheese	pasta, freshly cooked
(optional)	or leftover

Beat together the eggs, salt, pepper to taste, mozzarella and Parmesan. Heat the butter in a frying pan and add the spaghetti. Pour the egg mixture over the spaghetti and mix well with a fork. Cook until eggs are set and the frittata is golden brown and crisp at the bottom. Serve hot.

NOTE: There is no need to turn this frittata.

Baked Spinach Frittata   4 servings

Frittata di Spinaci al Forno   from Lombardy

3 pounds spinach,
   washed, drained and
   shredded
3 tablespoons butter
   salt
   freshly ground pepper
   dash of Tabasco

6 eggs
⅓ cup freshly grated
   Parmesan cheese
   Mushroom or Tomato
   Sauce (optional) (pp.
   288 and 135)

Cook spinach in the water that clings to it for 3 minutes. Drain spinach and squeeze it dry in a strainer, using a wooden spoon or hands. Return spinach to the saucepan. Add butter and cook over high heat, stirring constantly, until spinach is well coated with butter. Remove from heat and season lightly with salt (the cheese will be salty) and pepper to taste and the Tabasco. Beat together the eggs and Parmesan cheese. Butter a medium-deep 8-inch baking dish or deep 8-inch pie pan on all sides. Place it over direct low heat for a few moments to heat it up. Pour in half of the egg mixture. Cook like an omelet for 2 minutes, or until set. Remove from the heat. Spread the spinach evenly on top of the eggs. Top the spinach evenly with remaining eggs. Bake in a preheated moderate oven (350°F.) for about 15 minutes, or until set and golden. Unmold on a plate and serve hot with Mushroom or Tomato Sauce. Or serve lukewarm, with sliced tomatoes.

Onion Frittata   3 or 4 servings

Frittata di Cipolle   All-Italian

3 tablespoons olive oil   6 eggs, beaten
2 large onions, cut into   salt
   very thin slices   freshly ground pepper

Heat the olive oil in a deep frying pan. Add onion slices and cook over low heat, stirring frequently, until onions are very soft and golden; do not brown. Season the eggs with salt and pepper and pour over onions. Stir with a fork to distribute onions. Cook until golden brown and set on one side as described on page 156; turn and cook until golden brown and set.

Baking Powder Pizza   1 pizza, about 11 inches across

Pizza Fatta in Casa

Real pizza should be made with bread dough. In Italy bakers will sell you plain dough, and in America some ethnic bakers will do the same, though rather unwillingly. This is where a baking powder dough for pizza comes in; it is very acceptable indeed.

FOR THE DOUGH:
1 cup flour
½ teaspoon salt
1 tablespoon baking powder

3 tablespoons olive oil
⅓ cup water
olive oil

Into a bowl sift the flour, salt and baking powder. Combine 3 tablespoons oil and the water and stir the mixture into flour. Beat until well mixed; this should take less than 1 minute. Turn onto a lightly floured baking board or counter. Knead for about 1 minute, or until the dough forms into an easily handled ball. Pat the dough ball flat and place in the center of a lightly greased baking sheet; the sheet must be flat, without borders. Pat the dough into a circle ⅛ inch thick in the center and ⅜ to ½ inch thick at the edges. This is easiest done using fingers and starting from the center of the circle in a radiating pattern. The dough is very pliable; if it tears, the holes are easily repaired by pushing other dough over them. Brush olive oil around the edges of the circle.

FOR THE FILLING:
1¼ to 1½ pounds peeled fresh plum tomatoes or very well drained canned plum tomatoes (avoid canned if possible)
1 tablespoon salt
¼ pound fresh whole-milk mozzarella, approximately, to make 1 cup diced

freshly ground pepper
1 2-ounce can flat anchovy fillets, well drained
1 teaspoon dried oregano
3 tablespoons olive oil

To peel the tomatoes, spear each on a fork and dip quickly into rapidly boiling water; slip off peel. Do not let the tomatoes lie in the boiling water, or they will cook. Cut the tomatoes into halves. Or else, cut the tomatoes into halves and place them skin side down in a frying pan, preferably Teflon-coated. Place the pan over low to medium heat; after 3 to 4 minutes shake the pan to avoid sticking and scorching. The skins will begin to wrinkle. Remove from the heat and slip the skins off. With either method, turn the tomatoes into a colander and sprinkle them with the salt. Toss carefully in order not to break them. Stand the colander in the sink to let the tomatoes throw off excess liquid; this is important or you will have a wet pizza. If they are large, cut the tomato halves into 2 or 3 pieces. Dice the mozzarella.

TO ASSEMBLE:
A freshly baked pizza should be a lovely crazy quilt of white, red and golden brown, contrasting the soft shapes of tomatoes and cheese with the more clearly defined shape of the anchovies. By the spoonful, place the tomatoes in little round heaps in a circle on the bottom of the dough that has been patted out on the baking sheet. Fill the spaces between the tomatoes with the diced mozzarella, reserving a few pieces to scatter over the whole pizza. Season with freshly ground pepper. Cut the anchovies into halves and place them on both tomatoes and mozzarella. Sprinkle with oregano and olive oil. Bake in a preheated hot oven (450°F.) for 10 to 15 minutes, or until the dough is browned and the filling melted and bubbly.

NOTE: Most pizza, especially commercial pizza, is made with tomato sauce rather than with the vastly preferable fresh tomatoes. Reason: it is easier and quicker. There is a world of difference in the flavor of fresh tomatoes. It is essential that the oven be thoroughly preheated.

Fish and Seafood

Pesce e Frutta di Mare

Fish and seafood are an important part of the diet of a country surrounded on three sides by the sea. Italian fish is Mediterranean fish and enormously varied, depending on the various waters of that big inland sea, open to the Atlantic only at Gibraltar. Mediterranean fish markets are riots of shapes, colors and textures; they must be seen to be believed. I recommend a visit to the fish markets of Genoa or Venice, Palermo or Bari, to mention a few of the great Italian markets.

Fish, once Italy's cheapest protein food, is no longer as cheap or plentiful as it used to be and often as expensive as meat. Thanks to modern fishing methods the waters around Italy are being fished out; Sicily, for example, once abounded in giant tuna with its beef-red flesh. Today, tuna is becoming increasingly scarce.

Italian fish cookery is basically simple because it relies on the natural flavors of totally fresh ingredients. There are no complicated sauces or garnishes in regional Italian cooking. Popular eating does not require them although restaurants may offer more elaborate fish dishes. Generally speaking, little fish are fried; medium fish are boiled, broiled, baked stuffed or unstuffed as whole fish; and big fish get sliced and broiled or cooked in a simple sauce. Fish and seafood are added to other foods such as rice in Venice and in the North, and to pasta and vegetables in southern Italy. All kinds of fish are made into soups, with the addition of wine, or tomatoes and herbs. Their flavor depends on the local fish and they are not structured soups.

Italian fish has few counterparts in American waters. Even when the species are the same, their flavor will vary because of the different waters and climates. However, river and lake fish such as trout, pike or perch are more similar to our own, but again their flavor differs because of different surroundings.

Italians eat everything that comes out of the water, while Americans shudder at certain fish, such as eels and skate. In this chapter, I have chosen only recipes that can be duplicated with our own fish, omitting the more exotic kinds and indulging in my own preferences.

Grilled Fish   4 servings

Pesce in Gratella   All-Italian

This is a standard method for any small saltwater fish such as perch, mackerel, or red or gray mullet.

2 sea bass, each weighing about 1½ pounds, ready for cooking	salt
	freshly ground pepper
	dash of Tabasco
⅔ cup olive oil	lemon wedges
juice of 2 lemons	

Place the fish in a shallow baking dish. Combine olive oil, lemon juice, salt and pepper to taste and Tabasco, and pour over the fish. Cover and refrigerate for 1 to 2 hours. Drain and reserve marinade. At cooking time, oil the broiler grill and place the fish on it. Broil in a preheated broiler about 3 inches from the source of heat for 3 to 5 minutes on the first side. Turn carefully and broil for 5 to 6 minutes on the second side, or until the fish flakes; broiling time depends on the size of the fish. Baste the fish with the reserved marinade two or three times on each side during cooking time. Transfer carefully to a heated serving dish and pour the pan juices over the fish. Garnish with lemon wedges and serve hot or cooled, but not chilled.

Small Fish au Gratin   4 to 6 servings

Pesce Ammolicato   from Southern Italy

This dish is most frequently made with fresh anchovies, which are very small. In this country, it can be made with small sardines, smelts, whiting or any lean or oily small fish.

2½ pounds small fish
 1 cup olive oil
    salt
    freshly ground pepper
⅓ cup fresh white bread
    crumbs

3 garlic cloves, mashed
¼ cup minced parsley
1 teaspoon dried oregano
    (optional)
    lemon wedges

Scale and gut the fish, removing heads, tails and backbones. Place them in one layer in an oiled shallow baking dish. Sprinkle with ¾ cup of oil and season with salt and pepper to taste. Heat remaining oil in a small frying pan. Add bread crumbs, garlic, parsley and oregano and mix well. Cook, stirring constantly, for 2 to 3 minutes. Cool a little and spread the mixture evenly over the fish. Bake in a preheated hot oven (400°F.) for 10 to 15 minutes, depending on the size of the fish. Serve hot or cooled, with lemon wedges.

Fish Baked with Potatoes and Cheese 4 to 6 servings

Pesce al Forno from Southern Italy

This is a basic recipe for any lean, firm-fleshed fish. In Puglia, it is made with *orata* (gilt-head bream), a fish not available in the U.S. As in most Italian fish recipes, whatever fish is at hand can be used. I have made it successfully with red snapper.

1 cup olive oil
1 red snapper, 3 pounds, whole or in steaks, ready for cooking
1 cup minced parsley
¼ cup minced basil, or 1 tablespoon dried basil (optional)

6 medium-size potatoes, peeled and cut into thin slices
⅔ cup freshly grated Pecorino cheese
salt
freshly ground pepper

Pour about ⅔ cup oil into a baking dish that will hold the fish and potatoes. Sprinkle with half of the parsley and basil and top with half of the sliced potatoes and grated cheese. Place the whole fish or the fish steaks on the potatoes. Sprinkle with remaining parsley and top with remaining potatoes and cheese. Drizzle remaining oil over the top and season with salt and pepper. Cook in a preheated hot oven (400°F.) for 20 to 30 minutes, or until fish flakes and potatoes are tender.

Fish Stew or Fish Sauce   6 servings

Ciuppin   from Liguria

Since American fish is different from Mediterranean fish, any fish stew is bound to taste different in the United States. This dish, from Genoa, can be made into a soup or a stew, depending on the amount of liquid, or can be puréed into a sauce for pasta or rice.

1 medium-size carrot, chopped	3 or 4 large tomatoes, peeled and chopped
1 medium-size onion, chopped	6 cups boiling water, approximately
1 celery stalk, chopped	4 pounds mixed fish,
⅔ cup parsley sprigs, chopped	approximately (haddock, flounder,
⅓ cup chopped fresh basil, or 1 tablespoon dried basil	cod, perch, pollack, snapper, mackerel, bluefish, bass, etc.),
4 flat anchovy fillets, drained and chopped, or 1 tablespoon anchovy paste	boned and cut into pieces salt freshly ground pepper slices of Italian bread
½ cup olive oil	fried in oil
1 cup dry white wine	

Mince together into a paste the carrot, onion, celery, parsley, basil and anchovies. Heat the olive oil in a large heavy saucepan. Add the minced mixture and cook over medium heat, stirring constantly, for about 4 minutes, or until vegetables are soft. Add wine and cook for about 5 minutes longer. Reduce heat. Add tomatoes and 2 cups of the water if you want to make a fish sauce, 4 cups water if you want to make stew, and 6 cups water if you want to make soup. Bring to the boiling point, reduce heat, and simmer covered for 10 minutes. Add fish and simmer covered for 10 to 15 minutes, or until fish is tender. Season with salt and pepper. If to be used as a stew, serve as is over slices of Italian bread fried in oil. If to be used as a soup or a sauce, strain through a sieve or purée in a blender or in a food processor.

Brook Trout Baked with Marsala 4 servings

Trote al Marsala from Sicily

---

4 trout, about 10 ounces each, ready to cook	1 garlic clove, mashed
½ lemon	4 tablespoons minced parsley
salt	juice of ½ lemon
freshly ground pepper	⅓ cup dry Marsala
3 tablespoons olive oil	
½ cup fresh white bread crumbs	

Rub the trout lightly with the lemon on all sides. Sprinkle lightly with salt and pepper. Place side by side in an oiled shallow baking dish. Heat the olive oil in a frying pan. Remove from heat and stir in bread crumbs, garlic and parsley. Sprinkle the mixture over the trout. Sprinkle with lemon juice. Cook in a preheated moderate oven (350°F.) for 10 minutes. Sprinkle with the Marsala and cook for 5 to 8 minutes longer, or until fish flakes, basting frequently with the pan juices. Serve hot.

Striped Bass with Caper Sauce   4 servings

Spigola in Salsa di Capperi   from Liguria

FOR THE COURT BOUILLON:

10 or more cups water
¼ cup vinegar, preferably
   white-wine vinegar
1 small onion
1 celery stalk with leaves,
   cut into pieces
1 small carrot, scraped
3 parsley sprigs
2 bay leaves
1 sprig of fresh thyme, or
   ½ teaspoon dried
   thyme

½ lemon, sliced
2 tablespoons salt
1 dozen peppercorns
1 whole striped bass,
   approximately 3
   pounds
3 tablespoons butter
1½ tablespoons flour
3 egg yolks, beaten
½ cup drained small
   capers or chopped
   big capers

TO MAKE THE COURT BOUILLON:

Use a fish poacher, or a baking pan large and deep enough to
hold the fish submerged in the liquid. Or if necessary, cut the
fish into halves and cook in two parts. Combine the water,
vinegar, onion, celery, carrot, parsley, bay leaves, thyme,
lemon, salt and peppercorns. Bring to the boiling point. Cover
and reduce heat. Simmer for about 30 minutes. Strain the court
bouillon or remove the vegetables with a slotted spoon.

Carefully lower the fish into the liquid. Make sure that the
liquid barely simmers and that it covers the fish. If necessary,
add more hot water than the original 10 cups, bringing all the
liquid back to simmering. Poach the fish in the barely simmering water for 20 to 30 minutes, or until fish flakes when
touched with a fork. Using pancake turners or big cooking
spoons, carefully remove the fish from the liquid. Reserve the
liquid. Place the fish on a heated serving dish. Carefully pour
off any fish liquid that may have seeped into the dish; the fish
should be as dry as possible.

While the fish is poaching, prepare the sauce. Heat the butter
in a small saucepan and stir in the flour. Cook over low heat,
stirring constantly, until the mixture is smooth. Strain ½ cup
of the reserved liquid and stir it into the butter-flour mixture.

Cook, stirring constantly, for 3 to 4 minutes, or until the sauce is smooth and thickened. Remove sauce from the heat. Carefully, and a very little at a time, stir in the egg yolks, stirring until smooth after each addition. Stir in the capers and mix well. Spoon sauce over the fish, coating it; the liquid from the capers will thin the sauce sufficiently to make it cling to the fish. Serve immediately.

Halibut with Peas
4 to 6 servings

Palombo con Piselli
from Rome

This way of cooking fish is found throughout Italy.

¼ cup olive oil	salt
4 thick slices of halibut, approximately 2 pounds	freshly ground pepper
	1 pound fresh peas, shelled, or ½ 10-ounce package frozen peas
2 tablespoons minced parsley	
1 garlic clove, minced	
½ cup white vinegar	
2 pounds tomatoes, peeled, seeded and chopped	

Heat the olive oil in a large, heavy frying pan. Add fish slices and cook quickly over high heat, turning once, until golden brown. Add parsley, garlic and vinegar. Cook until the pan liquid has almost entirely evaporated. Add tomatoes and season with salt and pepper. Simmer covered for 5 minutes. Add the peas. Continue simmering for another 10 to 15 minutes, or until the fish flakes. Do not overcook. Transfer fish carefully to a heated serving dish, using a pancake turner, and pour the sauce over it. Serve with boiled potatoes.

Mackerel Sailor's Fashion   4 servings

Sgombro alla Marinara   from Puglia

1 mackerel, 3 pounds,
   split and cut into 4
   slices, or 2 smaller
   mackerel, split
   flour
4 tablespoons olive oil
3 or 4 garlic cloves
½ hot red pepper pod,
   seeded, or to taste
   salt

freshly ground pepper
grated rind of 1 lemon
juice of 1 lemon
¾ cup dry white wine
2 tablespoons minced
   fresh basil
3 tablespoons minced
   parsley
   lemon wedges

Dry the fish between sheets of kitchen paper. Coat the fish with flour on all sides and shake off excess flour. Heat the oil in a frying pan that will hold the 4 slices of mackerel, or divide it between 2 frying pans. Use 3 tablespoons of oil if only one pan is used, or use 2 tablespoons in each of 2 frying pans. Add garlic and hot pepper, again dividing the quantities if 2 frying pans are used. Cook over medium heat until garlic and pepper pod are browned. Remove garlic and pepper with a slotted spoon and discard. Place fish in the oil. Over high heat cook for 2 minutes, or until fish is golden; turn and cook for 2 more minutes on the other side. Reduce heat to low. Sprinkle with salt, pepper, lemon rind and juice, wine, basil and parsley. Cover and simmer for 2 minutes on one side. Turn and simmer for 2 minutes on the other side, or until fish flakes when tested with a fork. With a pancake turner, transfer fish slices to a heated serving platter. Bring pan juices to the boiling point, cook for 1 minute, and pour over fish. Serve immediately, with lemon wedges.

Marinated Sea Bass Baked in White Wine

4 to 6 servings

Branzino al Vino Bianco   from Venice

Any firm-fleshed fish may be used for this dish.

½ cup olive oil   flour
    juice of 2 lemons   4 tablespoons butter
2 garlic cloves, mashed   ½ cup dry white wine
2 bay leaves, crumbled   1 tablespoon lemon juice
    salt
    freshly ground pepper
1 sea bass, 3 pounds,
    ready for cooking
    and cut into 6 slices

Combine olive oil, lemon juice, garlic, bay leaves and a little
salt and pepper in a bowl and mix well. (Do not use aluminum
or other metal.) Place fish slices in the marinade, making sure
that the slices are coated with marinade on all sides. Cover and
refrigerate for 2 hours, turning once. Drain fish and dry it thoroughly between sheets of kitchen paper. Sprinkle lightly with
flour. Heat the butter in a deep frying pan large enough to
hold the fish slices in one layer. Over medium heat cook the
slices until golden on both sides, turning them over once with
a pancake turner. Season lightly with salt and pepper. Reduce
heat and add the wine. Cover tightly and simmer for 10 to 15
minutes, or until fish flakes easily. Transfer carefully to a
heated serving dish and spoon the pan juices over the fish.
Sprinkle lemon juice over the fish before serving.

Stuffed Baked Sardines   6 servings

Sarde a Beccaficcu   from Sicily

This famous Sicilian dish is named after a tiny bird, which the stuffed and rolled-up sardines are said to resemble.

6 tablespoons olive oil	1 garlic clove, mashed
1 cup fine fresh white	2 tablespoons minced
bread crumbs	parsley
½ cup currants, plumped	salt
in warm water and	freshly ground pepper
drained	dash of Tabasco
½ cup pine nuts (pignoli),	2½ pounds fresh sardines
chopped fine	(about 24 sardines)
¼ cup capers, drained	6 large bay leaves,
¼ cup pitted black olives,	shredded
chopped fine	¼ cup fresh lemon juice

Heat 2 tablespoons of the oil in a medium-size frying pan. Add ½ cup of the bread crumbs, stir well, and cook until crumbs are golden. Turn crumbs into a bowl. Add the currants, pine nuts, capers, olives, garlic, parsley, a little salt and pepper and the Tabasco. Mix until very well blended, using first a spoon and then the hands. Cut off the heads of the sardines, and scale them. Split them open on the belly side almost to the tail, but not dividing them completely. Carefully pull out innards and backbones. Wash sardines one by one in salted cold water and dry carefully between sheets of kitchen paper. Lay sardines opened flat on their backs. With the back of a knife, spread each sardine with a thin layer of the stuffing. Roll up the sardines, working toward the tail; if necessary, fasten with food picks. Oil a baking dish that will hold the sardines in one layer. Place the fish in tight rows, packed against each other, with the tails sticking up. Scatter the shredded bay leaves over the sardines. Top them with remaining ½ cup bread crumbs and sprinkle with remaining 4 tablespoons olive oil. Bake in a preheated hot oven (400°F.) for 15 to 20 minutes, or until crumbs are browned and fish will flake; baking time depends on the size of the fish. Serve immediately, sprinkled with the lemon juice.

NOTE: As in all traditional dishes, the ingredients and their amounts are not rigid; some people put cheese or anchovies into the dish.

Swordfish or Tuna Skewers

5 servings

Spiedini di Pesce

from Tuscany

1½ pounds swordfish, tuna or salmon, cut into 1-inch cubes

10 bay leaves, cut into halves or quarters, or 1 teaspoon ground bay leaf

35 fresh sage leaves

6 or more tablespoons olive oil

salt

freshly ground pepper

5 or 6 slices bacon, cut into 1-inch strips

4 tablespoons butter, melted

2 tablespoons fresh lemon juice

Dry fish cubes. Mix 5 bay leaves, 5 sage leaves, olive oil and salt and pepper to taste, making a paste. Rub into fish cubes and refrigerate them for 1 hour. On a skewer, place a piece of fish, a bay leaf, a strip of bacon and a sage leaf. Repeat until all the fish is used; these amounts make 5 skewers, each with 6 cubes of fish. Place in a single layer under the broiler or on a charcoal grill, about 3 inches from the source of heat. Brush with the butter. Cook for 5 or 6 minutes on the first side. Turn, brush again with butter, and broil for 4 or 5 more minutes on the second side, or until fork pierces fish easily. Remove from heat and place on a heated serving dish. Sprinkle with lemon juice and serve immediately.

Swordfish in Tomato Sauce

6 servings

Pesce Spada al Forno   from Sicily

½ cup olive oil
2 garlic cloves, mashed
1 cup minced parsley
¼ cup minced fresh basil
   (optional)
2 cups homemade
   Tomato Sauce (see
   p. 135, or 2 8-ounce
   cans canned tomato
   sauce

2 tablespoons lemon juice
   salt
   freshly ground pepper
3 pounds swordfish, or 2
   slices, each
   approximately 1½
   pounds and 1½
   inches thick

Heat the olive oil and add garlic, parsley and basil. Simmer over low heat for about 7 minutes. Add Tomato Sauce and cook for 5 more minutes. Stir in lemon juice and season with salt and pepper to taste. Place the fish in one layer in an oiled baking dish and pour the sauce over the fish. Cook in a preheated hot oven (400°F.) for 20 to 25 minutes, or until fish flakes when tested with a fork. Serve hot.

Sicily (Agrigento)

Swordfish Steaks with Lemon and Capers

6 servings

Pesce Spada al Limone   from Sicily

6 swordfish steaks, 1 inch
thick, about 3 pounds
total weight
salt
freshly ground pepper
flour

½ cup olive oil
juice of 2 lemons
½ cup minced parsley
½ cup drained capers
(chopped if large)

Dry the fish steaks between sheets of kitchen paper. Sprinkle both sides with a little salt and pepper. Dip each steak into flour, coating all sides and shaking off excess flour. Heat half of the olive oil in one deep frying pan and the other half in another deep frying pan. Add the steaks. Each piece should lie flat and not touch another piece. Cook over medium heat for about 8 minutes. Turn the steaks with a wide spatula. Cook for 6 to 8 minutes longer. The fish should be golden brown and crusty on both sides. Carefully transfer fish to a heated serving platter, laying the steaks side by side. Sprinkle each with a little lemon juice, a little parsley, and some capers. Serve immediately, very hot.

Marinated Swordfish or Tuna Steak   4 servings

Pesce al Forno Piccante   from Southern Italy

1 large swordfish or tuna
   steak, 1 to 1½ inches
   thick, about 2 pounds
   salt
   freshly ground pepper

1 tablespoon minced
   fresh fennel greens or
   wild fennel, or 2
   teaspoons fennel
   seeds, crushed

MARINADE:
¾ cup olive oil
3 tablespoons fresh
   lemon juice, or to
   taste
2 garlic cloves, mashed

GARNISH:
   lemon slices
⅓ cup capers, drained

Sprinkle fish on both sides with salt and pepper to taste and minced fennel. Place in an ungreased shallow baking dish. Combine olive oil, lemon juice and garlic and pour it over the fish. Cover and refrigerate for 3 to 4 hours. Baste occasionally with the marinade and carefully turn the fish over once. Cook covered in a preheated moderate oven (350°F.) for 15 minutes. Uncover and cook for about 15 minutes longer, basting frequently with the marinade, until fish will just flake. Garnish with lemon slices and sprinkle with the capers. Serve the fish from the baking dish, hot or cooled but not chilled, topping each serving with a little of the marinade.

Swordfish, Tuna or Halibut Steaks with Fennel

4 to 6 servings

Pesce al Finocchio   from Tuscany

2   pounds fish steaks,   6   tablespoons butter
      each 1 to 1¼ inches   salt
      thick   freshly ground pepper,
    flour   preferably white
1   teaspoon dried fennel   pepper
      seeds for each fish   1   cup dry white wine
      steak, approximately   lemon wedges
    olive oil

Dry the fish steaks between sheets of kitchen paper and coat
them evenly on all sides with flour. Scatter fennel seeds over
each steak and press them firmly into the fish. With a pastry
brush, brush each steak on both sides with olive oil. Heat the
butter in a large frying pan. Add as many steaks as pan will
hold side by side, without touching each other. Over medium
heat, cook for about 5 minutes on each side, turning over once,
or until fish flakes easily when tested with a fork. Sprinkle
lightly with salt and pepper. With a pancake turner, transfer
cooked fish to a heated serving platter and keep warm in a low
oven. Pour the wine into the frying pan. Cook over high heat,
stirring constantly, until wine is reduced by a third. Pour the
sauce over the fish and serve with lemon wedges.

Scungilli Marinara   4 servings

Scungilli alla Marinara   from Naples

Wrongly called conch, scungilli are knobbed whelk. This dish is frequently used as a pasta sauce.

1½ to 2 pounds scungilli
      pulp, cut into thin
      slices
      water
¼   cup olive oil
2   garlic cloves
1   small onion, diced
1   medium-size celery
      stalk, diced
1½ cups drained canned
      tomatoes
½   cup dry white wine

1   tablespoon tomato
      paste diluted with 2
      tablespoons warm
      water
½   teaspoon salt
½   teaspoon dried oregano
¼   teaspoon dried basil
1   large bay leaf
¼   teaspoon hot red
      pepper flakes, or to
      taste

Over medium heat, boil the scungilli in water to cover for 15 minutes. Drain. In a deep frying pan, heat the oil. Add the scungilli and all other ingredients. Simmer covered over low heat, stirring frequently, until scungilli are tender. Serve hot with a green vegetable or as a pasta sauce.

Fried Squid   4 servings

Calamaretti Fritti   from Rome and Southern Italy

Squid is not a pretty creature, but this recipe has the virtue of making it look neutral. Properly cooked, squid is tasty, delicate and tender.

2   pounds small squid   1   cup olive oil
    flour   lemon wedges
    salt

Have the squid dressed and skinned, or do it yourself. Wash under running cold water and dry thoroughly with kitchen paper. Cut the squid into ¼-inch rings and the tentacles into strips. Dip into flour seasoned with salt. Heat the olive oil to 375°F. on a frying thermometer. Drop in the squid without crowding the pieces. Fry until golden brown and crisp. Drain on kitchen paper. Serve hot with lemon wedges.

How to Dress Squid

It is quickly and easily done. Have ready a good-sized bowl filled with lukewarm water. Working *in* the water, remove the insides from the pocketlike part of the fish. Pull out the spinal bone. Remove the purple outside skin. Remove the ink bag from each side of the head, as well as the eyes and the hard core in the center of the tentacles. Rinse thoroughly under running cold water until free of all sand and grit. The dressed fish should be milky white. Dry with kitchen paper before using.

Mussels Marinara

4 servings

Cozze alla Marinara

from Puglia

2 quarts mussels
2 tablespoons olive oil
2 garlic cloves, crushed
1 cup chopped ripe
   tomatoes, or 1 cup
   canned plum
   tomatoes, drained

½ teaspoon dried oregano
1 cup dry white wine
   salt
   freshly ground pepper
¼ cup minced parsley
   toasted bread slices

Scrub mussels with a stiff brush under running cold water and remove the beards. Discard any that are open. Heat the olive oil in a saucepan large enough to hold the mussels. Add garlic and cook until garlic is browned; discard garlic. Add tomatoes, oregano, wine, and a little salt and pepper. Cook without a cover over medium heat for 5 minutes. Drop in the mussels. Cover tightly and cook for 5 to 10 minutes, or until all the shells are opened. Shake the pan frequently to prevent sticking. Remove the mussels to a heated deep serving dish and keep warm. Strain the cooking liquid over the mussels. Sprinkle with the parsley before serving with slices of toasted bread.

Shrimps in Cream   4 servings

Gamberetti alla Crema   from Venice

2 pounds medium-size shrimps	freshly ground pepper
4 tablespoons butter	1 cup heavy cream
½ teaspoon salt	2 garlic cloves, mashed
	¼ cup minced parsley

Shell and devein shrimps. Heat the butter in a large deep frying pan. Add shrimps and sprinkle with salt and pepper to taste. Over high heat, and shaking the pan frequently to prevent sticking, cook shrimps for about 5 minutes. While shrimps are cooking, combine cream, garlic and parsley in a small saucepan. Bring to the boiling point but do not boil. Pour cream over shrimps and cook for 1 more minute, shaking the pan all the time.

Broiled Lemon Shrimps   4 to 6 servings

Gamberetti alla Griglia   from Venice

2 pounds jumbo shrimps (25 to 28 shrimps)	4 garlic cloves, mashed
1 cup olive oil	¼ cup minced parsley
¾ cup fresh lemon juice	½ teaspoon hot red pepper flakes
grated rind of 1 lemon	

Shell and devein shrimps. Carefully wash shrimps and dry them between sheets of kitchen paper. Place shrimps in a large bowl; do not use metal or aluminum. Combine all other ingredients and mix well; pour over shrimps. Toss carefully with a fork to make sure that shrimps are coated with marinade on all sides. Cover and refrigerate for 4 hours or overnight, turning over once. Line the broiler pan with foil and preheat broiler. Drain shrimps, reserving the marinade. Place shrimps on the broiler pan. Broil about 3 inches from the source of heat on one side. Turn and broil for 3 to 5 minutes on the other side. Baste frequently with the marinade. Serve hot or chilled.

Meat

La Carne

Italian meat cookery was limited by the facts that meat was a luxury and that fuel was scarce. Compared to the country's size, there is little pasture, and much of the country is too hot for ordinary cattle. The heat-resistant cattle strains are new and seldom found in Italy which still has to import a large part of her meat. Cattle was also too costly an investment for small farmers; thus the prevalence of smaller animals such as pigs, sheep and goats which cost and demand little. Fuel also has always been expensive. As in other fuel-poor countries like China and Japan, it was essential in Italy that food could be cooked quickly, hence the endless small cuts of beef and veal. Even today a roast of beef or veal, a leg of lamb or a pork roast are considered serious, festive eating.

Italian meat is different from ours—both the meat itself and the way it is butchered. Italian meat is much leaner than the marbled American meat we admire and also has less water content. Italian butchers generally cut against the natural muscle divisions and the meat is usually deboned, making Italian cuts look unfamiliar to American eyes. Furthermore, meat cuts vary in different parts of Italy, or similar cuts are called by different names, with the exception of the *filetto*, the fillet.

Veal is the preferred Italian meat, basically because it is expensive to raise cattle to adult size. Adult cattle serve as work animals in some parts of Italy to this day. There are differences in veal: *vitello* is a calf that is two or three months old; in theory, it should never have been fed anything but its mother's milk. *Vitella* is really a heifer and *vitellone* is neither a baby nor an adult, but a teenager, virtually without fat. *Vitellone* makes the most famous Italian meat dish, Bistecca alla Fiorentina, which Italians like extremely underdone.

Lamb is cooked in many different ways throughout Italy, roasted on the spit or in the oven, or hunter style (*cacciatora*), to name a few. Lamb-eating country begins in Rome and goes south. The famous *abbacchio* of Rome is baby lamb, unweaned or only milk-fed; little legs of baby lamb weighing only two pounds are a common sight as are the skinned whole baby lambs that are sold especially at Eastertime.

Italian pork, unlike ours, is firm and lean. It is best when acorn-fed as in Umbria, which is famous for its pigs and pork products. Now, with improved butcher-shop hygiene and modern refrigeration methods, pork is sold throughout the year. But when I was a child in Rome, pork was sold only in the winter months, and the butcher shops sold straw hats in the summer. Whole, large roast pigs, called *porchetta*, seasoned with herbs and cooked over a spit, are a traditional sight in Central Italy where they appear in carts in the streets, especially on market days. The butcher-roaster will slice off any weight for the customer, who either takes the meat home or eats it on the spot in a sandwich made with a roll. The meat is moist and tasty, but on the fatty side.

Popular, regional Italian meat cookery is much more interesting than the short-order veal dishes or the eternal *bistecca*, a steak featured on restaurant menus. A highly individual flavor is achieved in home cooking due to the variety and quantity of herbs used, the cooking with prosciutto, and the piquancy provided by anchovies, capers, raisins and pine nuts. The meats of northern Italy are more plainly cooked, while the dishes with herbs and tomatoes and piquant ingredients come mainly from the South.

A word about innards. Wherever people are poor, all kinds of animal organs are eaten because meat is meat. This used to be so in Italy, where innards were part of ethnic cooking. But improved living conditions are changing this. Last summer, traveling through Italy, I made it a point to look at butchers' shops. Few had the ineffable tangle of miscellaneous innards I remember from my youth; only liver and kidneys, which are considered respectable innards, were prevalent. They are no longer cheap either, as progress marches on and on and on.

Stuffed Meat Roll

6 to 8 servings

Farsumagru   from Sicily

No one knows why this rich meat roll is called *farsumagru*, meaning "false lean," since it is neither. Have the butcher pound the meat to the thickness of ½ inch, or if you do it yourself, place the meat between two sheets of wax paper and pound it with a rolling pin, a filled bottle or a meat mallet.

1½ to 2 pounds lean veal or beef, such as boneless sirloin, in one piece
salt
freshly ground pepper
¼ pound mozzarella cheese, cut into ½-inch dice
2 sweet Italian sausages, skinned and chopped, or ¼ pound prosciutto, chopped, or lean pancetta, chopped, or lean salt pork, blanched and chopped

3 hard-cooked eggs, sliced
2 tablespoons minced parsley
1 garlic clove, minced
¼ teaspoon dried oregano
¼ cup olive oil
1 small onion, sliced
1 small carrot, sliced
2 bay leaves
¾ cup dry white wine
½ cup water

Season the meat on both sides with salt and pepper. In a bowl, combine mozzarella, sausages, hard-cooked eggs, parsley, garlic and oregano. Mix well; this is best done with the hands. Spread the filling on the meat slice and roll it up. Make sure none of the filling shows or it will ooze out during cooking. Tie the meat roll in several places with kitchen string to hold it together, and tie it also once lengthwise. Rub it on all sides with a little salt and pepper and with about 2 tablespoons of the olive oil. Place the meat roll in a baking pan; the pan should be no larger than necessary to hold the meat roll comfortably. Pour remaining oil into the baking pan, coating the bottom and sides with the oil. Arrange onion slices, carrot slices and bay leaves around the meat. Add ¼ cup of the wine and the water. Cook in a preheated moderate oven (350°F.) for about 1 hour, basting occasionally with the pan juices. When the meat is cooked, turn off the oven, transfer meat to a serving platter, and keep it warm in the oven. Take as much fat as possible off the pan juices. (Quantities of fat vary depending on whether sausages, prosciutto, pancetta or blanched salt pork have been used.) Add remaining wine and scrape up all the brown bits from the bottom. Cook over high heat, stirring constantly, for about 3 minutes. Strain the pan juices through a sieve, or purée them in a blender, and keep warm. Slice the meat, remove the strings, and arrange in overlapping slices on the serving platter. Drizzle pan juices over the meat. Serve hot, or cold.

Sautéed Small Steaks

Fettine in Padella   All-Italian

Thin little slices of boneless and very lean beef are standard family eating because they are thrifty. In this country, sandwich steaks and the rather amorphous little cuts of sliced beef sold in the supermarkets come closest to an Italian *fettina*, which in no way resembles an American steak.

One way of tenderizing the meat is to marinate it in a little olive oil at room temperature for 15 to 60 minutes.

To cook the beef, have it very sliced very thin and trimmed of all fat. Heat a very little olive oil in a frying pan. Over medium heat, cook the meat very quickly, for 2 to 3 minutes on each side. Season with salt and pepper and serve with the pan gravy and with lemon wedges. The flavors of the olive oil, meat and lemon juice are very agreeable together, and this is an easy way of utilizing inexpensive pieces of meat.

For a change, the steaks may be coated with a little flour; thin the pan gravy with a drop of wine before pouring it over the meat.

Beef Stew with Peas   6 servings

Spezzatino in Stufato   All-Italian

This is a basic Italian beef stew. In some regions, people leave out peas and add more tomatoes, depending on personal tastes. If you buy the standard American stew cuts (chuck, rump, brisket, or "beef stew") buy about ½ pound more since you will have to trim the meat of all fat; 2½ pounds of chuck, minus fat, come to 2 pounds. The recipe is easily halved or doubled.

2 tablespoons olive oil
1 medium-size onion, cut into thin slices
1 garlic clove, minced, or to taste
2 pounds beef stew, cut into 1½-inch pieces and trimmed of all fat
½ glass robust dry red wine
salt
freshly ground pepper

2 cups chopped, peeled, and seeded tomatoes, or drained canned plum tomatoes
2 tablespoons chopped fresh basil, or 1 teaspoon dried basil
1 to 1½ cups shelled fresh or frozen peas

Heat the olive oil in a large heavy saucepan. Add onion and garlic and cook, stirring constantly, until onion is soft. Add the meat. Over high heat, brown on all sides; the meat should be truly brown, the color of mahogany. Reduce heat to medium and add the wine. Cook, stirring frequently, until wine has evaporated and meat is almost dry. (Since the water content of meat varies, it is impossible to say how long this will take.) Reduce heat to low and add the tomatoes. Season with salt and pepper to taste and mix well. Simmer covered for about 1 hour, or until meat is almost tender; cooking time depends on the quality of the meat. Or preferably, cook in a low oven (300°F.) for 1½ hours, or until meat is almost tender. Stir occasionally. Add basil and peas and mix well. Cook for another 5 to 10 minutes, or until peas are tender. Do not overcook; even stews can be mushy.

Beef Stew with Onions

6 servings

Stufato alla Siciliana   from Sicily

4 tablespoons olive oil	2 garlic cloves
2½ pounds top round of beef, trimmed of all fat and cut into 2-inch pieces	2-inch piece of stick cinnamon
	6 whole cloves
	2 bay leaves
1 cup dry red wine	½ teaspoon dried oregano
2 cups canned plum tomatoes	salt
	freshly ground pepper
2 tablespoons tomato paste	⅓ cup minced parsley
2 pounds small whole white onions, peeled	

Heat 3 tablespoons of the olive oil in a heavy casserole or Dutch oven. Over high heat, brown the meat in it on all sides. Add ½ cup of the wine, reduce heat to low, and simmer for 10 minutes. Stir in tomatoes and tomato paste and continue to simmer covered. Heat remaining oil in a frying pan, and brown the onions in it very quickly. Add onions to meat, together with garlic, cinnamon, cloves, bay leaves, oregano and remaining wine. Season to taste with salt and pepper. Cover the pan and simmer over very low heat for 2 to 3 hours, stirring occasionally. The sauce should be a thick purée. Sprinkle with parsley before serving.

Piquant Pot Roast

4 to 6 servings

Manzo alla Certosina   from Lombardy

1 tablespoon butter	⅓ cup beef bouillon or water
1 tablespoon olive oil	
2 slices of lean bacon, cut into strips	4 to 6 flat anchovy fillets, drained, or 1 to 2 tablespoons anchovy paste
2 pounds beef round, trimmed of all fat	
salt	½ cup minced parsley
freshly ground pepper	1 teaspoon dried basil
⅛ teaspoon grated nutmeg	

Combine butter, olive oil and bacon in a saucepan just large enough to hold the meat. Heat and cook for 2 minutes. Add beef, and brown over high heat on both sides. Reduce heat to low and season meat with salt and pepper to taste and nutmeg. Add 2 tablespoons of beef bouillon. Simmer covered for about 1 hour, turning over twice. Check the liquid in the pan. Since meat contains a fair amount of water, there should be enough liquid to come up about ½ inch on the roast. If there is more liquid, cook without a cover in a low (325°F.) oven. Combine anchovies, parsley and basil and mash into a paste. Spread over the meat. Continue cooking for 30 more minutes, or until meat is tender, turning over once. Again, check the liquid as above; if necessary, add more bouillon, 1 tablespoon at a time. At the end of cooking, there should be 1 to 1½ cups pan juices. Transfer the roast to a platter and keep warm. Skim the grease off the gravy and keep warm. Slice the meat, not too thin, and lay it in overlapping slices on a heated platter. Strain the gravy over the meat. Serve hot or cold with boiled or mashed potatoes.

NOTE: Since the water content of meat varies greatly, it is impossible to give exact directions as to the amount of bouillon needed or the time required for cooking without a cover to reduce pan juices.

Pot Roast with Vinegar and Capers 6 to 8 servings

Manzo all'Aceto   from Lombardy

This is an old recipe, popular among the Milanese working classes. It is simple and tasty. Serve with mashed potatoes.

2	pounds beef round		salt
½	cup olive oil		freshly ground pepper
⅓	cup red-wine vinegar	½	cup drained capers

Trim all fat off the meat. Place meat, olive oil and vinegar in a saucepan that will just hold it and that has a tight-fitting lid. Season with a little salt and pepper. Simmer over low heat for about 2 hours, or until meat is tender. Slice the meat and place it in overlapping slices on a heated serving dish. Ladle a few soupspoonfuls of pan juices over the meat to keep it moist, and sprinkle with the capers. Good hot or cold.

NOTE: Chill remaining pan juices and strain off the fat. Use juices for soups, sauces or stews.

Beef Braised in Red Wine   6 servings

Bue al Barolo   from Piedmont

The best and most famous of all Italian pot roasts is marinated and cooked in Barolo, one of the very finest full-bodied red wines of Italy. Barolo is slow-maturing and compares favorably with the rich wines of the Rhône Valley. It is worth while making this dish with Barolo, but if not available, use another full-bodied wine such as a French Côte Rôtie, or a best-quality California Pinot Noir or Petite Sirah.

FOR THE MARINADE:
1 bottle Barolo or other full-bodied red wine (3 cups)
2 large carrots, chopped
2 medium-size onions, chopped
1 bouquet garni (¼ teaspoon dried thyme, 4 sprigs of parsley, 4 large celery leaves, 2 bay leaves, 3 cloves, ½ teaspoon whole peppercorns, wrapped and tied in cheesecloth)
1 teaspoon salt

FOR THE POT ROAST:
1 boned and rolled lean beef pot roast (rump, sirloin tip or eye of round), 2½ to 3 pounds
4 tablespoons butter
¼ cup brandy
salt
freshly ground pepper

Place all marinade ingredients in a bowl large enough to hold the meat; do not use aluminum. Mix the ingredients well. Add the beef and turn it in the marinade. Cover and refrigerate for no less than 6 hours and a maximum of 3 days, turning several times. Drain the meat, reserving the marinade. Dry the meat between sheets of kitchen paper; if not dry, it will not brown. Heat the butter in a Dutch oven. Over moderately high heat, brown the meat on all sides; this will take about 10 minutes. Pour off any fat in the Dutch oven. Pour brandy over the meat and ignite it. When flames have died down, add reserved marinade and vegetables. Bring to the boiling point, then reduce heat to lowest possible; you may have to use a flame guard. Cover the Dutch oven and simmer for 2 to 3 hours, or until meat is tender. Turn the meat every hour. Remove meat to a hot platter and keep warm. Remove and discard the *bouquet garni* from the pan juices. Blend the pan juices in a blender, or strain them through a sieve, to make a smooth sauce. Taste the sauce and add salt and pepper, if necessary. Return meat to the Dutch oven and pour sauce over it. Cover and continue cooking over lowest possible heat for 1 more hour, or until meat is very tender. Transfer meat to a heated serving platter and remove any strings. Slice across the grain in medium-thick slices. Pour the sauce over the meat. Serve very hot, with a dish of polenta or mashed potatoes.

Saltimbocca

4 to 6 servings

Saltimbocca   from Rome

The word means, literally, "they jump into your mouth."

2 pounds veal scaloppine, each piece about 5 inches square	3 tablespoons butter salt freshly ground pepper
1 teaspoon dried sage	½ cup dry white wine
¼ pound thin slices of prosciutto	

Sprinkle veal slices with sage. Cover each slice with a slice of prosciutto and trim this to the same size as the meat. (Reserve trimmings for sauces.) Pin prosciutto slices to the veal slices with food picks. Heat the butter in a large frying pan. Add meat in one layer, and cook for 2 to 3 minutes. Turn with a pancake turner and cook until golden on both sides. Season to taste. Place the slices of meat, ham side up, on a heated serving platter and remove the picks. Keep meat warm. Add the wine, scrape the brown bits from the bottom, and bring quickly to the boiling point. Pour the sauce over the meat and serve immediately.

Lemon Beef   6 to 8 servings

Manzo al Limone   from Lombardy

4	large juicy lemons	½	cup (¼ pound) butter
4	pounds beef round, in		salt
	one piece		freshly ground pepper
½	cup olive oil	2	cups cold beef bouillon

Cut 1 lemon into thin slices; remove any seeds. Squeeze another of the lemons and reserve juice. Trim all fat off the meat. Rub meat on all sides with the lemon slices, and reserve them. Put half of the lemon slices on the bottom of a bowl (not metal) large enough to hold the meat. Place meat on top of these lemon slices and top it with remaining lemon slices. Combine oil with the juice of the squeezed lemon and sprinkle over the meat. Cover the bowl and refrigerate for 3 days, turning the meat over once a day. At cooking time, drain the meat, reserving the marinade and discarding the lemon slices. Dry the meat thoroughly between sheets of kitchen paper. Place it in a baking dish and sprinkle lightly with salt and pepper. Cook meat in a preheated hot oven (400°F.) for about 1½ hours, or until it is tender. Combine marinade and beef bouillon. Baste the meat with some of the mixture every 10 minutes. If the pan liquid cooks down too much, add a little of marinade-bouillon mixture to prevent scorching. When the meat is cooked, transfer it to a hot serving dish, and keep hot. Squeeze remaining 2 lemons. Bring the pan juices to the boiling point and stir in the lemon juice. Check the seasoning and add, if necessary, a little salt and pepper. Cook the pan juices down to gravy consistency. There should be a moderate amount of it. Slice the meat, arrange it in overlapping slices on a heated serving platter, and spoon the gravy over it. Serve with a green vegetable, such as green beans or broccoli.

Teresa's Meat Loaf

6 to 8 servings

Il Polpettone di Teresa

from Rome

Teresa was one of my mother's cooks.

¼ cup dried mushrooms
warm water
2 slices of white bread,
crusts trimmed off
⅓ cup milk
½ pound beef round,
ground
½ pound lean pork,
ground
¼ pound Italian salami,
ground
1 medium-size onion,
minced

2 garlic cloves, mashed
½ cup minced parsley
1 teaspoon dried oregano
grated rind of 1 lemon
2 eggs
⅓ cup freshly grated
Parmesan cheese
⅛ teaspoon Tabasco, or to
taste
salt
freshly ground pepper
1 lemon, cut into thin
slices

Soak mushrooms in warm water to cover for 15 minutes. Drain and chop. Combine mushrooms and all other ingredients except sliced lemon. Mix well with a spoon and then with your hands. Place the mixture in a loaf pan, 9 × 5 × 2¾ inches. Top with the lemon slices. Cover with aluminum foil. Bake in a preheated moderate oven (350°F.) for 1 hour; uncover and bake for 15 more minutes. Serve hot or cold.

Piquant Meatballs with Capers

4 to 6 servings, 15 to 18 meatballs

Polpettine ai Capperi   from Southern Italy

1   to 1½ pounds beef,
    ground
2   eggs
¼   cup capers, chopped
⅓   cup freshly grated
    Parmesan cheese
2   tablespoons fine dry
    bread crumbs
¾   teaspoon salt

    freshly ground pepper
½   teaspoon ground
    marjoram
    flour
1   tablespoon butter
2   tablespoons olive oil
⅓   to ½ cup dry white
    wine
    lemon wedges

Combine beef, eggs, capers, Parmesan, bread crumbs, salt, pepper to taste and marjoram. Mix very thoroughly. With hands dipped into flour, shape the meat mixture into 1½-inch balls. Flatten balls out a little for quicker cooking. Coat meatballs with flour, shaking off excess flour. Heat butter and oil in a large frying pan. Cook the meatballs over medium heat for 5 to 7 minutes, turning once; cooking time depends on the thickness and desired doneness of the meat. A few minutes before meatballs are done, sprinkle them with the wine and reduce heat, letting the meat absorb the wine. Serve hot, with the pan juices poured over the meat, or cold. Accompany with a tossed green salad.

Quick Veal Scaloppine with Marsala   6 servings

Scaloppine al Marsala   All-Italian

2	pounds veal scallops, sliced ¼ inch thick and pounded thin salt	freshly ground pepper flour
		4 tablespoons butter
		1 cup Marsala wine
		juice of ½ lemon

Trim veal scallops so they are all approximately the same size. Reserve trimmings for sauces. Sprinkle a little salt and pepper on each slice of meat. Coat veal scallops on both sides lightly with flour, shaking off excess flour. Heat half of the butter in a large heavy frying pan until it is hot but not browned. Add a few scallops, taking care not to crowd them. Cook over medium heat for 2 to 3 minutes. Turn and cook for 2 minutes, or until golden on both sides. Transfer cooked scallops to a heated serving dish. Cover with a lid or a plate and keep warm in a low oven. Add remaining butter to the frying pan and continue to cook scallops until all have been cooked and are being kept warm. Add Marsala to the frying pan, and scrape up all the brown bits at the bottom. Cook over high heat until wine becomes syrupy. Remove from heat and stir in lemon juice. Spoon the sauce over the meat. Serve immediately, with a green vegetable such as beans, or in the Italian manner, with a tossed green salad.

Fancy Veal Birds   4 to 6 servings

Uccelletti alla Golosa   from Rome

3 large eggs
2 tablespoons freshly
   grated Parmesan
   cheese
⅓ teaspoon salt
   freshly ground pepper
4 tablespoons butter
8 equal-size slices of thin
   veal, each measuring
   5 to 6 inches in
   diameter
8 teaspoons tomato paste

½ pound mozzarella
   cheese, cut into 8
   slices
1 teaspoon dried oregano
   flour
1 tablespoon butter
2 tablespoons olive oil
3 tablespoons dry
   Marsala or sherry
¾ cup beef or chicken
   bouillon

In a small bowl, beat eggs with Parmesan, salt, and pepper to taste. Heat about ½ teaspoon butter in a very small frying pan. Add about 2 tablespoons of the egg mixture. Over medium heat, cook quickly for ½ minute on one side, then turn and cook for about 15 seconds on the other. There should be 8 small, flat omelets. Place the veal slices side by side on wax paper. Spread each with 1 teaspoon tomato paste. Top with a small omelet and top the omelet with a slice of mozzarella. Sprinkle ⅛ teaspoon oregano on each. Roll up the veal slices and fasten with food picks. Dust each lightly with flour on all sides. Heat butter and olive oil in a large, heavy frying pan. Add the veal birds in one layer, and season lightly with salt and pepper. Over medium heat, cook the veal birds, turning them over several times with a fork, for 10 to 15 minutes, or until golden brown on all sides. Add Marsala and bouillon. Simmer over low heat, without a cover, for about 15 more minutes, turning veal birds over frequently, until the pan juices are reduced by about half. Transfer the meat to a heated serving dish and spoon the sauce over it. Serve hot, with mashed potatoes.

Veal Birds from Genoa

6 servings

Saltimbocca alla Genovese from Liguria

2 pounds veal scallops, sliced ¼ inch thick and pounded thin
salt
freshly ground pepper
fresh sage or dried sage or ground sage

½ pound thin slices of prosciutto, approximately
flour
4 tablespoons butter
1 cup Marsala or dry white wine
½ cup hot beef bouillon

Trim the veal scallops so that they are approximately all of the same size. (Save trimmings for sauces.) Sprinkle a little salt and pepper on each slice of meat. Place 2 or more leaves of fresh or dried sage on each veal slice, or sprinkle about a scant ¼ teaspoon dried sage on each. Cut prosciutto to the same size as the veal slices. (Save trimmings for sauces.) Top each veal slice with a prosciutto slice. Roll up and secure with food picks, or tie with kitchen thread. Coat each veal roll lightly with flour, shaking off excess flour. Divide butter between two large frying pans; heat it without browning. Over medium heat, cook veal rolls for about 5 minutes, or until golden brown on all sides. Reduce heat and add ½ cup Marsala and ¼ cup beef bouillon to each frying pan. Cover frying pans and cook for 5 to 10 minutes longer; cooking time depends on the size and thickness of the rolls. Shake the pans frequently to prevent sticking. If necessary, add a little more beef bouillon; there should be 1 to 2 tablespoons sauce for each veal bird. Transfer the cooked veal birds to a heated serving dish and spoon the sauce over them. Serve immediately and very hot, with a tossed green salad.

Veal Cutlets Milanaise   6 servings

Cotolette di Vitello alla Milanese   from Milan

The real Milanaise veal cutlets are cutlets on the bone, that is, rib chops. *Scaloppine*, slices of veal cut from the fillet or leg, can be cooked in the same manner, and often are, since the meat is more readily available, hence the confusion between the two. The bread crumbs must be fine, dry and unflavored; they should be made at home from stale, crustless Italian bread, which assures a crisp, dry breaded cutlet. Commercial bread crumbs are generally made from American bread which contains shortening or even milk; they are never as firm or as dry as those made from the plain, crusty long Italian loaves, which contain no shortening, the reason they go stale so quickly. The blender makes bread crumbs in seconds; then they are sifted to get a uniform product. The cutlets or *scaloppine* should be prepared for cooking as short a time as possible before the actual cooking, so that the meat will not soak up the bread crumbs, which makes a limper cutlet. This, incidentally, holds true for all breaded and fried foods.

6 veal rib chops, about 1 inch thick	approximately
	3 tablespoons butter
2 eggs, beaten	2 tablespoons olive oil
½ teaspoon salt	lemon wedges
2 cups fine dry bread crumbs,	

Loosen the meat around the bone of the chop by pulling it a little and bending it back a little. Lay a piece of wax paper over the meat of each chop and pound it to about the thickness of ½ inch. Nick the edges of the meat to prevent curling during cooking. Combine eggs and salt in a shallow dish. Put bread crumbs on a dinner plate. Dip the chops, one at a time, into the beaten egg, shaking off excess moisture, coating them on both sides. Then dip them into the bread crumbs, making sure they are well coated on both sides, and shaking off excess crumbs. Lay chops side by side on a piece of wax paper. Heat butter and oil in a large, heavy frying pan. Cook the chops in a single layer until they are golden brown on one side. Turn them with tongs and cook until golden brown; the tongs will keep the golden crust intact. Again using the tongs, transfer cooked chops to kitchen paper to drain them; work quickly. Place drained chops in a heated serving dish. Keep hot until all the chops are cooked. Serve with lemon wedges and a tossed green salad.

NOTE: Properly cooked breaded cutlets are very good cold, but not chilled.

Veal Piccata

4 to 6 servings

Piccata di Vitello

All-Italian

2 pounds veal round or leg, cut into ¼-inch-thick slices and pounded thin for scaloppine salt freshly ground pepper	flour ½ cup (¼ pound) butter ¼ cup dry white wine 3 tablespoons fresh lemon juice ¼ cup minced parsley

Lay the scallops on a large platter. Sprinkle lightly with salt and pepper. Let stand at room temperature for 10 minutes. Dip into flour, coating on all sides and shaking off excess flour. Since scallops must be cooked in a single layer, divide the butter between two large frying pans and heat. Add the veal and cook over moderately high heat for about 2 minutes. Turn and cook for about 2 minutes longer. Transfer scallops to a heated serving dish and keep hot. Combine pan juices from the 2 frying pans in one, scraping up all the brown bits from the bottom. Stir in the wine and cook over high heat, stirring constantly, until wine has evaporated. Remove from heat and stir in the lemon juice and parsley. Pour over the veal and serve hot.

Veal Chops Braised with Wine and Lemon

4 servings

Braciole di Vitello al Vino e Limone   from Tuscany

As made by our Tuscan cook Isolina who knows that I like things cooked with lemon.

2 tablespoons olive oil
2 tablespoons butter
4 medium-size onions, cut into thin slices
4 loin veal chops, each about 2 inches thick, lightly floured
salt

freshly ground pepper
4 lemon slices, about ¼ inch thick, without rind
1 cup dry white wine
1 tablespoon minced fresh sage, or 1 teaspoon dried sage

Heat olive oil and butter in a large, deep frying pan that will hold the chops in one layer. Over medium heat, cook the onions until they are soft and golden; do not brown. Add the veal chops, increase heat to high, and brown chops on both sides. Reduce heat to low. Season the meat with salt and pepper. Place 1 lemon slice on each veal chop. Pour wine over meat and sprinkle with the sage. Simmer covered over very low heat for 45 to 60 minutes, turning once. Check the moisture; if too little, add a little hot water, 2 tablespoons at a time. If there is too much pan liquid, transfer cooked chops to a heated serving platter and keep warm, then reduce the pan juices over high heat. In any case, pour pan juices over the meat before serving.

Old-Fashioned Veal Stew

4 to 6 servings

Stufatino di Vitello all'Antica

from Tuscany

---

2 tablespoons olive oil	1 celery stalk, sliced
2 pounds lean boneless veal, trimmed free of fat and gristle and cut into 1½-inch cubes	3 medium-size tomatoes, peeled, seeded and chopped
1 tablespoon butter	1 medium-size carrot, sliced
¼ cup minced prosciutto or lean bacon	1 artichoke, cut into thin slices (see p. 248)
¼ cup minced parsley	½ cup dry white wine
½ medium-size onion, minced	½ cup chicken or beef bouillon
1 garlic clove, minced	salt
1 leek, white and green parts, sliced	freshly ground pepper

Heat the olive oil in a deep frying pan. Over high heat, quickly brown the veal in the oil. In a casserole or deep saucepan, combine butter, prosciutto, parsley, onion and garlic. Cook over medium heat, stirring constantly, for about 3 minutes. Add the veal and all the other ingredients. Simmer covered over low heat for about 25 minutes, or until meat is tender. Check the moisture; if necessary, add a little more bouillon; if too liquid, cook without a lid to reduce. Serve with boiled potatoes.

NOTE: A handful of peas or a few sliced mushrooms may be added to the stew.

Cold Veal and Tuna Fish   6 to 10 servings

Vitello Tonnato   All-Italian

This may be part of an antipasto or the main dish of a summer meal, with a salad. As with all popular dishes, there are small variations.

2 tablespoons olive oil
3 to 4 pounds boneless rolled leg of veal
1 large onion, sliced
1 can (2 ounces) anchovy fillets, drained
⅓ cup minced sour pickle
1 can (7 ounces) tuna fish, drained
1 cup dry white wine
2 garlic cloves, cut into halves
2 celery stalks, one with leaves, cut into thin slices

1 medium-size carrot, cut into thin slices
3 parsley sprigs
½ teaspoon dried thyme
1 teaspoon salt
¼ teaspoon freshly ground pepper
2 tablespoons lemon juice mayonnaise
¼ cup capers, drained

In a Dutch oven or a deep pot with a tight-fitting cover, heat the oil. Add the meat and over high heat quickly brown it *very lightly* on all sides. Add onion, anchovy, pickle, tuna, wine, garlic, celery, carrot, parsley, thyme, salt and pepper. Bring to the boiling point, skim, and reduce heat to very low. Simmer covered, skimming when needed, for about 2 hours, or until meat is tender but not mushy. Remove the meat and place it in a large bowl, not aluminum. Purée pan liquid and vegetables and pour the mixture over the veal. Cool, cover with plastic wrap, and refrigerate for 8 hours or overnight. At serving time, remove any fat that has risen to the top. Take out the meat and with a spoon scrape it clean of the marinade. Cut the meat into thin slices and arrange them overlapping on a deep serving platter. Stir the lemon juice into the marinade and thin it with mayonnaise to the consistency of thin cream. Spoon the sauce over veal slices and sprinkle with capers.

Braised Shin of Veal   4 servings

Ossibuchi alla Milanese   from Umbria

The classic version contains no tomato and should be finished off with *gremolata*, a mixture of parsley, garlic and minced lemon rind. This dish, traditionally served with risotto, is, to the best of my knowledge, the only Italian meat dish served with rice rather than a vegetable or salad.

2 tablespoons butter
4 veal shanks, about 4
   inches long and 2
   inches thick, with
   plenty of meat
2 tablespoons flour
   salt
   freshly ground pepper

1 cup dry white wine
   hot chicken bouillon
1 tablespoon minced
   parsley
1 garlic clove, minced
   minced rind of 1
   medium-size lemon

Heat the butter in a heavy casserole. Coat the shanks with flour and season with salt and pepper. Over high heat, brown quickly on both sides. Reduce heat to low. Stand the shanks upright so that the marrow won't fall out of the bones as they cook. Pour the wine over the meat and cook without a cover for about 5 minutes. Add ½ cup hot bouillon, cover pan, and simmer for about 1 hour, or until tender; do not overcook. Ten minutes before serving, combine parsley, garlic and lemon rind and sprinkle over the meat. Cover and cook for 5 minutes longer. Check the sauce. If too thick, add a little more bouillon; if too thin, thicken the sauce with 1 tablespoon butter and ½ tablespoon flour kneaded together and dropped into the sauce in pea-size pieces. Serve hot.

Pork Chops with Artichokes   6 servings

Coste di Maiale con Carciofi   from Rome

3 tablespoons olive oil	salt
6 loin pork chops,	freshly ground pepper
trimmed of excessive	2 garlic cloves, minced
fat	1 teaspoon dried sage, or
2 large or 4 medium-size	oregano, or basil
artichokes, sliced (see	2½ cups canned plum
p. 248)	tomatoes (1 No. 2 can)

Heat the oil in a deep frying pan large enough to hold the pork chops in a single layer, or use 2 frying pans. Over high heat brown the meat on both sides. Reduce heat. Place artichoke slices around chops; sprinkle with salt and pepper to taste, the garlic and sage. Pour the tomatoes over the meat. Simmer covered for 45 minutes, or until chops are tender. If the sauce is too thin (this depends on the tomatoes), simmer without a cover until sufficiently reduced.

Piquant Pork Chops

4 to 6 servings

Maiale Piccante

from Abruzzi

6 large loin pork chops, boned
salt
freshly ground pepper
3 teaspoons ground sage
2 tablespoons butter
¼ cup chicken or beef bouillon, or water
⅓ to ½ cup mild white vinegar, to taste

1 tablespoon anchovy paste, or 4 drained anchovy fillets, chopped
1 teaspoon butter (optional)
1 teaspoon flour (optional)

Trim any excess fat off the pork chops. Sprinkle each chop on both sides with salt and pepper. Rub each pork chop on both sides with about ½ teaspoon ground sage. Heat 2 tablespoons butter in a large deep frying pan with a tight cover. Brown pork chops on both sides. Pour bouillon and vinegar over pork chops, making sure that each gets some of the liquid; this is done by turning the chops in the pan juices, using a fork. Cover tightly and simmer over low heat for about 30 minutes, or until tender; cooking time depends on the thickness of the chops. Check liquid during cooking; if necessary, add a little more bouillon to prevent sticking.

Transfer the cooked pork chops to a heated serving platter. Stir anchovy paste or anchovies into pan juices until they have amalgamated with the sauce; there should be just enough to cover the chops. If too thin, work 1 teaspoon butter and 1 teaspoon flour into a paste, and drop it, a little at a time, into the hot sauce, until slightly thickened. Pour over the pork chops and serve hot, with mashed potatoes.

Pork Stewed with Tomatoes and Onions

4 to 6 servings

Spezzatino di Maiale al Pomodoro   from Rome

2 tablespoons olive oil
2 pounds lean boneless
   pork, trimmed of all
   fat and cut into 1-
   inch cubes
   salt
   freshly ground pepper
¼ teaspoon ground
   cinnamon
½ cup hot water or beef
   bouillon

1 pound small white
   onions, trimmed
2 garlic cloves
2 tablespoons wine
   vinegar
4 large tomatoes, peeled
   and chopped
¼ cup minced parsley

Heat the oil in a heavy casserole or saucepan. Add the meat
and sprinkle with salt and pepper to taste and the cinnamon.
Add the hot water. Simmer covered over very low heat for
about 45 minutes, stirring occasionally to prevent sticking. Add
onions, garlic, vinegar and tomatoes and mix well. Simmer
covered over low heat for 30 minutes. Uncover the casserole
and simmer for 15 to 25 more minutes, or until the meat is
tender. The sauce should have cooked down to the consistency
of a thick pancake batter; if too thick, add a little more hot
water, 1 tablespoon at a time. Serve hot, with plain boiled
potatoes.

Lazio (Rome)

Pork Arista   6 to 8 servings

Arista Fiorentina   from Florence

A dish that dates back to the Renaissance. *Arista* is a way of seasoning and cooking; I have made this dish successfully with a boned veal roast or a leg of lamb.

4 pounds loin of pork, cut to form chops but not through backbone	4 whole cloves salt freshly ground pepper olive oil
4 large garlic cloves, peeled and cut into quarters	dry white wine
3 tablespoons fresh rosemary, or 1 to 2 tablespoons crumbled dried rosemary	

Trim all excess fat from the meat. Wet the garlic pieces in water and roll them in the rosemary leaves to coat them with the rosemary. Insert some of the garlic quarters between the chops, together with the cloves. With a sharp knife, cut pockets into the meat and stuff each pocket with garlic. Rub the meat with salt and pepper. With your hands, rub a thin film of olive oil on the meat. Place the meat on a rack in a roasting pan. Add about 2 inches of wine. Cook without a cover in a preheated slow oven (300°F.). Baste occasionally. Allow 45 minutes of roasting time per pound. Cool the meat to lukewarm in its own juice; it should be moist. Slice and serve with a vegetable salad.

NOTE: Pour the pan juices into a bowl and chill. Remove any fat that has risen to the top and use as a sauce for spaghetti or rice.

Pork Cooked in Milk

6 servings

Arrosto di Maiale al Latte

from Florence

4 pounds loin of pork, boned
salt
freshly ground pepper
2 tablespoons crumbled dried rosemary

3 tablespoons butter
2 garlic cloves, crushed
3 to 4 cups milk
¼ pound mushrooms, cut into thin slices

Trim all fat from the meat. With your hands, rub in salt and pepper and the rosemary. Heat 2 tablespoons butter in a casserole into which the meat will fit snugly. Over high heat, and turning the meat over frequently, cook the pork for 4 to 5 minutes, or until golden brown on all sides. Reduce heat to very low. Add garlic and 3 cups of the milk. Cover tightly and simmer for 2 to 2½ hours. Check occasionally for moisture. The gravy should be thick, creamy and golden brown; if too thick, add a little more milk, 2 tablespoons at a time. While pork is cooking, heat remaining tablespoon of butter in a frying pan. Over medium heat, stirring constantly, cook the mushrooms in the butter for 2 to 3 minutes, or until golden. When the meat is ready, transfer it to a heated serving platter and slice it. Keep meat warm in a low oven. Beat the gravy until it is smooth and stir in the mushrooms. Ladle the gravy over the meat and serve hot.

Cotechino or Zampone Sausage

Cotechino or Zampone di Modena   from Emilia-Romagna

Both *cotechino* and *zampone* are salami that have been salted for only a few days; they have to be cooked for a long time and are usually eaten hot. These extremely tasty salami originated in the Emilia and the Romagna, two provinces famous for their excellent pork products. The difference between the two is that the *cotechino* looks like a fat, squat salami, whereas the *zampone* is stuffed into the skin of a pig's foot; the word itself means "big paw." These sausages are never made at home, but bought at the *salumerie* or cold-cut specialty shops. In the United States, practically all Italian butchers and grocers carry them. As with all sausages, they vary in quality and flavor, depending on how they were made, but invariably they are rich and flavorful. They must be cooked for a long time.

The classic accompaniment is a purée of lentils and mashed potatoes, as well as *frutta in mostarda*, fruits preserved in a sweet-sharp mustard sauce, which originally comes from Cremona. This, too, is never made at home. In its sweeter or sharper versions, it is imported to the United States in bottles or cans. *Frutta in mostarda* is also an excellent accompaniment for plain boiled, roasted, broiled or cold meats.

TO COOK:
Place the *cotechino* or *zampone* into a deep casserole. Cover with boiling water. Reduce heat to lowest possible and simmer covered for about 1 hour for every pound of meat. Save the liquid. Chill and degrease it and use for soups.

TO SERVE:
Cut the *cotechino* or *zampone* into thick slices. Arrange them on a heated serving platter and surround with lentil purée on one side and mashed potatoes on the other. Serve the *frutta in mostarda* separately. Serve mustards on the side.

NOTE: I find that lentil purée *and* mashed potatoes are too filling for one meal. I serve *cotechino* or *zampone* with one or the other and a green vegetable. Green beans, either buttered or vinaigrette, are a good accompaniment.

Calf's Liver with Vinegar

Fegato Piccante

4 servings

from Tuscany

2 tablespoons olive oil
2 tablespoons butter
1½ pounds calf's liver, ¼
to ½ inch thick, cut
into 2-inch squares
salt
freshly ground pepper

4 tablespoons wine
vinegar, or to taste
1 to 2 tablespoons
minced fresh sage, or
½ to 1 teaspoon
dried sage

Heat olive oil and butter in a large frying pan. Add the liver, preferably in one layer. Cook over medium heat for 2 to 3 minutes. Turn over with 2 forks or tongs and cook for 1 minute longer. Sprinkle very lightly with salt and pepper. Add vinegar and sage and bring quickly to the boiling point. Cook for 1 minute, no more. Serve immediately.

Panbroiled Veal Kidneys

2 servings

Rognone di Vitello alla Griglia   All-Italian

Washing veal kidneys with water robs them of their flavor, but milk preserves it.

1 to 2 cups whole milk
       or skim milk
2 veal kidneys, about ½
       pound each

4 tablespoons olive oil
   salt
   juice of 1 lemon

Pour the milk into a bowl. Cut kidneys lengthwise into halves. Trim off any outer fat, membrane and tubes. Quickly wash the kidneys in the milk in the bowl. Dry well with kitchen paper. Cut into thin slices and place in a deep serving dish. Pour olive oil over the kidneys, taking care that all the slices are coated with the oil. Let stand covered at room temperature for 30 minutes; if the day is hot, refrigerate for 1 hour. Heat a frying pan, preferably a black iron skillet. Add the sliced kidneys and cook over high heat, tossing the pan, for 3 to 4 minutes. Turn into a heated serving dish, and sprinkle with a little salt and the lemon juice.

Braised Lamb with Artichokes

4 to 6 servings

Abbacchio coi Carciofi

from Naples

3	pounds boneless lamb, cut into 1½-inch pieces	⅔	cup chicken or beef bouillon
1	tablespoon butter		salt
2	tablespoons olive oil		freshly ground pepper
1	large onion, minced	¼	teaspoon ground allspice
2	garlic cloves, minced	4	medium-size
½	cup minced parsley		artichokes, sliced (see
1 to 2	tablespoons flour		p. 248)
½	cup dry white wine		

Trim all fat, gristle and connective tissue from the meat. Wash and dry it thoroughly between sheets of kitchen paper. Heat butter and olive oil in a frying pan; over high heat, brown lamb pieces on all sides. Transfer meat to a 3-quart casserole. In the same frying pan cook onion, garlic and parsley, stirring constantly, until onion is soft. Stir in 1 tablespoon of the flour, and cook for 1 more minute. Stir in wine and cook, stirring constantly, for about 2 minutes. Stir in bouillon and season lightly with salt and pepper. Stir in allspice. Cook, stirring all the time, for about 2 minutes, or until the sauce is thickened. Pour sauce over the meat. Bring to the boiling point, reduce heat to very low, and simmer covered for about 30 minutes. Stir frequently; if sauce is very thin, mix remaining tablespoon flour with 2 tablespoons water to a paste and stir it into the sauce. Add the artichokes. Simmer for 15 more minutes, or until they are tender. Again, you have to adjust the sauce; if it is too thick, stir in a little hot water, 1 tablespoon at a time. Serve with mashed potatoes.

NOTE: After the meat has reached the boiling point, it may be transferred to a preheated moderate oven (350°F.) and cooked as above. For a party, the dish can be cooked in a very slow oven, at 275° or 300°F., taking into account that it will take a longer time to complete it.

Braised Lamb

4 to 6 servings

Abbacchio alla Romana

from Rome

Milk-fed Italian lamb is far more tender than ours. It is essential to use lard for this dish, and a good deal of pepper for the proper flavor.

2 pounds boneless lean lamb	2 tablespoons wine vinegar
¾ teaspoon salt	½ large garlic clove, mashed
¾ teaspoon freshly ground pepper, or to taste	1 teaspoon crumbled dried rosemary, or 1 tablespoon fresh rosemary
2 to 3 tablespoons lard	
1 tablespoon flour	3 drained anchovies, minced
⅔ cup dry white wine	
⅓ cup water	

Trim all fat and gristle from the lamb and cut it into 1½-inch cubes. Sprinkle with the salt and pepper. In a large, deep frying pan, heat the lard. Over high heat, brown the lamb quickly on all sides. Sprinkle the flour over the meat. Add all remaining ingredients. Reduce heat to lowest possible. Simmer covered, stirring occasionally, for about 20 minutes, or until lamb is tender. If sauce is too thick, add a little more wine, a tablespoon or two at a time; if too thin, cook without a cover until sauce reaches the desired consistency. Serve with home-fried potatoes.

Ragout of Lamb

6 servings

Ragù d'Agnello

from Puglia

⅓ cup olive oil
2½ to 3 pounds lean
    boneless lamb, cut
    into 1½-inch cubes
1 cup dry white wine
2 medium-size onions,
    cut into thin slices
2 garlic cloves, minced
2 green, red or yellow
    sweet peppers,
    seeded and cut into
    strips

1 cup canned plum
    tomatoes, drained
    salt
    freshly ground pepper
¼ cup minced fresh basil,
    or 1 tablespoon dried
    basil
1 cup pitted Italian black
    olives
¼ cup minced parsley

Heat 4 tablespoons of the oil in a large, deep frying pan. Add lamb and cook over high heat, stirring constantly, for about 5 minutes, or until meat is golden brown. Add wine and cook, stirring all the time, until wine has evaporated. Turn meat into a heavy saucepan or casserole. Heat remaining oil in the frying pan. Add onions, garlic and peppers. Cook over medium heat, stirring constantly, for about 3 minutes, or until vegetables are soft; do not brown. Pour over the meat in the casserole. Add tomatoes and mix well. Season with salt and pepper and stir in the basil. Bring quickly to the boiling point. Reduce heat to low and simmer covered for about 1 hour, or until meat is tender. Stir occasionally and check the moisture. If sauce is too thick, add a little hot water, 2 tablespoons at a time; if too thin, cook without a cover to reduce. Add the olives and cook for 2 more minutes. Turn into a heated deep serving dish and sprinkle with the parsley.

My Mother's Roast Leg of Lamb   8 to 10 servings

L'Abbacchio di Mamma   from Rome

This well-flavored well-done leg of lamb will appeal to those who don't like rare French lamb. Loin of pork can be treated in the same way.

1 leg of lamb, 6 to 7 pounds
8 garlic cloves, minced
2 cups parsley sprigs, chopped, freshly washed and still damp

⅓ cup crumbled dried rosemary, or ½ cup fresh rosemary leaves
salt
freshly ground pepper
olive oil
dry white wine

Cut every bit of fat, gristle and fell (skin) off the lamb; the meat must be totally bare; this is essential for the flavor of the dish. It takes time and patience and you will be surprised how much waste there is in a leg of lamb; most likely, you will be trimming off more than 1 pound of fat. The meat will partially hang in loose folds, but it will be tied up for cooking. Mince together until they are almost a paste the garlic cloves, parsley and rosemary; the dampness from the parsley will make the ingredients stick together. With a sharp knife, make little pockets all over the meat. Push a little of the parsley mixture into each pocket, using the point of a knife. Rub the meat with salt and pepper and with your hands coat it with a generous coat of olive oil; in fact, massage it with the oil. The meat can be cooked immediately, but it will be more flavorful if wrapped in plastic wrap and refrigerated overnight. Put the meat on a rack in a roasting pan and add 1 inch of dry white wine. Cook in a preheated hot oven (400°F.) for 15 minutes. Reduce heat to 325°F. and cook for about 3 hours, or until tender. Baste frequently with the pan juices. When they run dry, add more white wine, but no more than 1 inch. Do not add any wine during the last 30 minutes of roasting because the leg of lamb should be dry when finished. Serve warm or cold, but not chilled.

NOTE: Garlic and rosemary may be decreased or increased according to taste. A pleasant addition to the parsley mixture is 1 tablespoon grated lemon rind.

Lamb or Kid Stew with Marsala   4 to 6 servings

Spezzatino di Agnello o Capretto   from Sicily

---

3 pounds boneless lamb
    or kid
    equal parts of water
    and dry Marsala, or
    very dry Sherry
    salt
    freshly ground pepper
4 tablespoons olive oil

2 garlic cloves
2 medium-size onions,
    sliced
1 tablespoon flour
1 cup dry Marsala,
    boiling hot
¼ cup minced parsley

Trim all fat and gristle off the meat and cut it into 2-inch cubes. Place in a deep bowl, not aluminum. Add enough equal parts of water and Marsala to cover the meat; the quantity depends on the size of the bowl. Marinate for 2 hours. Drain and dry thoroughly between sheets of kitchen paper. Sprinkle with salt and pepper to taste. Heat the oil in a large heavy casserole. Add garlic cloves and brown them. Remove garlic and reserve it. Over high heat, brown the meat on all sides. Reduce heat to medium. Push the meat to one side of the casserole. Add onions and sprinkle them with the flour. Cook onions, stirring constantly, until they are golden brown. Mix meat and onions. Pour the boiling Marsala over the meat. Mash reserved garlic and add it to the casserole. Simmer covered over low heat, stirring frequently, for about 45 minutes, or until meat is tender. Check the pan juices; if too liquid, cook without a cover until reduced. Sprinkle with the parsley before serving.

Poultry and Rabbit
Pollame e Conigli

Until recently, chicken and other fowl were luxury eating in Italy, and compared to American eating habits, they still are in that category. The chickens were healthy outdoor birds, which were often brought to market alive by peasant women. City housewives like my mother usually had an agreement with a specific countrywoman who would raise especially fine birds for her. Now commercial chicken raising is increasingly on the rise since more people can afford to eat chicken, and frozen birds are also imported in large quantities from the United States. You have to be able to distinguish between naturally raised and commercial chickens if you want a good one. Commercial chickens are still not as inexpensive as American chicken, so that any kind of chicken is still considered a treat.

Italian chicken cookery is basically simple although fancy sauced-up chicken dishes can be found in expensive restaurants. Among the popular ways of preparing chicken the most delicious, to my mind, is spit-roasted chicken flavored with rosemary, now sold in supermarkets and rotisseries. It is said in Italy that you can recognize a man's emotional state from the little bundles he carries on Sundays. When he is in the courting stage, it will be a bunch of flowers; when a fiancé, a box full of *pâtisserie*; and when a husband, a carton with a roast chicken enthroned.

Italians like all sorts of birds and the widely raised capons and guinea fowl are more common on Italian tables than on ours. Italians are also merciless hunters; the country, once abundant in game (bear, boar, deer) is now practically hunted out. Their passion for tiny, innocent song-birds—larks and thrushes—has virtually silenced the skies of Italy.

A great deal of rabbit is eaten in Italy; whoever owns a plot of land will have, in addition to chickens, a rabbit hutch on it. Rabbit is meat, and meat, even rabbit in the shops, is expensive. Large numbers of rabbits are also raised commercially, as I know to my sorrow. In the plain under our hillside house in Tuscany, where white cows used to plow (cows provide meat and milk, and they are more useful than oxen) there now stands a red brick rabbit factory. Fortunately, it does not ruin the entire view. Rabbit meat is white and sweet, unlike the dark, gamy meat of the hare, which is also prized by Italian hunters.

Hunter's Chicken
3 to 4 servings

Pollo alla Cacciatora
from Tuscany

Another version of this dish is made with tomatoes and hot peppers. I prefer this more delicate version. The dish can also be made successfully with rabbit.

2 tablespoons butter
2 tablespoons olive oil
1 cup minced onion
½ cup minced parsley
1 broiler or fryer, 3 pounds, cut into pieces
½ cup water
1 cup sliced mushrooms
3 tablespoons minced fresh basil, or 1 tablespoon dried basil

1 teaspoon dried or fresh rosemary
1 bay leaf
salt
freshly ground pepper
½ to ¾ cup dry white wine

Heat butter and olive oil in a large frying pan. Cook the onion in it, stirring constantly, for 3 to 4 minutes, or until onion is soft and barely golden. Add parsley and cook for 1 more minute. Add chicken pieces and cook them over medium heat, turning pieces over with a fork, until golden. Add water, mushrooms, basil, rosemary, bay leaf, and salt and pepper to taste. Cover and simmer for 10 minutes. Add ½ cup of wine and cook for 10 more minutes, or until tender; if necessary, add a little more of the wine.

Piquant Chicken
4 to 6 servings

Pollo Piccante   from Abruzzi

One of the many ways, found especially in central and southern Italy, to make a common meat more interesting. See cooking instructions for Chicken in White Wine (p. 233).

4	large chicken breasts, halved and skinned flour	1	cup dry white wine
2	tablespoons olive oil	¼	cup drained small or chopped big capers (optional)
2	tablespoons butter		salt
3	garlic cloves, mashed, or to taste		freshly ground pepper
6	flat anchovy fillets, drained and chopped	2	sprigs of fresh rosemary, or 1 tablespoon crumbled dried rosemary
¼	cup white vinegar or white-wine vinegar		

Trim chicken breasts and remove any visible fat. Coat them lightly with flour, shaking off excess flour. Heat olive oil and butter in a frying pan. Cook chicken in it until golden brown on all sides. Transfer chicken to a wide casserole. Pour out all but 1 tablespoon of the fat in the frying pan. Add garlic and anchovies to frying pan. Stirring with a wooden spoon, cook until they have amalgamated into a smooth paste. Stir in vinegar and cook over medium heat, stirring constantly, until vinegar has evaporated and sauce is smooth. Stir in wine, bring to the boiling point, and reduce heat. Stir in the capers. Taste the sauce and see if it needs salt (anchovies and capers are salty), add pepper to taste. Pour sauce over chicken. Cook covered over low heat, or in a preheated moderate oven (350°F.), for 20 to 25 minutes, or until done; cooking time depends on the size of the breasts. Sprinkle with rosemary after 10 minutes of cooking. Check for moisture; add a little more wine to prevent scorching if necessary.

NOTE: For very large chicken breasts, increase the sauce ingredients to 8 anchovy fillets, garlic to taste, ⅓ cup vinegar and 1½ cups dry white wine.

Lemon Chicken   4 servings

Pollo al Limone   from Veneto

I always remove all chicken skin because it is fatty; if you do,
adjust cooking times. Generally, skinless chicken pieces cook
in a third less time. This recipe can be easily adapted to whole
or cut-up chickens. The finished dish should contain only a
few tablespoons of sauce, just enough to keep this delicate dish
moist.

1 large fryer, approximately 3½ pounds, cut into 4 pieces	1 tablespoon butter
	¼ cup chicken bouillon
	juice of 1 lemon
	grated rind of 1 lemon
salt	½ teaspoon dried thyme
freshly ground pepper	2 tablespoons minced parsley
flour	
2 tablespoons olive oil	

Trim any excess fat off the chicken pieces. Sprinkle them on
all sides with salt and pepper and coat them with flour, shaking
off excess flour. Heat olive oil and butter in a frying pan. Cook
chicken pieces in it until they are golden brown on all sides;
the color is important because the further cooking will not color
them any further; if the chicken is too pale, it is not appetizing.
Transfer browned pieces to a casserole with a tight-fitting lid;
the chicken is to be steamed rather than roasted. Add bouillon,
lemon juice and rind and the thyme. Cover the casserole; if it
is not absolutely tight, cover the top with a piece of foil and
then cover the foil with the lid. Cook over low heat for about
20 minutes, or until chicken is cooked but not overcooked.
Sprinkle with parsley and serve with boiled, buttered and pars-
leyed new potatoes.

Chicken in Red Wine   4 to 6 servings

Pollo Cotto nel Vino Rosso   from Tuscany

In Tuscany, this dish is made with wild mushrooms, which are very flavorful.

4 tablespoons olive oil	1 garlic clove, minced
2 frying chickens, 2½ pounds each, cut into pieces, all fat removed	1 tablespoon flour
	2 cups dry red wine such as Chianti
	salt
¼ pound lean prosciutto or smoked ham, chopped	freshly ground pepper
	2 bay leaves, crumbled
12 small white onions, peeled	¼ teaspoon ground sage or crumbled dried sage
½ pound small mushrooms, cut into 4 pieces each	¼ cup minced parsley
	¼ cup brandy (optional)

Heat olive oil in a large deep frying pan. Add chicken pieces, a few at a time, and brown on all sides. Transfer browned pieces to a casserole. Add prosciutto, onions, mushrooms and garlic to the frying pan. Cook over medium heat, stirring constantly, for about 3 minutes, or until vegetables are golden brown. Stir in the flour, add the wine, season with salt and pepper to taste, and mix well. Bring quickly to the boiling point. Pour the contents of the frying pan over the chicken pieces, scraping up all the brown bits at the bottom of the frying pan. Add bay leaves and sage. Simmer over low heat for about 30 minutes, or until chicken is tender. Stir occasionally and check the moisture. If the sauce is too thick, stir in a little hot water, 1 tablespoon at a time. If too thin, cook without a cover to reduce. Before serving, stir in the parsley and the brandy.

Chicken with Herbs   4 servings

Pollo in Padella con le Erbette   from Tuscany

1 cup dry white wine
⅓ cup olive oil
   grated rind of 2 large
   lemons
   juice of 2 large lemons
2 garlic cloves, minced
2 tablespoons minced
   parsley
2 tablespoons minced
   fresh sage, or 1
   teaspoon dried sage

1 tablespoon fresh
   thyme, or ½
   teaspoon dried thyme
1 chicken, 3 to 4 pounds,
   cut into 4 pieces
4 tablespoons butter
   salt
   freshly ground pepper

Combine wine, olive oil, lemon rind and juice, garlic, parsley, sage and thyme in a bowl, not aluminum; mix well. Remove all fat from the chicken and, if desired, remove skin and wing tips. Wash chicken and place it in the bowl with the marinade, coating each piece well on all sides. Cover and refrigerate for 2 to 4 hours, turning several times. Drain and reserve the marinade. In a frying pan large enough to hold chicken pieces in one layer, heat the butter. Add chicken pieces, skin side up. Cook over medium heat until golden brown; turn and brown the other side. Pour off any fat in the frying pan. Add the marinade and season chicken lightly with salt and pepper. Cook over medium heat, without a cover, for 15 to 20 minutes, depending on whether the chicken is skinned. Serve hot or lukewarm, with the pan juices spooned over the meat.

Chicken Fricassee with Tomatoes, Peppers and Capers

4 servings

Spezzatino di Pollo Piccante   from Southern Italy

6 tablespoons olive oil
2 garlic cloves
1 medium-size onion, cut into thin slices
4 large sweet peppers, preferably red or yellow ones, skinned and cut into strips
3 large tomatoes, peeled, chopped fine and drained (about 2 cups)
¼ cup minced fresh basil, or 1 tablespoon dried basil

salt
freshly ground pepper
Tabasco
1 frying chicken, 3 pounds, cut into serving pieces
flour
1 cup dry white or red wine
⅓ cup pitted black olives, cut into halves
2 to 4 tablespoons drained capers

Heat 3 tablespoons of the olive oil in a deep frying pan. Add garlic and cook until garlic is browned; discard garlic. Add onion and peppers to oil. Cook over low heat for about 5 minutes, or until peppers are beginning to get tender. Add tomatoes and basil. Season lightly with salt (olives and capers are salty) and with pepper and Tabasco to taste. Mix well. Simmer covered for about 30 minutes, stirring frequently. During this time, heat remaining olive oil in a large frying pan. Coat chicken pieces very lightly with flour and add them to the frying pan. Cook over medium heat, turning frequently, until pieces are golden on all sides. Transfer chicken to a 2½-quart casserole that can go to the table. Add the wine and spoon vegetables over chicken, making sure that all the pieces are covered by sauce. Stir in olives and capers. Simmer covered over very low heat for 30 to 40 minutes, or until chicken is very tender. Serve hot or lukewarm.

NOTE: If the dish looks very liquid, cook it without a cover for the last 10 to 15 minutes. Skinless chicken cooks faster; shorten the total cooking time by 5 to 10 minutes.

Chicken in White Wine   4 to 6 servings

Pollo al Vino Bianco   from Rome

As with practically all chicken recipes, this dish can be made
with chicken pieces, chicken breasts or boned chicken breasts.
The procedures are the same, but the butter and oil and the
cooking times may have to be adjusted.

4 large chicken breasts,
  halved, skinned and
  boned
  flour
2 tablespoons olive oil
2 tablespoons butter
  salt
  freshly ground pepper

1 cup dry white wine
6 scallions, white and
  green parts, or 2
  small leeks, white
  and green parts, cut
  into thin slices
  grated rind of 1 lemon

Trim chicken breasts and remove any loose or visible fat. Coat
lightly with flour, shaking off excess flour. Heat olive oil and
butter in a frying pan. Cook chicken until golden brown on all
sides. Season with salt and pepper and add wine. Cook for
about 5 minutes, or until about half of the wine has evaporated.
Sprinkle the scallions or leeks over the top of the chicken.
Cover tightly and cook over low to medium heat for about 10
minutes for boned chicken breasts, or until tender. Check the
liquid occasionally; if necessary, add a little more wine to prevent sticking. There should be 1 to 2 tablespoons of sauce for
each chicken piece in the finished dish. At serving time, sprinkle grated lemon rind over the chicken and serve very hot.

Stuffed Roast Chicken   4 servings

Puddighino a Pienu   from Sardinia

The chicken may also be spit-roasted.

STUFFING:

2 tablespoons olive oil
2 teaspoons grated onion
1 garlic clove, mashed
  chicken liver and
  gizzard, chopped
2 hard-cooked eggs,
  sliced
¼ cup dry or fresh white
  bread crumbs
12 pitted black olives,
  chopped
2 tablespoons minced
  parsley
1 tablespoon minced
  fresh basil, or ½
  teaspoon dried basil

1 sprig of fresh thyme, or
  ¼ teaspoon dried
  thyme
  grated rind of 1 lemon
2 to 3 tablespoons dry
  Marsala
  salt
  freshly ground pepper

1 roasting chicken, 3 to 4
  pounds
  salt
  pepper
½ to ⅔ cup olive oil,
  approximately

TO MAKE THE STUFFING:

Heat the olive oil in a small frying pan. Add onion and garlic and cook for 2 minutes. Add chicken liver and gizzard and cook, stirring constantly, for 2 more minutes. Turn the mixture into a bowl. Add hard-cooked eggs, bread crumbs, olives, parsley, basil, thyme and lemon rind, and mix well. Stir in the Marsala, enough to bind the mixture without being too moist. Taste for seasoning and, if necessary, add a little salt and some pepper.

Wash and dry the chicken inside and out. Remove any fat and cut off the wing tips. Season the cavity with salt and pepper and spoon in the stuffing. Do not pack too tight. Truss the chicken. With a pastry brush, brush chicken on all sides, under the legs and under the wings, with olive oil. Sprinkle with salt and pepper. Place on a rack in a roasting pan, laying the bird on one side. Roast in a preheated hot oven (400°F.) for 10 minutes, basting twice with remaining olive oil. Protecting your hands with thick wads of kitchen towels, turn chicken on the other side. Roast for 10 more minutes, basting twice. Turn the chicken breast side up and baste. Roast for 40 to 50 more minutes, or until the drumsticks are loose. Baste frequently; toward the last 20 minutes of roasting time, baste thoroughly every 5 minutes. If the bird is browning too quickly, tent it loosely with aluminum foil, or just cover the drumsticks with foil. Remove the trussing strings and serve chicken hot or lukewarm, but not chilled.

NOTE: The more you baste, the juicier the chicken, which will turn a delicious golden brown color.

Chicken Livers with Sage

Fegatini di Pollo alla Salvia

3 to 4 servings

from Tuscany

It is worth the effort to find fresh sage for this dish.

1 pound chicken livers salt freshly ground pepper	4 tablespoons (¼ cup) butter
12 to 15 fresh sage leaves, chopped, or 1 to 2 tablespoons dried sage	¼ cup minced prosciutto, or 2 slices of bacon, minced ¼ cup dry white wine

Trim chicken livers; if large, cut into halves. Season with salt and pepper and sprinkle with the sage. Heat butter and prosciutto in a frying pan. Cook the livers in the pan over moderate heat, stirring frequently, for about 5 minutes, or until browned. Add wine and simmer for 2 to 3 minutes longer. Serve hot, with polenta.

Chicken and Veal Roll   6 to 8 servings

Polpettone di Pollo e Vitello   from Emilia

A good dish for an antipasto, a picnic, or a party dinner. There should be roughly the same amounts of boneless chicken and veal, that is, about 1 pound each.

1 pound lean boneless veal from the leg	⅛ teaspoon grated nutmeg
2 large chicken legs and 1 large chicken breast	2 to 4 tablespoons dry Marsala or brandy
½ pound sausage meat	salt
2 large eggs, beaten	freshly ground pepper
⅓ cup flour	butter
¾ cup freshly grated Parmesan cheese	1 quart chicken bouillon, approximately
⅓ cup chopped pistachio nuts	1 cup dry white wine

Trim all fat and gristle from the veal and take skin and fat off chicken pieces. With a sharp knife, cut off all the meat from the bones. Cut the veal into pieces. Put veal and chicken through the fine blade of a meat grinder twice, or process it in a food processor. If you are grinding the meat, add the sausage meat the second time around and grind it along with the meat. If using a food processor, add the sausage meat before the veal is completely ground. Turn the mixture into a bowl and mix thoroughly with your hands. Blending well after each addition, add eggs, flour, Parmesan, pistachios, nutmeg and 2 table-spoons of the Marsala; if this is not enough, add the rest of the Marsala. The mixture should be firm, not soupy or weeping. Season lightly with salt and pepper.

On a lightly floured baking board or kitchen counter, spread the mixture into a rectangle, 8 × 12 inches. (A floured rolling pin is helpful.) Roll up like a jelly roll. Pat firm and smooth into the shape of a sausage. Take 3 thicknesses of cheesecloth or a clean kitchen towel. (Rinse the towel in hot water to make sure that no trace of soap or detergent remains or it will flavor the meat.) Cut the cheesecloth into a piece large enough to wrap around the meat roll. Allow an overlap of 2 inches at each end which will serve as handles. Spread the cloth generously with butter. Place the meat roll on it, roll up tightly into a smooth and even roll, and tie both ends, leaving handles for lifting the roll. Place the roll in a kettle large enough to hold it and add bouillon to cover. Bring to the boiling point, then reduce heat to lowest possible. Add the wine. Simmer covered for about 1½ hours. Lift out by the handles; drain. Reserve the broth for soup. Place the meat roll between 2 plates and put a heavy weight (a heavy can or electric iron) on the top plate to press the meat down. Cool the meat roll. After 4 hours, remove the cloth. Wrap the meat roll in aluminum foil until serving time. Cut into thin slices and serve with other cold cuts, with pickles and a salad.

NOTE: If used as an antipasto, the roll may be glazed with a clear aspic or served with a herb-lemon mayonnaise.

Deviled Broiled Chicken
2 servings

Pollo alla Diavola   from Rome

1 broiler chicken, 2½
   pounds
   olive oil
   salt
2 teaspoons crushed hot
   red pepper flakes, or
   to taste

¼ cup dry white wine,
   approximately
   lemon wedges

Split chicken lengthwise into halves, or have the butcher do it. Remove any fat. Put a sheet of wax paper over the chicken. With a meat mallet or a rolling pin, crush the chicken, bones and all, flat. Brush both sides of the chicken lavishly with olive oil. Sprinkle with salt and the red pepper flakes. Preheat the broiler. Place the chicken, skin side down, on a lightly oiled broiler rack. Broil at about 6 inches from the source of heat for 15 minutes on the first side, brushing twice with more olive oil. Turn the chicken and broil for 10 more minutes, brushing twice with more olive oil. Transfer cooked chicken to a heated serving dish and keep hot. Place the broiler pan with the chicken juices over direct heat and stir in the wine. Bring quickly to the boiling point and pour over the chicken. Serve hot, with lemon wedges. In Rome, this would be served with a tossed green salad.

NOTE: For a change, instead of hot red pepper flakes, scatter 1 tablespoon dried or fresh rosemary leaves over the chicken. Or use both seasonings.

Grilled Deviled Squabs

4 servings

Piccioni alla Diavola

from Rome

The original recipe calls for doves; they are hard to find unless you shoot them yourself. Since squabs are extremely expensive, you may wish to use small Cornish hens or chickens.

4 squabs, each ¾ to 1 pound
⅔ cup minced parsley
⅓ cup minced fresh basil
2 tablespoons minced onion
2 garlic cloves, mashed
2 tablespoons minced fresh sage, or 1 teaspoon dried sage
½ teaspoon dried oregano
1½ tablespoons salt

½ teaspoon crumbled dried hot red chili pepper (remove seeds and membranes), or to taste, or ¼ teaspoon Tabasco, or to taste
1 cup dry white wine
½ cup olive oil
1 teaspoon freshly ground pepper

Cut squabs into halves. Wash and dry thoroughly between sheets of kitchen paper. Spread squabs, skin side up, on a clean counter or kitchen table. With a meat mallet, a rolling pin or a bottle, pound the birds to flatten them out, taking care not to tear them. Combine all other ingredients in a bowl, not aluminum, and mix well. Turn the flattened squab halves into the bowl, a few at a time, and coat them with the marinade. Put them all into the bowl and refrigerate for 2 to 3 hours. At cooking time, drain squabs, reserving the marinade. Grill or broil squabs, skin side down, about 3 inches from the source of heat for about 20 minutes on the first side and 15 minutes on the other. Baste frequently with the marinade; the birds should be dark golden, with a crusty surface, even a little charred.

NOTE: The broiling times will have to be adjusted according to the birds.

Roast Marinated Guinea Hen or Pheasant

4 servings

Faraona o Fagiano Arrosto   from Marche

This is a good way of treating birds of an uncertain age. Adjust cooking times and test for doneness as follows: protect forefinger and thumb with a wad of kitchen paper and pinch the thickest part of the thigh. If the meat feels very tender, the bird is done. Or wiggle the drumsticks; if they wiggle easily, the bird is done.

½ cup olive oil
1 cup dry white wine
   grated rind of 1 lemon
   juice of 1 lemon
3 tablespoons fresh
   rosemary, or 2
   tablespoons crumbled
   dried rosemary

1 guinea hen or
   pheasant, 3 to 4
   pounds
   salt
   freshly ground pepper
¼ pound sliced bacon
   olive oil

To make the marinade, combine olive oil, wine, lemon rind and juice and rosemary in a deep bowl, not aluminum; mix well. Add the bird and coat it well on all sides with the marinade. Refrigerate for 2 hours, or longer if the bird is old. Remove bird from the marinade, scrape off rosemary leaves and lemon rind, and dry between sheets of kitchen paper. Sprinkle with salt and pepper. Cover the bird with bacon slices, both under and over the legs and wings. Truss the bird. Place on a rack in a baking pan in a preheated moderate oven (350°F.). Roast for 1 to 1½ hours, or even longer, depending on the age and size of the bird. With a pastry brush, baste frequently with olive oil the parts of the bird that are not covered by bacon; the bacon shrinks in cooking. At serving time, remove trussing strings and serve bird hot or lukewarm, with a tossed green salad.

Marches (Ascoli Piceno)

Sweet-Sour Rabbit   6 servings

Coniglio Agrodolce   from Southern Italy

1 fresh or frozen rabbit, 3
   pounds, disjointed (if
   frozen, thawed)
2 cups dry red wine
2 medium-size onions,
   minced
4 whole cloves
2 garlic cloves
1 cup chopped parsley
4 bay leaves
¼ teaspoon freshly
   ground pepper
   flour
4 tablespoons olive oil

3 slices of fat bacon,
   shredded
   salt
   freshly ground pepper
½ to 1 cup beef bouillon
2 tablespoons sugar
½ cup wine vinegar, or
   more if vinegar is
   mild
⅓ cup currants, plumped
   in warm water and
   drained
⅓ cup pine nuts (pignoli)

Carefully wash the rabbit and dry the pieces between sheets
of kitchen paper. Put the meat into a bowl, not aluminum.
Combine wine, 1 onion, the cloves, garlic, parsley, bay leaves
and pepper in a saucepan. Heat, but do not boil. When mixture
is very hot, pour it over rabbit pieces, turning them so that
they are coated on all sides. Cover and refrigerate for 4 hours
or overnight, turning the pieces twice. Drain rabbit pieces,
straining and reserving the marinade. Dry the meat carefully
between sheets of kitchen paper. Coat it on all sides with flour,
shaking off excess flour. In a large, deep frying pan, or in a
saucepan large enough to accommodate all the rabbit pieces, heat
oil and bacon. Add remaining onion and cook until golden.
With a slotted spoon, remove bacon and onion pieces, reserving them. Add rabbit pieces, a few at a time; over high heat,
turning them constantly, cook them until evenly golden but
not browned. When golden brown on all sides, begin adding
the strained marinade, 1 tablespoon at a time, until 6 to 8 tablespoons have evaporated in the pan and the rabbit pieces are
dark brown. Reduce heat to very low. Season the meat with
salt and pepper and add ½ cup of the bouillon. Simmer covered for about 1½ hours, or until rabbit is tender; if necessary,

add a little more bouillon, 2 tablespoons at a time. The sauce should be very thick; keep on skimming all fat that rises to the surface. (Do not overcook the meat.) Put the 2 tablespoons of sugar into a small frying pan. Over low heat, heat until sugar is melted and golden; take care not to burn it. Stir in the vinegar. Stirring constantly, blend sugar and vinegar. Pour the mixture over the meat and mix carefully with a fork. Sprinkle currants and pine nuts over rabbit and stir into the sauce. Cook over medium heat for 3 to 4 more minutes, or until thoroughly heated through. Serve hot or lukewarm, but not chilled.

Rabbit with Egg and Lemon Sauce   6 servings

Coniglio alla Friulana   from Veneto

1 fresh or frozen rabbit, 3
  pounds, disjointed (if
  frozen, thawed)
2 tablespoons olive oil
2 tablespoons butter
1 medium-size onion,
  minced
  salt
  freshly ground pepper
1½ cups minced parsley

2 ounces (½ cup)
  julienne strips of
  prosciutto or smoked
  ham
1 tablespoon flour
½ cup dry white wine
  hot water
2 egg yolks
  juice of 1 large lemon

Carefully wash rabbit pieces and dry them between sheets of
kitchen paper. Heat olive oil and butter in a large saucepan.
Add rabbit pieces, a few at a time, and cook over medium heat,
turning the meat with 2 wooden spoons, until meat is golden;
it must not brown. Transfer cooked pieces to a platter and keep
hot; repeat until all rabbit pieces are cooked to a golden color.
Add onion to the pan juices and cook until soft; do not brown
it. Return all the meat to the saucepan. Season with salt and
pepper to taste. Sprinkle with ½ cup of the parsley. Add prosciutto and stir in flour. Add wine and another ½ cup of the
parsley. Cook over medium heat, turning meat frequently, until all the wine has evaporated. Then add enough hot water to
reach three quarters of the height of the meat. Simmer covered
over low heat for 1½ to 2 hours, or until rabbit is tender; cooking time depends on its age. Check the moisture; although the
sauce should be on the thick side, you may have to add a little
more water, 2 tablespoons at a time, to prevent scorching.
When the rabbit is tender (do not overcook), beat egg yolks
until fluffy. Beat in lemon juice and remaining parsley, and
pour the mixture over the rabbit; mix, using wooden spoons.
Simmer covered over low heat for 5 minutes, or until thoroughly heated through. Turn into a heated serving dish and
serve very hot.

Vegetables
Verdure, Legumi

Vegetables are one of the cornerstones of Italian cookery, and the Italians are very particular about their size, taste and freshness. Vegetables grow in profusion from the Alps to the Ionian Sea the year round, and their quality is a revelation to many American travelers. They have not yet succumbed to the demands of agrobusiness as have most American vegetables, so that in Italy it is still possible to obtain vegetables grown by hand, so to speak, and naturally matured. And of course, there is the difference of soil and climate, and the way the land is worked in truck gardening.

Italian vegetable cookery can be very simple. The various greens such as spinach, chard, green beans, broccoli and asparagus are often cooked with a little water or bouillon or in their own juices, and served hot or cold with olive oil and lemon. Vegetables also make up elaborate, composed dishes that are served as main dishes, especially in southern Italy, where meat used to be of poor quality and scarce.

In Italy, mushrooms are important as both food and flavoring. There are many varieties, gathered wild, and incredibly delicious. How safe are these wild Italian mushrooms? I would buy them in reputable market stalls and shops and eat them in restaurants but I would not buy unknown mushrooms at the roadside. Italian dried mushrooms are very flavorful. Here in America, where only cultivated and bland mushrooms are available, I add some dried Italian mushrooms to any mushroom dish to pep up its flavor.

Vegetables are served as part of an antipasto, as a first course (especially asparagus), as a *contorno* (a side dish to a meat course), as a *sformato* (a vegetable pudding), in combination with other vegetables, in soups, and on pasta and rice. I think they are the best stretchers in any eating.

Tossed green salads are not part of the meal as they are in the United States; they take the place of a vegetable. Potatoes are secondary in Italian cookery, especially in the southern parts of the country where it is too hot to grow them. They are not served if a pasta or rice dish precedes the meat course.

Frozen vegetables are produced in Italy, but the nation still prefers the fresh product, bought daily at the market, the smaller, the better. Since our own vegetables, with the exception of homegrown ones, or those of a good farmer's market, have so much less flavor than their Italian counterparts, I compensate for this by increasing the flavoring ingredients, such as herbs, when preparing Italian dishes.

Globe Artichokes

Carciofi   All-Italian

Globe artichokes belong to the thistle family; the other vegetable called "artichoke," the Jerusalem artichoke, is a tuber which has no relation to the globe artichoke. Globe artichokes are among the most popular Italian vegetables. They are cooked in many ways, and often with other ingredients. In Italy, there are more artichoke varieties than in the United States, since most Americans favor the large ones. Some small artichokes can be found in our Italian markets, but unfortunately not the small, purple and deliciously tender artichokes of Venice.

Some famous Italian artichoke dishes, such as the deep-fried *carciofi alla Giudea* do require small, very tender specimens and unfortunately they cannot be made with our varieties.

Most Americans know only one way of eating artichokes, that is, boiled, with a sauce to dip leaves in; this is good. When the artichoke is young and tender, it also tastes good raw, dipped into a sauce. The generally inhospitable look of the vegetable discourages people from preparing it for other kinds of cookery. Yet it is simple, if two points are kept in mind. First, most of the artichoke is waste; there is more volume when the edible parts have been eaten. Second, artichokes discolor very easily; as soon as they are cut up, they should be dropped into acidulated water, that is, water mixed with lemon juice preferably, or vinegar.

How to Prepare Artichokes

ACIDULATED WATER:
To each quart of cold water, add 3 tablespoons lemon juice or white vinegar.

HOW TO CUT UP ARTICHOKES:
Prepare acidulated water. Have a sharp kitchen knife ready. Tear off and throw away the artichoke's outer leaves, until you reach leaves that are greenish-white two thirds of the way up from the base. Lay the artichoke on its side. Cut off the green part of the leaves with the spikes with one stroke, leaving only the light part. Dip the artichoke into the acidulated water. Now cut off the stem, leaving about ½ inch from the base. Peel the base and remaining stem as you would peel an apple. Cut artichoke into 4 parts, again as you would quarter an apple. Drop all the pieces into acidulated water to prevent darkening. Take one quarter and cut off the fuzzy center part, again as you would core an apple. Drop the artichoke quarter again into acidulated water.

When artichokes are very small and very tender, they may be cooked whole and then cut into quarters. However, most American artichokes are large and not tender, so that the trimmed quarters must be cut into thin slices; the tougher the artichoke, the thinner the slice. Drain and dry artichoke quarters or slices thoroughly on kitchen paper before using further.

FATS TO USE IN ARTICHOKE COOKERY:
Artichokes have a robust flavor, and I think they are better cooked with a somewhat robust fat such as olive oil, lard, pancetta or bacon. When olive oil is used in braising artichokes (which to my mind is the best fat for the purpose), it is better to use equal parts of olive oil and water since olive oil alone would make too rich a dish.

Any dipping sauce for cold artichokes should be piquant.

Fried Artichokes

4 servings

Carciofi Fritti

from Rome

4 medium-size artichokes acidulated water olive or peanut oil flour	2 eggs, beaten with 1 tablespoon olive oil salt

Prepare artichokes and cut them into thin slices. Drop the finished slices into acidulated water. In a deep frying pan, heat about 2 inches of olive or peanut oil to the smoking point. As the oil heats, drain artichokes and dry them thoroughly between sheets of kitchen paper. Dip a few slices at a time first into the flour and then into the beaten eggs. Fry in hot oil until crisp and golden. Remove with a slotted spoon and drain in a serving dish lined with a triple layer of kitchen paper. Keep fried artichokes warm in a low oven as you fry remaining slices. When all the slices are fried, blot the top layers in the dish with kitchen paper to drain them thoroughly. Pull the paper which lines the dish out from under the artichokes, sprinkle them with salt, and serve very hot.

Artichoke Flan   4 servings

Tortino di Carciofi   from Tuscany

Serve as a main luncheon dish, with a tomato salad. Instead of nutmeg, use any favorite herb in desired amounts.

6 medium-size artichokes
  acidulated water
  flour
1 cup olive oil
  butter for baking dish
6 eggs

⅓ cup light or heavy cream or milk
  salt
  freshly ground pepper
⅛ teaspoon grated nutmeg

Prepare artichokes and cut them into thin slices. Drop finished slices into acidulated water. When ready to use, drain artichokes and dry thoroughly between sheets of kitchen paper. Coat the pieces with flour and shake off excess flour. Heat the olive oil to the smoking point, and fry artichokes until crisp and golden. Drain on kitchen paper. Butter a shallow 1½-quart baking dish and put artichokes into it. Beat together the eggs and cream; season with salt and pepper to taste and nutmeg or herbs. Pour the mixture over artichokes. Cook in a preheated moderate oven (350°F.) for 15 to 20 minutes, or until golden and puffy. Serve immediately.

Artichokes and Peas   4 to 6 servings

Contorno di Carciofi e Piselli   from Rome

Serve as a first course or as a vegetable with any meat dish.

3 slices of lean bacon,
minced, or ¼ cup
minced pancetta
½ medium-size onion,
minced
¼ cup minced parsley
1 small garlic clove,
minced
2 tablespoons butter
2 tablespoons olive oil
6 medium-size
artichokes, trimmed
and thinly sliced (see
p. 248)

2 tablespoons minced
fresh basil, or 1
teaspoon crumbled
dried basil
salt
freshly ground pepper
⅓ to ½ cup hot chicken
bouillon
2 pounds fresh peas,
shelled (about 2
cups), or frozen peas,
barely thawed

Combine bacon, onion, parsley and garlic on a chopping board
or in a food processor and mince together to a paste. Heat
butter and olive oil in a heavy casserole and add bacon mixture.
Cook over medium heat, stirring constantly, for about 3 minutes. Add artichokes, basil, salt and pepper to taste and ⅓ cup
of the bouillon. Simmer covered over low heat, stirring frequently, for about 10 minutes. Add peas; if necessary to prevent scorching, add a little more bouillon, 1 tablespoon at a
time; the dish should not be soupy. Simmer covered for 5 to
10 more minutes, or until vegetables are tender but still firm.

Baked White Beans with Tomatoes   6 to 8 servings

Fagioli al Forno   from Tuscany

These beans may be reheated successfully.

1 pound dried small white beans (navy or pea beans)
1 large smoked ham hock, or ¼ pound bacon
1 pound tomatoes, peeled and chopped
freshly ground pepper
1 leek, white and green part, cut into very thin slices, or 1 large onion, cut into very thin slices
3 garlic cloves, mashed
2 tablespoons olive oil
salt

Put beans in a bowl and add enough water to cover them by 2 inches; soak them overnight. At cooking time drain beans and transfer them to a 2½- to 3-quart ovenproof casserole. If you are using a ham hock, scrape it if necessary and scald it with boiling water. If you are using bacon, tie the slices together with a string to facilitate later removal. Add either ham hock or bacon to beans, with tomatoes, leek or onion, and garlic; stir in the oil. Add enough water to cover the beans by about 1 inch. Bring to the boiling point, cover, and transfer to a preheated slow oven (325°F.). Cook for 50 to 60 minutes, depending on the beans. Check occasionally for moisture. If beans look too dry, add a little more hot water, ¼ cup at a time. The beans should not be soupy, and the moisture depends on the amount of liquid in the tomatoes. If too soupy, cook without a cover to evaporate liquid. When beans are almost cooked, taste and season with salt and pepper. (Adding salt earlier in the cooking toughens the beans.) At serving time, remove ham hock or bacon. The beans should be soft, but still retain their shape.

NOTE: If you are planning a later use of the beans, cook until half done. Refrigerate after cooking and finish cooking later.

VARIATION:

Baked White Beans with Tomatoes and Mushrooms
8 servings

Fagioli al Forno con i Funghi

Sauté ½ pound thin slices of mushrooms in 3 tablespoons butter over medium heat until mushrooms are somewhat dry. (If they retain too much of their liquid, they will make the beans soupy.) Stir the mushrooms into the cooked beans.

Beans with Sage
4 to 6 servings

Fagioli all'Uccelletto
from Tuscany

1½ cups dried white beans, soaked and ready to cook
2 tablespoons butter
3 tablespoons olive oil
2 to 3 tablespoons minced fresh sage, or 1 to 1½ teaspoons dried or ground sage

salt
freshly ground pepper
⅓ cup fresh tomato sauce or drained chopped tomatoes

Cook beans in boiling water to cover plus 3 inches for 45 minutes to 1 hour, or until beans are tender. This must be done over very low heat to prevent the beans bursting open. Do not add salt or the beans will be tough. Drain the beans. Heat together butter and olive oil. Add beans, sage, and salt and pepper to taste. Cook over medium heat for about 3 minutes, stirring with a fork so as not to break the beans. Add tomato sauce and cook for 3 minutes longer, or until sauce and beans are very hot.

Braised Fresh Fava (Broad) Beans with Lettuce

4 servings

Fave Fresche Stufate   from Rome

Shelled mature fava beans have a coarse skin, which careful cooks slip off before cooking, as cooking hardens it.

4 pounds fava beans in the pod	salt
	freshly ground pepper
2 tablespoons butter	1 large or 2 small heads
1 tablespoon olive oil	of romaine lettuce,
1 small onion, cut into thin slices	cut into ¼-inch shreds
¼ pound prosciutto or smoked ham, cut into ¼-inch dice	½ cup beef bouillon or water, approximately

Shell fava beans; if necessary, slip off the coarse skins of the mature beans. Heat butter and olive oil in a heavy saucepan or casserole. Add onion and cook, stirring constantly, until onion is soft. Stir in prosciutto and cook for 3 minutes longer. Add fava beans and a little salt and pepper. Cook over medium heat, stirring constantly, for about 3 minutes. Add lettuce and half of the bouillon; mix well. Cook covered, stirring frequently, for 5 to 10 minutes, or until beans are soft; cooking time depends on their size and age. Serve hot.

NOTE: The dish should not be soupy. Since lettuce has varying degrees of moisture, the dish needs to be watched. If it is drying out, add more bouillon; if too liquid, cook without a cover.

Asparagus Milanese

4 servings

Asparagi alla Milanese   from Milan

The eggs make this a main course.

2   pounds fresh asparagus   ⅓   cup hot browned butter
    butter for baking dish   4   or 8 butter-fried eggs
¾   cup grated Parmesan or   (optional)
    Swiss cheese

Cook asparagus until just tender; drain carefully. Butter a shallow baking dish generously and heat it in a low oven. Lay half of the asparagus in the dish. Sprinkle the tips with half of the grated cheese. Repeat with remaining asparagus and remaining cheese. Drizzle browned butter over asparagus tips. Lay fried eggs on top of asparagus, if you use them, and serve very hot.

Carrots Cooked with Marsala

4 to 6 servings

Carote al Marsala   from Sicily

1½   pounds medium-size   freshly ground pepper
     carrots (10 to 12   ⅓   cup dry Marsala or
     carrots)   Sherry
2   tablespoons butter
    salt

Scrape or peel the carrots and cut them into the thinnest possible rounds. Heat butter in a heavy saucepan with a close-fitting lid. Add carrots and cook over medium heat, stirring constantly, for about 2 minutes. Season lightly with salt and pepper. Add Marsala, cover tightly, and simmer over very low heat for 10 to 15 minutes, or until tender.

Broccoli with Oil and Lemon   4 servings

Broccoli all'Olio e Limone   All-Italian

Broccoli, cauliflower, green beans, chard, spinach—practically all vegetables are cooked *al dente* and served as in the following recipe; it is perhaps the favorite Italian way of eating greens. Serve either hot or cold.

1 large or 2 small bunches of broccoli	salt freshly ground pepper
½ to ⅔ cup olive oil	
juice of 1 large lemon, or to taste	

Trim broccoli and cut heads into flowerets. Cut off the stems and discard the hard part. Peel the remaining part of stems and cut them into 3-inch pieces. Wash and drain. Cook in just enough boiling salted water to cover for 4 to 5 minutes, or until tender but still crisp. Drain and put into a serving dish. Combine oil, lemon juice, and a little salt and pepper, and pour over the broccoli. Serve hot or cold.

Cardoons au Gratin
4 servings

Cardi al Gratin
from Lombardy

The cardoon is a whitish-green thistlelike plant which looks like an overgrown bunch of celery. The edible parts are the fleshy stalks and midribs which have to be peeled to remove the stringy parts; they are cut into pieces and blanched before being eaten in soups, in salads and as a vegetable. The flavor is delicate, reminiscent of oyster plant and artichokes. It is worthwhile to prepare this elegant and interesting vegetable which is found here in Italian vegetable markets.

Since cardoons discolor the way artichokes do when exposed to the air during trimming, have a bowl of acidulated water ready (3 tablespoons lemon juice to 1 quart water). Remove blemished outer stalks and strip the leaves off the tender inner stalks. Remove stringy parts as if you were trimming celery stalks. Cut stalks into 2- to 3-inch pieces and drop them into the acidulated water. Trim the heart and cut it into pieces, dropping them immediately into acidulated water. Cook cardoons in boiling salted water to cover until tender but still crisp; average cooking time is 5 to 10 minutes, depending on the age of the vegetable. Drain and dress with salt and pepper, melted butter and lemon juice, or any of the asparagus or artichoke sauces; or bread and deep-fry.

1½ pounds edible cardoon parts, approximately, cut into 2- to 3-inch pieces, cooked and drained
salt
freshly ground pepper

4 tablespoons butter, cut into pieces
1 cup grated Swiss cheese
¼ cup fine dry bread crumbs

Butter a 1½-quart serving dish generously. Line it with half of the cardoons. Season very lightly with salt (the cheese will be salty) and pepper. Dot with half of the butter and sprinkle with half of the grated cheese. Top with the remaining cardoons, butter and grated cheese. Sprinkle with the bread crumbs. Cook in a preheated moderate oven (350°F.) for 15 minutes, or until golden.

Golden Cauliflower   4 servings

Cavolfiore Dorato   from Veneto

1 cauliflower, about 1½   3 tablespoons butter
   pounds   freshly ground pepper
   flour   lemon wedges
1 egg, beaten

Divide cauliflower into equal-size flowerets. Trim off hard
stems and leaves; wash and drain. Place in a deep frying pan
or shallow saucepan in one layer. Cover with boiling salted
water and cook for about 5 minutes, or until just barely tender;
the vegetable will be cooked further and it easily gets mushy.
Drain cauliflowerets and dry them thoroughly between sheets
of kitchen paper. Dip them into flour, coating them lightly on
all sides and shaking off excess flour. Dip them into the beaten
egg. Heat butter in a large deep frying pan. Add cauliflowerets
in one layer, and cook them until they are golden, turning over
as needed with two forks. Turn the vegetable into a heated
serving dish, sprinkle with pepper, and serve hot, with lemon
wedges.

Cauliflower Milanaise

3 to 4 servings

Cavolfiore alla Milanese from Milan

1 cauliflower, about 1½ pounds
4 to 6 tablespoons butter
1 small onion, minced

½ cup freshly grated Parmesan cheese
1 tablespoon minced parsley

Trim cauliflower, removing coarse leaves and trimming the stem. Wash in several changes of cold water; drain. Place in a deep saucepan, head uppermost. Cover with boiling salted water; the water should cover the cauliflower. Cook for about 10 minutes, or until barely tender; do not overcook; drain and cool. Divide cauliflower into flowerets. In a shallow baking dish that can go to the table and will hold the cauliflowerets tightly packed in one layer, heat 2 or 3 tablespoons of the butter. Add the onion and cook for about 3 minutes, or until onion is just beginning to get tender. Add flowerets in neat, tight rows, flower part up. Sprinkle with Parmesan cheese. Melt remaining butter and drizzle it over vegetable. Sprinkle with the parsley. Cook in a preheated hot oven (425°F.) for about 10 minutes, or until golden and bubbly. Serve hot.

Baked Eggplant, Mozzarella, Eggs and Tomatoes

3 to 4 servings

Tortino di Melanzane e Mozzarella   from Naples

4 small eggplants, each
   about 6 inches long
  salt
2 large ripe firm
   tomatoes, peeled and
   cut into ¼-inch slices
4 anchovies, drained and
   minced
  butter for baking dish
3 hard-cooked eggs,
   sliced
1 mozzarella cheese, 8 to
   12 ounces, cut into
   ¼-inch slices

  salt
  freshly ground pepper
1 cup Italian parsley
   sprigs
¼ cup fresh basil leaves,
   or 2 tablespoons
   dried basil
2 garlic cloves
¼ cup olive oil

Trim and peel eggplants, and cut into ¼-inch slices. Put the slices on a large platter and sprinkle each slice with about ⅛ teaspoon salt. Let stand at room temperature to draw excessive moisture. Drain eggplant slices and dry between sheets of kitchen paper. Spread a little minced anchovy on each tomato slice. In a buttered shallow ovenproof dish which can go to the table, or a pie plate, make well-overlapping rows of eggplant, egg, tomato and mozzarella slices, in that order. Sprinkle with very little salt (the eggplant slices and the anchovies are salty) and pepper. Mince together the parsley, basil and garlic. Sprinkle the mixture over vegetables and cheese, and sprinkle everything with olive oil. Cover the dish with aluminum foil. Bake in a preheated moderate oven (350°F.) for 30 minutes. Remove aluminum foil and bake for about 10 minutes longer, to let excessive moisture in the dish evaporate. Serve hot, lukewarm or cold, but not chilled.

Stuffed Eggplant

4 servings

Melanzane Imbottite   from Southern Italy

2   eggplants, each about
    1½ pounds
½   cup olive oil
1   cup minced onion
2   garlic cloves, minced
1   cup drained chopped
    fresh tomatoes or
    drained canned plum
    tomatoes
½   cup minced parsley
1   teaspoon crumbled
    dried oregano

1   cup drained cooked rice
    (about ⅓ cup
    uncooked)
½   cup ricotta cheese
    salt
    freshly ground pepper
    dash of Tabasco
1   cup fine dry bread
    crumbs
2   tablespoons butter, plus
    butter for baking dish

Cut eggplants lengthwise into halves. Scoop out the centers, leaving a ½-inch-thick shell; be careful not to pierce the shell. Cut scooped-out eggplant centers into ½-inch dice. Heat the oil in a large frying pan. Add onion and garlic, and cook, stirring constantly, until onion is soft. Add diced eggplant. Cook over medium heat, stirring all the time, for 3 to 4 minutes, or until eggplant is soft and wilted. Add the tomatoes, parsley and oregano, mix well, and cook for 3 more minutes. Stir in rice and ricotta and season with salt and pepper to taste and the Tabasco; mix well. Remove from heat and cool for 5 minutes. Stuff eggplant shells with this mixture, leveling it with the blade of a knife. Sprinkle the tops with bread crumbs and dot with butter. Place eggplant shells side by side in a greased shallow baking dish. Pour about ½ inch of water around the eggplant halves. Cook in a preheated moderate oven (350°F.) for 30 to 40 minutes, or until tops are golden brown. Serve hot or lukewarm.

Sautéed Fennel

4 to 6 servings

Finocchio alla Casalinga

from Puglia

4 large or 6 small or medium-size heads of fennel	3 garlic cloves salt freshly ground pepper
½ cup olive oil	½ cup dry white wine

Cut the "fingers" with their green tops flush off the fennel heads; trim the base; remove tough outer leaves. Cut large fennel heads lengthwise into 8 pieces, or cut small or medium-size fennel into quarters. Place in a saucepan and barely cover with boiling salted water. Cook covered for 3 to 5 minutes; do not overcook; the fennel should be barely tender. Drain fennel. Heat olive oil in a large heavy frying pan. Cook garlic cloves in the oil until they are browned; discard garlic. Add fennel, sprinkle with salt and pepper, and add wine. Reduce heat to low, cover the frying pan, and cook for 5 to 10 minutes; the vegetable should still be firm. Serve hot.

Gratin of Fennel   6 servings

Finocchio alla Parmigiana   from Emilia

Serve with broiled or roasted meats.

4 large heads of fennel	⅔ cup melted butter
salt	⅔ cup freshly grated
freshly ground pepper	Parmesan cheese

Cut the "fingers" with their green tops flush off the fennel
heads; trim the base; remove tough outer leaves. Cut fennel
heads lengthwise, from top to bottom, into ¼-inch slices. Place
in a saucepan and barely cover with boiling salted water. Cook
covered for 3 to 5 minutes; do not overcook. Drain fennel.
Butter a shallow baking dish and place half of the fennel slices
on it. Season with salt and pepper, drizzle half of the melted
butter over the fennel, and sprinkle with half of the grated
Parmesan. Top with remaining fennel, butter and cheese. Bake
in a preheated hot oven (425°F.) for 5 to 10 minutes, or until
the top is golden brown and bubbly. Or run quickly under the
broiler about 6 inches from the source of heat. Serve immediately.

Baked Mushroom Pudding   6 servings

Sformato con Funghi   from Rome

One of the many vegetable puddings that are baked and then
turned out on a dish, to be served as a first course with a sauce
or as a side dish with meats.

5 tablespoons butter	2 cups milk
1 pound mushrooms, cut into thin slices	4 ounces mozzarella cheese, diced (about ¾ cup)
6 tablespoons flour	
6 tablespoons Marsala wine	⅓ cup freshly grated Parmesan cheese
salt	butter for baking dish
freshly ground pepper	fine dry bread crumbs
⅛ teaspoon grated nutmeg	4 eggs, separated

Heat 2 tablespoons of the butter in a large frying pan. Add
mushrooms and cook over medium heat, stirring constantly,
for about 3 minutes. Stir in 1 tablespoon of the flour and cook
for 2 more minutes. Stir in the Marsala. Continue cooking
over medium heat, stirring constantly, for 5 to 7 minutes, or
until mushrooms have released most of their liquid and are on
the dry side, still retaining their shape. If not dry enough,
they will water down the pudding in baking. Season mushrooms with salt, pepper and nutmeg, and set aside. Heat remaining 3 tablespoons of butter in a saucepan. Stir in remaining 5 tablespoons flour. Cook, stirring constantly, for 1 to 2
minutes, then add the milk. Cook, stirring all the while, until
sauce is thick and smooth. Reduce heat to lowest possible.
Stir in mozzarella and cook, stirring, until it has dissolved in
the sauce. Stir in Parmesan, and remove pan from heat.
Check the seasoning; if necessary, add a little more salt, pepper and nutmeg. Cool the sauce. Generously butter an 8-cup
baking dish with straight sides. Coat it thoroughly with bread
crumbs on bottom and sides. Shake off any excess bread
crumbs. Beat egg yolks into cooled sauce, stir in mushrooms,
and mix well. Beat egg whites until stiff and fold them into

the sauce. Turn into the baking dish, smoothing out the top with a wet knife or metal spatula. Bake in a preheated hot oven (400°F.) for 15 to 20 minutes, or until pudding is browned and puffy. Remove from the oven and let stand for a few minutes. Turn out on a heated serving dish. Serve immediately with a tomato sauce or plain.

Braised Leeks with Tomatoes and Olives

4 to 6 servings

Porri in Umido from Southern Italy

---

2 bunches of leeks (6 to 8 medium-size leeks)
⅓ cup olive oil
1 garlic clove
4 large tomatoes, peeled, seeded and chopped, or 1½ cups drained canned plum tomatoes

1 cup small black Italian olives, pitted
salt
freshly ground pepper
juice of 1 lemon

Trim leeks, cutting off all but 2 inches of the green part. Cut into 2-inch pieces and drop into a bowl of cold water. Wash thoroughly to remove all sand, changing the water as needed; drain. Put leeks into a saucepan and add boiling water to cover. Cook over medium heat for 3 minutes; drain. Heat the oil in a large, deep frying pan. Add garlic and cook until browned; discard garlic. Add leeks and cook for 3 minutes, shaking the pan to prevent sticking. Add tomatoes and olives and season with salt and pepper. Simmer covered over low heat for 7 to 10 minutes, shaking the pan frequently to prevent sticking. If necessary, add a little hot water, 2 tablespoons at a time. Stir in lemon juice before serving.

Mushrooms with Garlic and Herbs   4 to 6 servings

Funghi al Funghetto   All-Italian

6 tablespoons olive oil
2 pounds mushrooms,
  cut into thin slices
3 garlic cloves, mashed
2 teaspoons dried thyme,
  or to taste, or any
  other preferred herb

salt
freshly ground pepper
juice of ½ lemon

NOTE: The mushrooms must be cooked a few at a time, so that they will sauté and not steam, as they do when crowded.

Heat olive oil in a large, deep frying pan. Over high heat, sauté mushrooms in several batches for 3 to 4 minutes or until golden brown. Transfer cooked mushrooms with a slotted spoon to a bowl and keep hot. When all the mushrooms are browned, return them all to the frying pan. Over low heat, stir in garlic and thyme. Season with salt and pepper. Cook for 3 to 4 minutes, stirring frequently. Turn onto a hot serving dish and sprinkle with lemon juice.

Piquant Sautéed Mushrooms

4 servings

Funghi Trifolati alla Fiorentina

from Tuscany

Trifolati does not mean truffled but cut into thin slices, and the term applies to all foods so cut up.

1 pound mushrooms	1 tablespoon butter
3 tablespoons olive oil	4 anchovy fillets, minced
1 garlic clove	3 tablespoons minced
salt	parsley
freshly ground pepper	juice of 1 small lemon

Trim the mushrooms and cut them into very thin slices. Heat the oil in a deep frying pan. Brown the garlic in it; remove and discard garlic. Add mushrooms and a little salt (anchovies are salty) and pepper. Cook over high heat, stirring constantly, until all the mushroom liquid has evaporated. Stir in butter, anchovies and parsley, and cook 2 minutes longer. Remove from heat and stir in lemon juice. Serve very hot.

Onions with Ham and Rosemary   6 servings

Cipolline al Prosciutto e al Rosmarino   from Abruzzi

3 cups boiling water
½ cup white vinegar
2 pounds small white
   onions, the smaller
   the better, peeled
2 tablespoons butter
2 tablespoons olive oil
¼ pound prosciutto or
   smoked ham, cut into
   julienne strips

2 to 3 tablespoons
   crushed dried
   rosemary, or 2 sprigs
   of fresh rosemary, 3
   inches long
salt
freshly ground pepper

Combine boiling water and vinegar in a saucepan large enough to hold the onions. When it is at the boiling point, add onions. Cook over medium heat for 3 to 4 minutes; drain. Heat butter and olive oil in a large frying pan. Add prosciutto and cook, stirring constantly, for 1 to 2 minutes. Add onions and rosemary and season with salt and pepper to taste. Cook over medium heat, stirring all the time, for about 3 minutes. Reduce heat to lowest possible. Simmer covered, shaking the pan frequently, for about 45 minutes. Check the moisture; if necessary, add a little warm water, 2 tablespoons at a time.

NOTE: Avoid aluminum saucepan if possible; vinegar may cause discoloration of pan.

Abruzzi (l'Aquila)

Onions and Mushrooms

4 to 6 servings

Contorno di Cipolle e Funghi

from Abruzzi

I had this in Scanno, near the Abruzzi National Park, with marvelous wild mushrooms.

1 pound onions, cut into thin slices	1 pound mushrooms, cut into thick slices
3 tablespoons olive oil	1 tablespoon wine vinegar, or more to taste
1 garlic clove, minced	
¼ cup minced parsley	
¼ teaspoon dried hot red pepper flakes, or to taste	

Put onions into a saucepan and barely cover with boiling water. Cook covered for 3 to 5 minutes, or until barely tender. Drain and reserve. Heat olive oil in a deep frying pan. Add garlic, parsley and hot red pepper flakes. Cook, stirring constantly, for about 2 minutes. Add mushrooms. Cook over medium heat, stirring constantly, until mushrooms are tender and their liquid has evaporated except for 2 to 3 tablespoons. Add onions and simmer covered for 5 minutes. Remove from heat and stir in the vinegar. Serve with roasted meats.

Onion Stew

4 to 6 servings

Cipolline d'Ivrea

from Piedmont

1½ pounds small white
    onions
3 tablespoons butter
1 tablespoon olive oil
2 bay leaves
1 cup onion broth or
    chicken bouillon

½ cup dry white wine
    salt
    freshly ground pepper
¼ cup minced parsley

Choose onions of a similar size so that they will be cooked in the same length of time. Put onions in a saucepan and add enough boiling water barely to cover them. Bring to the boiling point, reduce heat, and cook until onions are about three-quarters tender. Drain and reserve the cooking liquid. Peel the onions. Heat butter and olive oil in a deep frying pan. Add onions and cook over high heat for 1 to 2 minutes, or until barely golden. Reduce heat and add bay leaves, 1 cup of onion cooking liquid and the wine. Season lightly with salt and pepper. Simmer without a cover until onions are tender and cooking liquid has reduced to a few spoonfuls. Shake the pan frequently to prevent sticking. Sprinkle with parsley before serving.

NOTE: Do not overcook or the onions will fall apart. Cooking time depends on their size.

Peas with Prosciutto

4 servings

Piselli con Prosciutto   from Rome

3 tablespoons butter
3 tablespoons minced
   onion
½ cup minced prosciutto
¼ cup minced parsley
2 pounds fresh peas,
   shelled, or 1 to 2 10-
   ounce packages
   frozen peas, thawed

2 to 4 tablespoons
   chicken or beef
   bouillon
salt
freshly ground pepper
1 tablespoon minced
   fresh mint (optional)

Combine butter, onion, prosciutto and parsley in a heavy saucepan. Cook over medium heat, stirring constantly, for 3 to 4 minutes. Add peas and bouillon, 2 tablespoons if you are using fresh peas or 10 ounces of frozen peas, 4 tablespoons if you are using 2 10-ounce packages of frozen peas. Season with salt and pepper to taste. Cook covered over low heat for 10 minutes, or until peas are tender. Check for moisture; if necessary, add 1 or 2 more tablespoons of bouillon to prevent scorching. Sprinkle mint on top before serving.

Potato Pudding

6 to 8 servings

Gatto di Patate

from Campania

Use this traditional Neapolitan dish as a first course, with a tomato or mushroom sauce, or as a main dish with a tossed salad. The word comes from the French "gâteau".

2 pounds potatoes (about 6 medium-size potatoes), peeled
6 tablespoons butter, at room temperature
freshly ground pepper
1 cup freshly grated Parmesan cheese
3 eggs, separated
¼ pound prosciutto or salami, cut into ¼-inch dice

½ pound fresh or smoked mozzarella cheese, cut into ½-inch dice
2 hard-cooked eggs, cut lengthwise into 8 wedges each
butter for mold
fine dry bread crumbs

Cook potatoes in salted water until they are soft. Put 4 table-spoons of the butter in a large bowl. Drain the potatoes and push them through a ricer or a food mill into the bowl with the butter. Stir to mix well. Season with pepper and stir in the Parmesan cheese; mix well and cool. Beat in the 3 egg yolks, one at a time, beating well after each addition. Beat in prosciutto or salami and mozzarella. Mix to distribute prosciutto and cheese dice evenly through the potatoes. Add hard-cooked egg pieces carefully, distributing them through the pudding without breaking them into too many pieces. Beat egg whites until stiff and fold them into the pudding. Generously butter an 8-cup mold with straight sides and coat bottom and sides with fine dry bread crumbs, shaking off excess bread crumbs. Turn the mixture into the mold and smooth out the top. Sprinkle with 4 tablespoons fine dry bread crumbs and dot with remaining 2 tablespoons of butter. Cook in a preheated hot oven (400°F.) for 45 to 55 minutes, or until well set and golden. Turn off the oven, open the door, and let the pudding stay in the oven for 5 minutes. Then serve from the dish or unmold on a round platter.

Potato Stew   4 to 6 servings

Patate in Umido   from Rome

2 pounds potatoes (6 to 7   1 garlic clove, minced
    medium-size   2 to 2½ cups canned
    potatoes)   plum tomatoes
¼ cup minced pancetta or   ¼ cup minced fresh basil,
    blanched salt pork   or 1 tablespoon dried
2 tablespoons butter   basil, or to taste
1 medium-size onion, cut   salt
    into thin slices   freshly ground pepper

Peel potatoes and cut them into 1-inch cubes. In a heavy saucepan, heat together pancetta and butter. Add onion and garlic,
and cook over medium heat, stirring constantly, for 2 minutes,
or until onion is soft. Add potatoes and cook, stirring all the
time, for 2 minutes. Add tomatoes, basil, and salt and pepper
to taste. Simmer covered over low heat, stirring frequently,
until potatoes are tender. Check the liquid since tomatoes have
different water content; if necessary, add a little hot water, 1
tablespoon at a time, to prevent scorching, or cook without a
cover to reduce the sauce. The dish should not be soupy.

NOTE: ¼ cup dried mushrooms, soaked in lukewarm water for
15 minutes, may be added with their liquid to the dish along
with the tomatoes.

Spinach Genoa, with Pine Nuts and Currants

3 to 4 servings

Spinaci alla Genovese coi Pignoli   from Liguria

2 pounds fresh spinach
⅓ cup dried currants or
  seedless raisins,
  plumped in warm
  water, drained
⅓ cup pine nuts (pignoli)
¼ cup olive oil

1 garlic clove
2 teaspoons anchovy
  paste (optional)
  salt
  freshly ground pepper
  dash of ground nutmeg

Wash the spinach in several waters. Put washed spinach into a large saucepan and cook covered with just the water remaining on the leaves for 3 minutes, or only until spinach is getting soft. Drain spinach in a strainer, pressing out excess liquid with the back of a spoon. Chop spinach into coarse pieces. Add currants and pine nuts to spinach and mix well. Heat the olive oil in a frying pan, add garlic, and cook until garlic is turning brown. Take garlic out with a slotted spoon and discard it. Add anchovy paste and cook, stirring constantly, until it is dissolved. Add the spinach mixture. Stir with a fork to blend oil and spinach. Cover the frying pan. Simmer over very low heat for 5 to 10 minutes to heat through thoroughly and to blend the flavors. Season with salt and pepper to taste and add nutmeg. Serve very hot, immediately.

Swiss Chard and Mushroom Pudding   6 servings

Polpettone di Bietole alla Genovese   from Genoa

2 bunches of Swiss
   chard, 2 to 2½
   pounds
2 tablespoons butter
2 tablespoons olive oil
2 garlic cloves
½ pound mushrooms, cut
   into thick slices
4 tablespoons (¼ cup)
   grated Parmesan
   cheese

   salt
   freshly ground pepper
½ teaspoon dried thyme
   dash of Tabasco
3 eggs
   oil for baking dish
4 tablespoons fine dry
   bread crumbs

Trim the Swiss chard and cut it into ¼-inch strips. Wash thoroughly; drain. Place in a saucepan with the water clinging to the leaves. Cook covered over high heat for 3 to 4 minutes. Drain and first squeeze dry with a wooden spoon against the sides of the strainer, and then with your hands. Heat butter and olive oil. Add garlic and cook until garlic is browned, then discard it. Add mushrooms and cook over high heat, stirring constantly, for 3 to 4 minutes, until mushrooms are golden but still firm. Add the Swiss chard and 2 tablespoons of the Parmesan. Cook over medium heat, stirring constantly, for 3 to 4 minutes. Remove from heat and season with salt and pepper to taste and the thyme. Stir in the Tabasco. Cool. The chard and mushrooms will release a certain amount of juices; pour them off. Beat eggs with remaining Parmesan, combine with the vegetables, and mix well. Oil a deep 8-inch baking dish and coat it with 2 tablespoons of the dry bread crumbs on the bottom and sides. Pour in the vegetable mixture and smooth out the top with a spatula. Sprinkle with remaining bread crumbs. Bake in a preheated moderate oven for 20 to 30 minutes, or until firm and golden brown on the top. Serve hot or cool, but not chilled.

Tomatoes Stuffed with Mozzarella   4 to 6 servings

Pomodori Riempiti di Mozzarella   from Naples

4 to 6 large, ripe but
 firm tomatoes
 oil for baking dish
 salt
 freshly ground pepper
3 tablespoons olive oil
¼ to ½ pound
 mozzarella cheese
 (amount depends on
 size of tomatoes)

2 tablespoons minced
 fresh basil, or 2
 teaspoons dried basil

Cut a slice from the top of each tomato. Using a teaspoon, scoop out the pulp and seeds. Turn tomatoes upside down on a platter and let them stand for 15 minutes to drain. Place tomatoes in an oiled baking dish just large enough to hold them. Season each tomato cavity with salt and pepper. Drizzle 1 teaspoon of oil into each tomato. Chop the mozzarella fine and mix it with the basil. Stuff tomatoes with mozzarella. With a pastry brush, brush the outside skin of tomatoes with remaining olive oil. Bake in a preheated moderate oven (375°F.) for about 20 minutes, or until mozzarella has melted. Serve hot.

Zucchini and Egg Loaf

6 servings

Timballo di Zucchini   from Tuscany

6 large zucchini, washed and trimmed salt 2 tablespoons olive oil 6 tablespoons butter 1 large onion, cut into thin slices 3 slices of white bread, crusts removed, soaked in milk, drained and mashed 4 eggs, beaten	½ cup freshly grated Parmesan cheese ½ cup minced parsley 3 tablespoons minced fresh marjoram, or 3 teaspoons dried marjoram freshly ground pepper dash of Tabasco oil for baking dish 1 cup fine dry bread crumbs

Do not peel zucchini. Cut them lengthwise into quarters; if very large, halve the quarters lengthwise. Scrape off the seeds with a sharp spoon. Cut the strips into ¾-inch pieces. Spread a clean kitchen towel on the counter and lay zucchini pieces on it. Sprinkle lightly with salt. Tie the four ends of the kitchen towel together and hang it over the kitchen sink to drain, or place it in a strainer set in a dish. Let stand for 45 minutes. The zucchini will start losing their moisture. Squeeze and twist the towel to extract as much moisture as possible; you will be surprised at the amount. In a large, deep frying pan, heat the olive oil and 4 tablespoons of the butter. Over medium heat, cook onion until it is soft but still white. Add the zucchini and cook, stirring frequently, for about 5 minutes. Remove from heat and cool. Stir in bread, eggs, Parmesan, parsley and marjoram. Check the seasonings; the zucchini may be sufficiently salty; if not, add a little more salt, pepper to taste and Tabasco. Blend the mixture thoroughly. Sprinkle an oiled 2-quart baking dish, or a pan 13 × 9 × 2 inches, with half of the bread crumbs. Turn the vegetable mixture into the dish. Sprinkle with remaining bread crumbs and dot with remaining 2 tablespoons butter. Bake in a preheated moderate oven (350°F.) for about 30 minutes, or until well set and golden on top. Serve warm or cooled, but not chilled, cut into slices.

Cold Soused Zucchini

4 to 6 servings

Zucchini alla Scapece

from Naples

2 pounds medium-size
zucchini
½ to 1 cup olive oil
½ to ⅔ cup fresh mint
leaves, stems
removed

3 garlic cloves, minced
salt
freshly ground pepper
⅓ cup wine vinegar

Scrape and wash the zucchini. Cut them into ½-inch slices, one at a time, so that the slices keep dry. Heat some of the olive oil in a large frying pan. When it is just beginning to smoke, add zucchini slices, a few at a time; they must not touch each other as they fry. Fry until golden on one side, then turn with 2 forks and again fry until golden. Remove zucchini with a slotted spoon and drain the slices on several thicknesses of kitchen paper. Cut up the next zucchini and repeat. If necessary, add a little more olive oil as you fry remaining zucchini. When all zucchini are fried, turn off the heat under the frying pan and pour off the oil into a little bowl and save for further cooking use. Layer the fried zucchini slices in a glass or china serving dish. Between layers, place some of the mint leaves and a little garlic, and sprinkle with salt and pepper. Heat 3 to 4 tablespoons fresh oil in the frying pan and add the vinegar. Cook for 2 minutes and pour over the zucchini. (For a tarter dish, use vinegar to taste.) Chill well before serving with roast or broiled meats or broiled fish.

Zucchini Stuffed with Meat   4 to 6 servings

Zucchini Imbottite con la Carne   from Rome

Good-sized zucchini, cut into pieces, are easier to stuff than small, whole zucchini. Since the size of zucchini varies, as does the way they are hollowed out, the quantities indicated for the stuffing ingredients have to be flexible.

THE STUFFING:
- ½ to ⅔ cup lean ground beef, veal or pork
- 3 tablespoons grated Parmesan cheese
- 3 tablespoons minced pancetta or lean bacon
- 1 to 2 tablespoons fresh white bread crumbs grated rind of 1 lemon
- ¼ cup capers (if large, chopped)
- 1 egg
  salt
  freshly ground pepper

ZUCCHINI:
- 5 large zucchini, each about 7 inches long
- 2 tablespoons olive oil
- 1 small onion, minced
- 2 cups plain tomato sauce or tomato juice
  salt
  freshly ground pepper
- ¼ cup minced parsley

Combine all the stuffing ingredients, using ½ cup ground meat and 1 tablespoon bread crumbs; mix well. If zucchini are large, use all the ground meat and bread crumbs.

Trim zucchini and cut each into 3-inch pieces. Scoop out the pulp with an apple corer, taking care not to break the shells. Since the apple corer will not scoop out a large enough cavity, scoop out some more with a teaspoon. Push some of the stuffing into each zucchini piece, packing it tight. Heat the oil in a large, wide frying pan which will take all the zucchini pieces. Or use 2 frying pans, using 2 tablespoons of oil in each. Cook the onion, stirring constantly, until it is barely golden. Add zucchini pieces. Over medium heat, cook zucchini until they are golden on all sides. Using a wooden spoon, turn zucchini pieces so that they are cooking on all sides. Pour tomato sauce over zucchini. Check seasoning and add the parsley. If you are using 2 frying pans, you will need more tomato sauce; add 1½ cups to each pan. Cook covered over low heat for 15 to 20 minutes, or until zucchini are tender. Check the moisture; if too dry, add a little hot water. The finished dish should have just enough sauce to top the zucchini. Transfer carefully to a heated serving dish and pour the sauce over the vegetable.

Zucchini in Cream with Rosemary — 4 servings

Zucchini alla Crema — from Piedmont

The dish should have a pronounced rosemary flavor.

2 pounds zucchini, each 6 to 7 inches long	1 cup heavy cream
1 tablespoon salt	1 to 2 tablespoons fresh or dried rosemary (crumbled if dried)
2 tablespoons butter freshly ground pepper	

Trim zucchini and wash them. Cut lengthwise into 4 strips. With a sharp paring knife, remove most of the seeds in each strip, coring them as you would an apple. Cut zucchini into 1-inch pieces. Place pieces in a bowl and sprinkle the salt over them, mixing well. Let stand at room temperature for 15 to 30 minutes. The vegetable will yield its surplus moisture; pour it off. Dry zucchini between sheets of kitchen paper. Heat the butter in a large deep frying pan or shallow saucepan. Add the zucchini. Over medium heat, and stirring constantly, cook for 2 to 3 minutes. Check seasoning; if necessary, add a little more salt and add pepper to taste. Pour the cream over the zucchini and sprinkle with the rosemary; mix well. Over high heat, stirring frequently, cook for 4 to 5 minutes, or until cream has reduced to sauce consistency. Serve immediately.

Quick Shredded Zucchini   4 servings

Zucchini alla Svelta   from Lombardy

2   pounds zucchini   freshly ground pepper
1   tablespoon salt   juice of ½ lemon
2 to 4   tablespoons butter

Wash and trim zucchini but do not peel them; however, remove all blemished skin. Shred on the coarse side of a cheese grater or in a food processor. Place zucchini in a colander and sprinkle with the salt. Stand in the sink and let zucchini throw off excess moisture for 3 to 4 minutes. Drain. Place zucchini in a deep frying pan. Cook over high heat, stirring once or twice, for 3 to 4 minutes or even less, depending on the age of the zucchini. The vegetable must remain green and crisp. Remove from heat and stir in the butter, pepper to taste and lemon juice. Serve immediately.

Sauces

Salse

Italian food is not sauced up as in French cuisine; the sauces are either inherent to the dish or simple accompaniments to add zest to the food rather than to mask it. Especially in popular regional cooking the sauces are not elegant in nature, being piquant rather than rich with butter, cream and eggs. Oil and lemon juice combine in the most popular of all sauces; capers, anchovies, herbs, nuts and the like serve as additions. Above all, lemon juice must not be missing; on Italian steak or meats, it takes the place of Béarnaise sauce.

Contrary to the practice of many American-Italian restaurants, not all Italian food is doused in tomato sauce. Even in southern Italy, where tomato sauce figures prominently in regional cookery, it is used with a good deal of discretion. It is used very little in northern Italian cooking, where the tomato sauces are also lighter than those of the South.

A number of sauces are found in the chapters on Pasta, Rice, Polenta and Dumplings, with the dish of which each is a component, and other sauces follow those chapters in a chapter of their own. All are listed under sauces in the index.

White-Wine Salad Sauce

about 1¾ cups

Salsa per Insalate al Vino Bianco

from Tuscany

For vegetable salads, green and mixed salads, and seafood.

¾ cup dry white wine
½ cup olive oil
¼ cup white-wine vinegar
  (preferably tarragon
  vinegar)
¼ cup grated onion

½ garlic clove, mashed
salt
freshly ground pepper
sprinkle of any
  preferred herb

Combine all the ingredients and blend thoroughly. Use while foods to be dressed are still hot.

Simple Caper Sauce

about ⅔ cup

Salsa Semplice con i Capperi

All-Italian

For fish and seafood, plain meats and cooked vegetables.

½ cup olive oil
juice of 1 large lemon
½ cup drained capers

freshly ground pepper
dash of Tabasco

Combine olive oil, lemon juice and capers and mix well. Season with pepper to taste and stir in the Tabasco.

Bagna Cauda

about ¾ cup

Bagna Cauda

from Piedmont

A famous Piedmontese sauce used as a dip for raw vegetables such as celery, peppers, carrot strips, and cauliflowerets. A chafing dish is practical for this sauce which must be kept hot, but must *never* boil.

½ cup (¼ pound) butter
¼ cup olive oil
4 garlic cloves, sliced very thin, or garlic to taste

6 anchovy fillets, drained and chopped
1 small white truffle, cut into thin slices (optional)

Heat butter and olive oil in a chafing dish or a small shallow pan that can go to the table. Add the garlic. Cook over very low heat for 5 minutes, or until garlic is soft; it must not brown, nor must the mixture boil. Remove from the heat. With a wooden spoon, stir in the anchovies; return sauce to the heat and cook, stirring constantly, until anchovies have dissolved into the sauce. Add the truffle slices and serve hot.

NOTE: Keep the sauce hot at the table on a candle-warmer, an electric hotplate or a fondue heating unit.

Uncooked Piquant Green Sauce   about 2½ cups

Salsa Verde Piccante   All-Italian

The consistency of a sauce is a matter of personal preference; the egg and/or the walnut make a thicker sauce. Serve with hot or cold fish and seafood, with cooked vegetables such as artichokes, cauliflower and broccoli, and with broiled or boiled meats.

2 cups parsley leaves, without stems, tightly packed, or 1 cup parsley leaves, without stems, tightly packed, *and* 1 cup watercress leaves, tightly packed
2 tablespoons drained capers
1 tablespoon minced onion
1 garlic clove, chopped
2 teaspoons dried basil, or 1 to 2 tablespoons fresh basil

2 teaspoons anchovy paste, or 2 anchovy fillets, minced (optional)
1 hard-cooked egg, chopped (optional)
⅓ cup chopped walnuts (optional)
¾ cup olive oil
juice of 2 large lemons
salt
freshly ground pepper

Put the parsley, or parsley and watercress, into a bowl. Add enough boiling water to cover; let stand for 2 minutes. Drain and place in a blender container. Add all the other ingredients. If you are using anchovy paste, go easy on the salt. Blend at low speed until thoroughly mixed. If the mixture appears to be too thick, add a little more olive oil, 1 tablespoon at a time. Chill before using.

Thin Egg and Lemon Sauce   about ½ cup

Salsa per Verdure Lessate   All-Italian

One of the simplest and best sauces for cooked vegetables and boiled fish.

In the serving dish in which the vegetable will be served, beat together 2 egg yolks, the juice of 1 large lemon, and salt and pepper to taste. Add the drained hot vegetables and toss. If the sauce looks too thick, beat 1 or 2 tablespoons of the vegetable cooking liquid into it. If the sauce is to be used for fish, beat the ingredients in a bowl. Place the fish on a serving platter and pour the sauce over it.

Almond Sauce for Plain Boiled Fish   about 1⅓ cups

Salsa di Olio, Mandorle e Limone per il Pesce Bollito   from Sicily

12 blanched almonds,   2 to 3 tablespoons fresh
    chopped   lemon juice
 2 garlic cloves, chopped   1 cup olive oil
 ½ teaspoon salt

Put almonds, garlic, salt and lemon juice into a blender container. Whirl at slow speed; while the blender is whirling, slowly pour in the olive oil. Blend until smooth.

Mushroom Sauce   about 2⅔ cups

Salsa di Funghi   All-Italian

1 tablespoon chopped onion	1 small tomato, peeled, seeded and chopped, or 2 canned plum tomatoes, drained
2 tablespoons parsley heads without stems	
½ cup chopped prosciutto or lean bacon	1 cup dry white wine
	½ cup chicken or beef bouillon
2 tablespoons olive oil	salt
2 tablespoons butter	freshly ground pepper
½ pound mushrooms, sliced thin	¼ teaspoon dried thyme
1 tablespoon flour	

Combine onion, parsley and prosciutto on chopping board. Chop and mince together so that ingredients are well blended and pasty. Heat olive oil and butter. Cook prosciutto mixture over low heat, stirring constantly, for 5 minutes. Add mushrooms. Cook over high heat, stirring constantly, for about 3 minutes. Lower heat to low and stir in flour. Add tomato, wine, bouillon, salt and pepper to taste and thyme. Simmer without a cover for 10 to 15 minutes, stirring frequently.

Sarmoriglio

about 1⅓ cups

Salsa Sarmoriglio

from Sicily

Used on roasts, it is also good for boiled fish and seafood and cooked vegetables.

1 cup olive oil	4 tablespoons hot water
juice of 2 lemons	salt
2 tablespoons minced parsley	freshly ground pepper
	dash of Tabasco
½ teaspoon dried oregano	(optional)

Combine oil, lemon juice, parsley and oregano in the top part of a double boiler and beat together. Add the hot water and beat until the sauce is smooth. Season with salt and pepper to taste and stir in Tabasco. Heat the sauce over, not in, hot water. When it is very hot, pour it over slices of roast lamb, veal or chicken or freshly cooked vegetables such as broccoli and green beans. Serve immediately.

Uncooked Sweet Pepper Sauce   about 1½ cups

Salsetta ai Peperoni   from Puglia

For broiled fish and seafood, meats and fowl.

2 very large green, red or   1 tablespoon mild vinegar
     yellow sweet   or lemon juice, or to
     peppers, or 4   taste
     medium-size peppers   salt
1 medium-size onion   freshly ground pepper
½ to ⅔ cup olive oil

To peel the peppers, place them over high heat, directly on the
burners, until the skin is black and blistered. Turn peppers
frequently so that the skin will cook on all sides. Under running cold water, using your fingers and a paring knife, peel
and scrape off the blistered and blackened outer skin. Trim the
peppers free of seeds and membranes and dry them well with
kitchen paper. Chop together the peppers and the onion until
bits are the size of peas. Add olive oil, vinegar, and salt and
pepper to taste; mix well.

Desserts
Dolci

Italians usually end their meals with fresh fruits. Yet throughout Italy we find an enormous number of varied desserts, from homemade creams, tarts and fried cookies to sophisticated ices and pastry shop creations. Who eats all these sweet things?

A dessert may be served at the end of a family meal on Sunday to make it more festive, or on a religious holiday. Desserts are served to guests invited to dinner, or to people who drop in between meals. Desserts are eaten in cafés and pastry shops, at fairs, or from the stand of a street vendor. Like many dishes in regional cooking, some desserts are made but once a year, on a specific day.

Ever since the introduction of sugar into Italy the Italians have made good use of it, becoming renowned in all of Europe as pastry cooks and confectioners. Sweets were festive, sweets were beautiful, sweets were something special within a simple diet. They became regional like other cookery. In northern Italy, where milk and cream are abundant, desserts were also inspired by French cookery. In the South, where milk and cream were not common, almonds, in milk or paste, took their place, substituting also for butter. The sweets of the Italian South and Sicily are part of the Saracen heritage of these regions, and the Spanish heritage, which was also influenced by the Saracens. And the Bourbons brought Frenchified notions to Naples.

There is a sharp division in Italy between professional desserts and homemade ones. The first have increased in popularity. It is more elegant to order a party dessert from the best pastry shop in town; and the products of the Italian *pasticcerie* are at times sublime, from the tiny pastries to St. Honorés glittering with spun sugar. The second, desserts made at home, for street fairs and markets and for special holidays, are on the decline. One reason is that commercial desserts, cakes and ice creams are now distributed on a national basis and are found even in remote little cafés and local markets.

Yet many of the traditional sweets of the Italian regions, no longer found except possibly in homes, deserve to remain part of Italy's living cuisine. In view of this, rather than dividing desserts into categories such as puddings, cakes, and cookies, I have split them into two groups. The first includes customary desserts that are still made in homes, that will be successful, and that are not too complicated or demanding in terms of expense and time. They are, in other words, desserts for family meals and informal entertaining. The second group includes rare and occasional desserts, some curiosities, and recipes for sweets usually bought in shops or stalls, such as Cannoli alla Siciliana. I have included the latter because I know from experience that there are always nostalgic cooks who want to reproduce something they had in Italy which they cannot find available for purchase at home.

DESSERTS FOR FAMILY AND FRIENDS

Strawberries with Wine
6 servings

Fragole al Vino
All-Italian

---

dry white wine
2 quarts strawberries, hulled

superfine sugar to taste
1 cup dry or sweet white wine or Marsala

Pour enough inexpensive dry white wine into a bowl to half-cover the strawberries. Add strawberries, rinse quickly, and drain them. Place in a glass serving dish and sprinkle with sugar. Add 1 cup wine and toss gently. Chill before serving.

VARIATION I: *Strawberries with Lemon*
Proceed as above, but substitute the wine with the juice of 2 to 3 large lemons, strained. This is the preferred way of serving the fragrant wild strawberries of Italy, and it is good with all strawberries.

VARIATION II:
In place of lemon juice, use fresh orange juice to taste.

Sliced Oranges in Marsala   4 to 6 servings

Arance al Marsala   from Sicily

6 large oranges,   sugar to taste
   preferably blood   ⅔ to 1 cup sweet Marsala
   oranges

Peel oranges carefully over a plate, to catch the juices. Discard all the white pith. Cut oranges into thin slices, and place them and the juice in a glass serving dish. Sprinkle with sugar to taste. Add Marsala and toss gently with a fork. Chill well before serving.

Chestnuts with Marsala and Wine   6 servings

Castagne al Marsala   from Abruzzi

1½ pounds fresh chestnuts   1 cup dry red wine
½ cup sugar   1 cup Marsala

Score the chestnuts across the flat sides with a sharp knife. Place in boiling water to cover plus 2 inches of water and simmer for 15 minutes. Taking out a few chestnuts at a time, remove outer shells and inner skins; they will come off if the chestnuts are warm. Work carefully, since chestnuts break very easily. Combine sugar, red wine and Marsala in a wide, shallow saucepan. Simmer over low heat for about 5 minutes. Carefully add the chestnuts and simmer over low heat for 5 to 10 minutes, or until they are tender. Shake the pan occasionally to prevent sticking. With a slotted spoon, transfer chestnuts to a glass or silver serving dish. Bring pan liquid quickly to the boiling point and cook for 1 to 2 minutes. Cool a little and pour over the chestnuts. Serve warm or cold with plain heavy cream and thin, crisp cookies.

Baked Stuffed Peaches   6 servings

Pesche Ripiene   All-Italian

6 large, ripe but firm
   peaches, preferably
   Freestone peaches
½ cup almond macaroon
   crumbs (4 to 5
   macaroons), or
   ground almonds
¼ cup mixed glacé fruit,
   shredded fine

butter for baking dish
12 blanched almonds
½ to ¾ cup dry white
   wine, or equal
   quantities of Marsala
   and water

Wash peaches and cut them into halves. Remove pits. Using a teaspoon, scrape and slightly enlarge the cavity. Mash the pulp obtained and put into a bowl. Add macaroon crumbs and the glacé fruit; mix well. Fill peach cavities with the mixture. Butter a deep baking dish just large enough to hold the peach halves, and arrange them in the dish in one layer. Top each half with an almond. Sprinkle with ½ cup of the wine. Bake without a cover in a preheated moderate oven (375°F.) for 15 to 20 minutes, depending on the ripeness of the fruit. After 10 minutes of baking, sprinkle with the remaining wine. Serve warm or cold, but not chilled.

Fried Cream

about 2 dozen

Crema Fritta

from Lombardy

Delicious and old-fashioned.

½ cup granulated sugar
4 whole eggs
4 eggs, separated
  grated rind of 1 lemon
2 cups flour

4 cups milk
  fine dry bread crumbs
  olive oil for deep-frying
  confectioners' sugar

In the top part of a double boiler, beat together very thoroughly the granulated sugar, whole eggs, separated egg yolks and lemon rind. Combine flour and milk to make a smooth paste. Stir it gradually into the egg mixture. Put the double boiler top over boiling water, reduce heat and cook, stirring frequently, for 1 to 1½ hours. Rinse a shallow baking dish with cold water. When the mixture is very thick and comes away from the pan, spread it into the baking dish in a layer about 1 inch thick. Cool completely. When cold and firm, cut the paste into diamond shapes; 2 inches is a good size. Dip the creams into egg whites and then into bread crumbs. Make sure creams are well coated with egg white and bread crumbs on all sides or they will ooze during frying. Heat abundant olive oil to 375°F. on a frying thermometer. Fry a few pieces at a time until golden, turning them over once or twice. Drain on paper towels. Pile on a hot serving dish lined with a napkin and sprinkle with confectioners' sugar before serving.

Mont Blanc of Chestnuts
6 to 8 servings

Monte Bianco
from Lombardy

A classic dessert, and one of the best in the world. It should be very light and fluffy. Make this a short time before serving. Some recipes advocate simmering the chestnuts in sugar syrup, but I find this impairs the lightness of the dessert.

1½ to 2 pounds chestnuts
3 cups milk
¾ cup sugar
1 piece of vanilla bean, 3 inches

2 cups heavy cream, whipped

With the point of a sharp knife score the chestnuts across the flat sides. Put them into a saucepan, cover with water plus 2 inches of water, and bring to the boiling point. Simmer for 15 minutes. Taking out a few chestnuts at a time, remove outer shells and inner skins; they will come off if the chestnuts are warm. Combine milk, sugar and vanilla bean and scald. Drop peeled chestnuts into the milk. Simmer without a cover over lowest possible heat until chestnuts are very tender and falling to pieces. Drain, reserving the milk for custard or other puddings, and remove the vanilla bean. Over a large serving dish, preferably a silver one, force the chestnuts through a potato ricer, a food mill or a coarse sieve in a circular motion. Start at the edges of the dish and move toward the center and up. You should have a cone-shaped mound. Do not try shaping the mound in any way; the chestnuts must remain loose and fluffy. Lightly spoon the whipped cream over the chestnut mound, letting it stream casually down the sides. Do not press it down. The Mont Blanc, as its name indicates, should resemble a brown mountain (the chestnuts) streaked and topped with snow (the whipped cream). Refrigerate for 15 to 20 minutes, but no longer.

Rich Chocolate Dessert

8 to 10 servings

Dolce Torino

from Piedmont

Use, if possible, the ladyfingers sold in Italian pastry shops or by Italian bakers, which are firmer than commercial American ladyfingers. If the latter are used, reduce the amount of brandy or rum sprinkled over the ladyfingers or they might become mushy. This is a winter dessert.

24 ladyfingers
1 cup Maraschino
   liqueur, rum or
   brandy
8 ounces (8 squares)
   semisweet chocolate
3 to 4 tablespoons light
   cream
½ teaspoon vanilla
   flavoring
1 cup (½ pound) unsalted
   butter (it must be
   unsalted butter)

⅓ cup superfine sugar
2 egg yolks, lightly
   beaten
   blanched almonds
   glacé cherries, cut into
   halves
½ cup heavy cream,
   whipped

Split the ladyfingers and place the halves on one or two platters. Sprinkle with the Maraschino and let stand for 30 minutes. They should be moist but still retain their shape. Combine the chocolate, 3 tablespoons of the cream and the vanilla in the top part of a double boiler. Cook over hot, but not boiling, water, stirring constantly, until chocolate is melted and the mixture is smooth. If too thick to stir, stir in remaining tablespoon of cream. Remove from heat and cool. Cream the butter until soft and fluffy. Gradually beat in the sugar, beating well after each addition. Use an electric beater or mixer; the mixture must be very smooth and no longer grainy. Beat in the egg yolks, a little at a time, beating well after each addition. Gradually add chocolate mixture to butter mixture, a little at a time, blending thoroughly, until soft and creamy.

On a platter or preferably a silver serving dish, and using a spatula, arrange 12 ladyfinger halves in the shape of a square.

Using a spatula dipped into cold water, spread a thin layer of chocolate cream over the ladyfingers. Top with 12 more lady-fingers and more chocolate cream until all the ladyfingers are used, ending with a layer of chocolate cream and coating the sides of the confection. Smooth the surface and decorate with the almonds and glacé cherries. Cover lightly with wax paper and let ripen in a cool place for at least 6 hours. At serving time, pipe decorative swags of whipped cream around the edges of the cake.

NOTE: The reason for keeping the Dolce Torino in a cool place rather than in the refrigerator is that too cold a temperature congeals the butter. However, if the Dolce Torino has to be refrigerated, let it stand at room temperature for at least 30 minutes before serving.

Ricotta Pudding   4 to 6 servings

Budino di Ricotta   from Rome

Some ricotta is softer and moister than others. This pudding requires dry ricotta, so that it may be advisable to line a strainer with cheesecloth and place the moist ricotta on it to drain.

2 cups ricotta cheese	¼ cup glacé citron, cut
1 whole egg	into tiny dice
4 eggs, separated	grated rind of 1 lemon
½ cup sugar	¼ cup rum or Maraschino
¼ cup flour	liqueur
¼ teaspoon grated	butter for mold
nutmeg	confectioners' sugar
¼ cup glacé orange rind,	ground cinnamon
cut into tiny dice	

Put the ricotta into a large bowl. Beat in, one at a time, the whole egg and the 4 egg yolks, beating well after each addition. Beat in the sugar, flour, nutmeg, glacé fruits, lemon rind and rum, and beat until very smooth. Beat the 4 egg whites until very stiff and fold them into the ricotta mixture. Generously butter a 2-quart mold with smooth sides. Spoon in the batter; the mold should not be more than half full. Bake in a preheated moderate oven (350°F.) for about 30 minutes, or until well puffed and golden. Sprinkle with confectioners' sugar and a little ground cinnamon, and serve hot. Or cool and then sprinkle with confectioners' sugar and ground cinnamon.

Trifle

10 to 12 servings

Zuppa all' Emiliana

from Central Italy

This type of dessert is the official sweet at rural feasts such as weddings, first communions and christenings. Slight variations exist depending on the locality and the cook, but this version, from the Romagna, is typical.

3 egg yolks
3 tablespoons sugar
¼ cup flour
2½ cups milk
3 ounces sweet or semisweet chocolate, cut into small pieces
butter for pan
2 spongecake layers, about 8 inches in diameter

¼ cup rum or Maraschino liqueur
¼ cup Morello or sour cherry preserve
multicolored sprinkles

In the top part of a double boiler and using a wire whisk, beat the egg yolks with the sugar until they are light. Alternately, stir in the flour and the milk, beating the mixture smooth. Cook over boiling water, stirring frequently with a wooden spoon, for about 20 minutes, until the mixture has begun to thicken and has almost reached the boiling point. Remove from heat and transfer half of the custard to a bowl. Stir chocolate into remaining half. Return to heat and cook, stirring frequently, until chocolate has melted. Remove from heat. Chill both custards until thickened. Lightly butter an 8-inch springform pan. Cut each spongecake layer horizontally into halves, making 4 pieces. Put 1 piece into the springform pan and sprinkle with 2 tablespoons of the rum. Top with the yellow custard. Cover with another piece and spread the preserve on top. Cover with the third piece and top it with the chocolate custard. Cover with the last sponge piece and brush this piece with the remaining rum. Chill the trifle for at least 4 hours. Unmold on a platter and decorate with the sprinkles.

Rice Torte   8 to 10 servings

Torta di Riso   from Bologna

Rice cakes are made frequently in Italy. Most are stodgy because of too much rice and too few eggs.

½ cup each of finely diced
    glacé lemon, orange
    and citron peel
½ cup Maraschino,
    Strega, rum or other
    preferred liqueur
½ cup Carolina or Italian
    rice (do not use
    converted or instant rice)
4 cups boiling water
4 cups milk

   yellow peel of 1 lemon,
    cut into 1 long twist
¾ cup sugar
6 eggs, well beaten
½ cup shredded blanched
    almonds
1 teaspoon almond
    flavoring
   butter for baking dish
   fine dry bread crumbs
   confectioners' sugar

Combine the glacé fruits and the liqueur in a small bowl and
mix well. Let stand for 1 hour or overnight. Sprinkle rice into
the boiling water and boil for 2 minutes, no longer. Drain. This
removes any excess starch.) Combine rice, milk and lemon peel
in a saucepan. Bring to the boiling point, reduce heat to lowest
possible, and cook covered, stirring frequently, until rice is
very soft and has absorbed almost all the milk. There must be
still a little milk left, a few tablespoons, so that the rice will
stay moist in cooling. Remove lemon peel and discard. Stir in
the sugar. Turn rice into a bowl and cool. Beat in the eggs, the
glacé fruits and their liquid, the almonds and almond flavoring,
and mix thoroughly. Butter a 9-inch round or square baking
dish and sprinkle the bottom and sides with bread crumbs.
Turn the rice mixture into the baking dish. Bake in a preheated
slow oven (300°F.) for about 1 hour, or until a knife inserted in
the middle of the torte comes out clean. Cool the torte and
turn out on a serving dish. The rice torte may be chilled, or,
once thoroughly cooled, can be kept in an airtight container.
Before serving, sprinkle confectioners' sugar through a doily
onto the top of the torte; this makes a pretty pattern. Cut into
diamonds and serve with a sweet dessert wine, such as Marsala, Asti Spumante, Muscatel or Sherry.

Emilia-Romagna (Bologna)

Cold Zabaglione Cream   6 to 8 servings

Semifreddo di Zabaglione   from Lombardy

A *semifreddo*, literally, half cold, meaning half frozen, is a popular dessert, made in many ways. Its name distinguishes it from ice cream, which is frozen hard.

1 envelope unflavored gelatin	1 egg white 1½ cups heavy cream,
4 tablespoons cold water	whipped and
5 egg yolks	sweetened to taste
5 tablespoons superfine	½ cup heavy cream,
sugar	whipped, for garnish
⅔ cup Marsala wine	candied violets

Have ready a bowl filled with ice cubes and water that is large enough to hold the top of a 1½- to 2-quart double boiler. Sprinkle the gelatin over the cold water in a small bowl, and set the bowl in a pan of hot water until gelatin is dissolved, stirring once or twice. Keep the gelatin liquid. Combine egg yolks and sugar in the top part of a 1½- to 2-quart double boiler. Beat with a wooden spoon, a whisk or, best, an electric beater at medium speed until the mixture is pale and thick. Beat in the Marsala, about 2 tablespoons at a time, continuing to beat as you add the wine. Place over, *not in*, hot but *not boiling* water. Continue beating until the mixture is thick and has risen almost to the top of the pan. Beat in the liquid gelatin. Remove from heat and set the double boiler top into the bowl filled with ice cubes and water. The mixture will collapse on contact with the cold. Continue beating until the zabaglione is thoroughly cold. Beat the egg white until stiff and fold it gently into the mixture. Fold in the 1½ cups whipped sweetened cream. Pour into a serving dish or individual sherbet or soufflé dishes. Chill for about 2 hours before serving. At serving time, decorate with rosettes or swirls of whipped cream and candied violets.

Apple Cake   6 servings

Dolce di Mele   from Tuscany

2 or 3 large, firm tart apples	grated rind of 1 lemon
⅓ cup rum	3⅓ cups flour
4 eggs	2 teaspoons baking powder
1¾ cups sugar	butter and flour for pan

Peel and core the apples and cut them into very thin slices. Put the slices in a bowl and pour rum over them. Make sure all the slices are moistened with rum. Beat the eggs with 1½ cups of the sugar until thick and light. Beat in the lemon rind. Sift together the flour and baking powder; stir gradually into the batter. Butter and flour a baking pan, 7 × 11 × 1¼ inches. Turn the dough into the pan and smooth out. Place the apple slices in orderly rows or circles on top of the dough. Sprinkle with remaining ¼ cup sugar. Bake in a preheated moderate oven (350°F.) for 35 to 40 minutes, or until the cake tests done. Serve warm or cold but not chilled.

Cassata Christmas or Easter Cake   one 10-inch cake

Cassata alla Siciliana   from Sicily

A *cassata* may be vanilla ice cream filled with whipped cream, chocolate bits and candied fruits, which is never made at home, but eaten in cafés and *gelaterie*, ice-cream parlors. Or it may be a cake, as it is here. There is also a Neapolitan *cassata*, a spongecake filled with custard and garnished with nuts and candied fruits. The Sicilian *cassata* gets its typical flavor from the ricotta, an essential ingredient.

3 cups (1½ pounds) fresh
     ricotta
⅓ cup superfine sugar   ¾ cup fine dice of mixed
2 tablespoons milk   glacé fruit
6 tablespoons Maraschino   1 spongecake, 10 inches,
     liqueur or rosewater   homemade or
     or orange-flower   purchased
     water   Frosting (recipe follows)
1 ounce (1 square) bitter   strips of glacé orange
     or semisweet   peel
     chocolate, chopped   glacé cherries, cut into
     fine   halves

Beat the ricotta until it is fluffy. Gradually beat in the sugar, beating well after each addition. Beat in the milk and 3 table-spoons of the Maraschino. Beat until mixture is light and fluffy. Beat in chocolate and glacé fruit. Cut the spongecake into 3 layers. Sprinkle 1 tablespoon of remaining Maraschino on each of the layers. Spread half of the filling on one cake layer, top with another layer, spread remaining filling on it, and top with the third layer. Chill. Frost just before serving time.

FROSTING:
2 to 3 cups sifted   1 to 2 tablespoons
     confectioners' sugar   lemon juice
1 egg white, unbeaten   red and green food
2 teaspoons almond   coloring
     flavoring

Put 2 cups of the confectioners' sugar, the egg white, almond flavoring and 1 tablespoon of the lemon juice into a bowl. Beat to spreading consistency. If too thin, beat in a little more confectioners' sugar; if too thick, add a little more lemon juice, ½ teaspoon at a time. Reserve one third of the frosting. Frost the sides and top of the cake. Divide remaining third of the frosting into two parts, and tint one with a drop of red food coloring and the other with a drop of green food coloring. Decorate the top of the cake with swirls of the colored frostings, strips of glacé orange peel and halves of glacé cherries.

Chestnut Flour Tart
8 to 10 servings

Castagnaccio
from Central Italy

An ancient Italian sweet, and the joy of my childhood. It was baked on an open grill in the street and sold hot in thick slices in the fall and winter, when the chestnut flour was fresh. Or vendors sold it from a big tray, covered by a white napkin. Light brown chestnut flour, imported from Italy, can be found in Italian groceries during the fall and winter months.

1 pound chestnut flour	2 tablespoons fennel seed
½ teaspoon salt	¼ cup pine nuts (pignoli)
water	
olive oil for pan	
⅔ cup currants, plumped in warm water and squeezed dry	

Sift the chestnut flour into a bowl to remove all lumps. Stir in the salt. Stirring with a wooden spoon, add just enough cold water to make a very stiff batter. Oil a 10- or 12-inch layer-cake pan with olive oil and pour in the batter. Sprinkle on top the currants, fennel seed, pine nuts, and enough olive oil to moisten lightly the whole surface of the cake. Bake in a preheated moderate oven (375°F.) for about 40 minutes, or until the top is crisp. Serve warm or cold, but not chilled.

Sour Cherry Tart

one 8-inch tart

Crostata di Visciole

from Rome

The cherries used in Rome are dark red and sweeter than our sour cherries. They resemble Morello cherries, but are larger and more flavorful. Morello cherries can be found in gourmet fruit markets, and are preferred for any cooking use since the usual sour cherries are insipid and too acid. *Crostate*, found throughout Italy, are made with different fruits or jam.

FOR THE PASTRY SHELL:
- 2 cups flour
- 6 tablespoons butter
- 4 tablespoons (¼ cup) lard
- ⅔ cup sugar
- 1 egg
- grated rind of 1 lemon

FOR THE FILLING:
- 3 to 4 cups Morello cherries, stoned
- ½ cup water
- ½ cup sugar
- ¼ teaspoon ground cinnamon
- 1 egg yolk, beaten

TO MAKE THE PASTRY SHELL:
Put the flour into a bowl and cut the butter and lard into it until the mixture resembles small peas. Stir in the sugar, egg and lemon rind. Stir with a spoon to make a ball; at the end you may have to use your hands. Wrap the dough in plastic wrap and chill. Reserve one third of the dough to make lattice strips. Roll out remaining dough and line an 8-inch pie pan with it in the usual manner. Chill both the reserved dough and the dough-lined pan.

TO MAKE THE FILLING:
Put the cherries with water, sugar and cinnamon into a saucepan. Bring to the boiling point, reduce heat, and cook, stirring constantly, for about 10 minutes, or until cherries have cooked down into a medium-thick jam. Cool. Spoon the cherry jam into the tart shell. Roll out remaining dough and cut it into ½-inch-wide 9-inch-long strips. Weave the strips into a lattice and place the lattice on the jam. Press down the edges, pinching them onto the tart shell. With a pastry brush or with your finger, paint the lattice strips with the beaten egg yolk. Bake

in a preheated hot oven (425°F.) for about 25 minutes. Cool
thoroughly before serving.

NOTE: The tart improves if it rests overnight or for 24 hours.
If necessary, frozen red sour cherries may be substituted for
the fresh Morello cherries. Mix 2 pounds thawed, drained red
sour cherries, ½ cup cherry juice, ½ cup sugar and ¼ teaspoon
ground cinnamon in a saucepan. Proceed as directed above.

Chocolate Icebox Cake   8 servings

Cassatella   from Emilia-Romagna

---

5 ounces sweet chocolate, shredded	3 eggs, separated
1 cup crushed sweet cookies, such as vanilla wafers	1 cup sifted confectioners' sugar
¾ cup macaroon crumbs (about 5 macaroons)	1 cup (½ pound) butter, cut into little pieces, at room temperature
⅓ to ½ cup rum, brandy or Sassolino liqueur (a regional specialty)	butter for loaf pan
	3 ounces ladyfingers

Combine chocolate, crushed cookies and macaroon crumbs in
a paper bag. Shake to mix. Crush with a rolling pin or the
bottom of a heavy plate to make a fine mixture. Turn chocolate
into a bowl and sprinkle with 2 tablespoons of the rum. Beat
egg yolks with sugar until they are thick and lemon-colored.
Beat in the ½ pound butter. Stir in the chocolate mixture and
blend thoroughly. If too thick, add 1 or 2 more tablespoons
of the rum. Beat egg whites until stiff. Fold them gently into
the chocolate-egg mixture. Line a lightly buttered 1¾-quart
(7-cup) loaf pan or round mold with the ladyfingers, covering
the bottom and the sides. Sprinkle remaining rum over ladyfingers. Spoon in the chocolate mixture and smooth the top
with a spatula dipped into cold water. Chill for 2 hours, or
until very firm. Unmold on a serving platter only at serving
time.

Hazelnut Cake

one 8-inch cake

Torta di Nocciuole

from Piedmont

butter and flour for pan
3 eggs
1 cup sugar
grated rind of 1 lemon
½ cup (¼ pound) butter,
at room temperature,
cut into small pieces
1⅔ cups flour

1 teaspoon baking
powder
1¼ cups hazelnuts, ground
fine in a blender,
food processor or nut
grinder
1 tablespoon olive oil
⅓ to ½ cup milk

Generously butter and flour an 8-inch springform pan. With an electric beater, beat together the eggs and sugar until very thick. (The longer the eggs are beaten, the lighter the cake.) Beat in lemon rind and butter, piece by piece. Sift together the flour and baking powder. Fold gently into the batter. Add the hazelnuts, olive oil and ⅓ cup milk, mixing well to make a medium-soft batter. If necessary, add another spoonful or two of milk. Turn into the springform pan. Bake in a preheated moderate oven (350°F.) for 50 to 60 minutes, or until the cake shrinks from the sides of the pan and tests done.

Bread and Grape Cake

2 to 3 servings

La Miascia di Tremezzo

from Lombardy

A specialty from Lake Como and an old, rustic recipe.

2 cups stale firm white-
   bread crumbs
⅔ cup milk
   salt
   grated rind of 1 lemon
¼ cup sugar
1 tablespoon flour
1 tablespoon cornmeal
1 egg, slightly beaten
1 handful stemmed fresh
   green seedless grapes
   (about 1 cup)

1 tablespoon currants,
   plumped in warm
   water and squeezed
   dry
   butter for mold
1 tablespoon butter
1 tablespoon olive oil
1 tablespoon sugar made
   from crushed sugar
   cubes
1 tablespoon crumbled
   dried rosemary

Put the bread crumbs into a bowl and pour the milk over them. Let stand for about 15 minutes. Beat in a little salt, the lemon rind, ¼ cup sugar, the flour, cornmeal and egg; beat to mix well. Stir in the grapes and currants and mix, taking care not to break the grapes. Generously butter a 1-quart mold. Turn the bread mixture into it, smoothing the top with a metal spatula dipped into cold water. Dot with 1 tablespoon butter and sprinkle with olive oil, crushed sugar and rosemary. Bake in a preheated moderate oven (350°F.) for about 45 minutes, or until golden brown. Serve lukewarm. Or if served later, reheat in a moderate oven for 10 minutes.

NOTE: Crushed sugar cubes have a brilliance not found in ordinary sugar. In Italy, sugar can be bought specifically for such uses, but here the closest substitute is made by crushing cube sugar.

Ricotta Pie

one 9-inch pie

Pizza Dolce

from Campania

Lard is the traditional shortening for this pie.

FOR THE DOUGH:
1¾   cups flour
½   cup sugar
8   tablespoons (½ cup)
     lard (preferably) or
     butter, at room
     temperature
3   egg yolks

FOR THE FILLING:
⅓   cup sugar
¼   cup flour
½   cup milk
1   whole egg
1   egg yolk
     grated rind of 1 lemon
1   cup (½ pound) ricotta
     cheese
¾   cup (¼ pound) ground
     almonds
     butter and flour for pan
     confectioners' sugar

TO MAKE THE DOUGH:
Sift together the flour and sugar into a bowl. Cut in the lard until the mixture resembles small peas. Stir in the egg yolks. Mix with your hands just sufficiently to blend the ingredients. Shape the dough into a ball, wrap in plastic wrap, and chill.

TO MAKE THE FILLING:
Sift together the sugar and flour into the top part of a double boiler. Stir in the milk to make a smooth paste. Beat in the whole egg. Cook over hot water, stirring frequently, until thickened and smooth. Remove from the heat. Immediately beat in the egg yolk and the lemon rind. Beat the ricotta into the mixture and mix well. Beat in the almonds. Generously butter a 9-inch pie pan and flour it. On a lightly floured baking board, divide the dough into a larger and a smaller piece as if making a regular American pie. Roll out the two pieces of dough. Line the bottom of the pie pan with the larger piece. Spoon in the filling. Cover with remaining piece of dough and crimp the edges of the two pieces together. Cut a small cross into the top crust. Bake in a hot oven (400°F.) for about 30 minutes. Cool, and sprinkle with confectioners' sugar before serving.

The Nun's Eggs
6 servings

Uova da Monacella
from Naples

An old-fashioned recipe, taught to my mother by her god-mother, a nun in Naples. It is quite typical of the fancy confections made in the old convents of southern Italy.

6 hard-cooked eggs
1 cup sweet cocoa, or 4
   ounces (4 squares)
   semisweet chocolate,
   grated
⅓ cup superfine sugar

¾ teaspoon ground
   cinnamon
1 egg, separated
1 tablespoon water
   oil for deep-frying

Shell the eggs and cut them lengthwise into halves. Remove the yolks, taking care not to tear the whites, which will have to be stuffed. Press yolks through a sieve or mash them until very smooth. Stir in ⅔ cup of the cocoa, the sugar, ½ teaspoon cinnamon and the raw egg yolk, mixing to a smooth paste. Stuff the cooked egg whites with this mixture, smoothing it out to be level with the white. Add remaining ¼ teaspoon cinnamon to remaining ⅓ cup cocoa and coat each stuffed egg half with it. Beat the raw egg white with the water until foamy. Dip each stuffed egg half into the beaten egg white, coating it well and shaking off excess egg white. Heat oil to 375°F. on a frying thermometer. Drop 2 or 3 egg halves into the hot oil and fry until golden, turning once. Drain on kitchen towels and serve very hot, as a dessert.

St. Joseph's Day Fritters   2½ to 3 dozen

Zeppole di San Giuseppe   from Southern Italy

Frying the fritters in lard gives them a characteristic flavor.

1 envelope dry yeast   4½ cups flour
2 eggs   lard or olive oil or fat
⅔ cup sugar   for frying
½ teaspoon ground   confectioners' sugar
   cinnamon
1 teaspoon salt
6 tablespoons butter, at
   room temperature
   and cut into pieces

Measure ¼ cup lukewarm water into a small bowl and sprinkle the yeast over it. Let stand for 3 or 4 minutes. Meantime,
measure ¾ cup warm water into a bowl. Add the eggs, sugar,
cinnamon, salt and butter. Mix well. Beat in 1 cup of the flour,
a little at a time, beating well after each addition. Beat in dissolved yeast and remaining 3½ cups of flour. Mix thoroughly.
Knead until smooth and elastic. Put the dough into a greased
bowl, cover it with a kitchen towel, and let it rise in a warm
place until doubled in bulk. Punch down and let rise again
until doubled in bulk. Punch down again. Roll out the dough
on a floured board to the thickness of about ¼ inch. With a
doughnut cutter, cut into 3-inch rings. Place rings on greased
cookie sheets, cover with kitchen towels, and let rise in a
warm place for 30 minutes. In a deep-fryer, heat the lard to
375°F. on a frying thermometer. Fry a few fritters at a time,
turning them once, until golden brown on both sides. Drain
on paper towels. Sprinkle with confectioners' sugar and serve
immediately.

Fried Honey Cookies

about 6 dozen small cookies

Strufoli di Natale

from Campania

Fried cookies are common in all of Italy; in the South, they are often combined with honey, as in Mideastern pastries.

5	cups flour	¾	cup honey
½	teaspoon salt		grated rind of 3 oranges
1	tablespoon sugar	1¼	cups glacé citron, cut
	grated rind of 1 lemon		into tiny dice
8	whole eggs	1¼	cups glacé orange peel,
2	egg yolks		cut into tiny dice
⅓	cup lard or butter		
	lard or olive oil for		
	deep-frying		

Put the flour into a deep bowl and stir in the salt, sugar and lemon rind. Mix well. Make a well in the middle and add whole eggs, egg yolks and ⅓ cup lard. Stir with a fork until the mixture begins forming a ball. Then knead with lightly floured hands until the dough is smooth. Snip off pieces of dough; again with lightly floured hands, roll the dough pieces between your hands into little rolls the size of your little finger. Cut these diagonally into little diamonds. Heat lard or olive oil to 375°F. on a frying thermometer. Drop in only a few pieces of dough at a time to fry until golden. The cookies should not touch each other while frying or they will be soggy. Take out the fried cookies with a slotted spoon and drain on kitchen paper. Pour the honey into a wide, heavy saucepan. Cook over medium heat until honey is liquid and almost makes a soft ball at 234°F. on a candy thermometer. Remove from heat and stir in grated orange rind, citron and orange peel. Mix well. Drop all the cookies into the honey mixture. Stir with 2 forks to make sure that cookies are well coated with honey, taking care not to crush them. Turn the whole mixture onto a large serving dish slightly moistened with cold water. With hands dipped into cold water, shape the mixture into a pyramid, the traditional shape, or more easily, into ring shape. Let stand at room temperature for 2 to 3 hours before serving.

Sweet Ravioli

about 4 dozen

Piconi

from Marche

These are little baked turnovers filled with ricotta which are made all over Italy.

FOR THE DOUGH:
- 4 cups flour
- 1¼ cups sugar, preferably superfine sugar
- grated rind of 1 lemon
- 12 tablespoons (1¼ cups) chilled butter
- 5 egg yolks, lightly beaten

FOR THE FILLING:
- 1 cup (½ pound) very dry ricotta or farmers' cheese
- 3 egg yolks
- 2 tablespoons confectioners' sugar
- ¼ teaspoon ground cinnamon
- grated rind of ½ lemon
- 1 tablespoon rum or brandy
- 1 teaspoon water

TO MAKE THE DOUGH:
Sift together flour and sugar and mix in the lemon rind. Cut in the butter with a pastry blender until the mixture resembles fine bread crumbs. Add the egg yolks. Mix with a fork until the pastry forms a ball. If you have to use your hands at the end to shape the pastry, work as lightly and rapidly as possible. Wrap the pastry ball in plastic wrap and chill for 1 hour.

TO MAKE THE FILLING:
Beat the ricotta until soft and creamy. Beat in 2 egg yolks, the confectioners' sugar, cinnamon, lemon rind and rum. Beat until the mixture is smooth.

TO ASSEMBLE:
Roll out the dough on a very lightly floured board with short, light strokes to the thickness of ¼ inch. Cut it with a cookie cutter (or the edge of a small glass dipped frequently into water) into 3-inch rounds. Put a level measuring teaspoon of filling in the middle of each round. Fold over to make a half-

moon shape. Press down the edges so that the filling won't ooze out during baking. Beat remaining egg yolk with the teaspoon of water. Using a pastry brush or your finger, coat the sweet ravioli with it on top. Place on a lightly greased and floured baking sheet. Bake in a preheated hot oven (425°F.) for 8 to 10 minutes. Cool slightly before removing from baking sheet.

Fried Ribbon Cookies
4 to 5 dozen cookies

Crostoli
from Friuli

One version of the numerous and similar fried cookies that were popular throughout Italy; nowadays, they are found less often. They were quick and easy to make and did not require baking.

	¼ cup warm milk
2 eggs	2½ cups flour
¼ cup sugar	⅓ cup butter, melted
grated rind of 1 lemon	olive oil or fat for deep-
½ teaspoon salt	frying
3 tablespoons rum or	confectioners' sugar
grappa	

Break the eggs into a bowl. Add sugar, lemon rind, salt and rum, and beat thoroughly until light. Stir in 2 tablespoons of the milk. Put the flour into another large bowl and make a well in the middle. Pour in the egg mixture and the butter. Stir to mix well, making a dough that is on the soft side. If necessary, add remaining milk, a little at a time. On a lightly floured board, roll out the dough as thin as possible or to the thickness of ⅛ inch. Cut the dough into strips ½ inch wide and 7 inches long. Tie the strips loosely into knots. Heat deep oil or fat to 375°F. on a frying thermometer. Fry a few cookies at a time until they are golden and come to the surface. Remove with a slotted spoon and drain thoroughly on paper towels. Sprinkle with confectioners' sugar before serving them piled up high on a serving plate lined with a table napkin.

Water Ices

Granite   from Rome and Southern Italy

Granite are made only with water and flavorings, unlike sherbets, which contain egg white to make them smooth. *Granite*, the most refreshing refreshment on a hot day, are easily made in the refrigerator since they do not have to be stirred as often as cream ices to avoid the formation of ice crystals. These crystals are part of a *granita*, which is stirred several times during freezing, to emerge neither solid nor runny, but as a kind of solid mush. The freezing time and the number of times a *granita* needs to be stirred depend on the coldness of the refrigerator or freezer. The amount of sugar depends on individual taste; a larger quantity of sugar needs a longer freezing time.

Coffee Ice with Whipped Cream   4 to 6 servings

Granita di Caffè con Panna   All-Italian

1½ cups ground Italian-
       style coffee
⅓ cup sugar, or more to
       taste

5 cups boiling water
1 cup heavy cream,
      whipped with 1
      tablespoon sugar

Combine coffee, sugar and water in the top part of a double boiler. Steep covered over simmering water for about 30 minutes. Cool. Strain through a strainer lined with a triple layer of cheesecloth. Pour into ice trays and freeze as in Strawberry Ice (next page). Serve in highball glasses, topped with whipped cream.

Strawberry or Raspberry Ice

4 to 6 servings

Granita di Fragole o di Lamponi

from Rome

1 cup water
1 cup sugar
2 quarts fresh
  strawberries or
  raspberries

juice of 1 medium-size
lemon

Combine water and sugar. Simmer over low heat for about 5 minutes, or until syrupy. Cool. Purée the berries in a blender or strain through a fine sieve. Stir in the sugar syrup and the lemon juice. Pour into ice-cube trays. Freeze until frozen crystals have formed around the edges of the trays. Stir with a fork, breaking the crystals. Freeze again for 1 more hour, again breaking the crystals with a fork. Freeze for 1 more hour, or until the *granita* is all frozen into crystals. Then stir once more. Serve in individual sherbet glasses or from a glass serving dish.

Watermelon Ice   6 servings

Gelato di Cocomero   from Sicily

Colorful and easy.

4 cups watermelon flesh
1 to 1½ cups superfine
  sugar
2 tablespoons orange-
  flower water or
  rosewater or jasmine
  water
4 ounces sweet chocolate,
  shredded or chopped

⅓ cup shelled pistachios,
  chopped
1 cup glacé citron or
  orange peel, cut into
  tiny dice
½ teaspoon ground
  cinnamon

Remove the black watermelon seeds and strain the flesh into
a bowl. Stir in ½ to ¾ cup of the sugar, depending on the
sweetness of the watermelon. Stir until the sugar has completely dissolved. Pour into the ice-cream freezer bowl or into
refrigerator ice-cube trays. Freeze until almost solid. Turn into
a bowl and beat to a mush. Beat in remaining ½ or ¾ cup
sugar, the orange-flower water, chocolate, pistachios, citron or
orange peel and cinnamon. Mix well. Turn the mixture into a
melon-shaped or a round mold and freeze until solid. At serving time, run cold water over the mold and unmold it on a
serving platter. To serve, cut into slices.

Biscuit Tortoni

6 servings

Gelatini di Crema   All-Italian

2 eggs, separated	¼ cup Maraschino
½ cup confectioners'	cherries, drained and
sugar	chopped
2 tablespoons Maraschino	1 cup heavy cream,
liqueur or rum	whipped
½ teaspoon vanilla extract	
⅔ cup crushed Italian	
macaroons (amaretti)	

Beat the egg yolks until light. Gradually beat in the sugar, beating well after each addition. Beat in Maraschino and vanilla. Reserve about 3 tablespoons of the crushed macaroons. Stir remaining macaroons and the Maraschino cherries into the egg mixture. Fold in the whipped cream. Beat the egg whites until stiff and standing in peaks. Carefully fold into the cream. Turn the mixture into individual 4-ounce soufflé dishes or paper cups, the kind used for baking cupcakes. Sprinkle each with a little of the reserved macaroons. Freeze until firm. Serve in the dishes.

Homemade Ice Cream with Almonds 6 to 8 servings

Semifreddo di Crema   from Tuscany

1¼ cups sliced almonds
     (about 5½ ounces)
3 cups chilled heavy
     cream
¾ cup superfine sugar
4 ounces (4 squares)
     semisweet chocolate,
     chopped fine

¼ cup glacé cherries,
     chopped into coarse
     pieces
1 tablespoon brandy
     chocolate curls for
     garnish (optional)
     Chocolate Sauce (recipe
     follows)

Spread the almonds on a jelly-roll pan or baking sheet. Bake in a preheated moderate oven (350°F.) for 6 to 7 minutes, or until golden brown. Cool thoroughly. Grease a loaf pan, 9 × 5 × 3 inches, or an 8-cup mold and line it with wax paper. Whip the cream with an electric beater or electric mixer until stiff. Gradually beat in the sugar. Do not overbeat or the cream will turn to butter. Carefully fold in the almonds, chocolate, glacé cherries and brandy. Turn the mixture into the prepared pan. Cover with plastic wrap or wax paper fastened with a string. Freeze in the freezing compartment of the refrigerator or in a freezer for 4 to 5 hours or overnight, until the mixture is firm. Remove from the pan onto a chilled platter. Decorate with chocolate curls. To serve, cut into thick slices and accompany with Chocolate Sauce.

TO MAKE CHOCOLATE CURLS:
Using a vegetable peeler, shave a square of semisweet chocolate in long, thin strokes, letting the curls fall onto a piece of wax paper.

Chocolate Sauce

about 1 cup

This is a bittersweet sauce.

4 ounces (4 squares) semisweet chocolate	⅔ cup water 1 tablespoon brandy

Heat chocolate and ⅔ cup water in a small heavy saucepan. Stir until chocolate is melted. Remove from heat and stir in the brandy. If the sauce thickens too much in cooling, stir in a little hot water, 1 tablespoon at a time.

Frozen Punch

1 quart

Ponce Gelato alla Romana   from Rome

An old-fashioned refreshment.

1 cup water	¼ cup rum
1 cup sugar	1 egg white
¼ cup dry white wine	¼ cup confectioners'
⅓ cup lemon juice	sugar
¼ cup orange juice	sprigs of fresh mint

Pour the water into a saucepan and stir in the sugar. Boil over low heat for about 5 minutes, stirring constantly, until sugar is completely dissolved. Remove from heat and cool for 5 minutes. Add the wine and lemon and orange juices. Cover the saucepan and let stand at room temperature for 1 hour. Freeze as usual in an ice-cream freezer until solid. Or turn into a 1-quart ice-cube tray and freeze in the refrigerator freezing compartment set at the coldest temperature until firm. Break up the frozen mixture in a large bowl and beat until smooth. Stir in the rum. Beat the egg white with the confectioners' sugar until stiff and glossy. Fold the beaten egg white into the frozen mixture. Return to ice-cube tray and freezing compartment and freeze again until solid. Serve in sherbet glasses, each topped with a little sprig of mint.

DESSERTS FOR SPECIAL OCCASIONS

Cannoli alla Siciliana   8 or 9 cannoli

Cannoli alla Siciliana   from Sicily

This most famous of all Sicilian dessert cakes consists of a pastry shell called popularly *scorza*, or skin, filled with ricotta cream. Cannoli bought at a fine pastry shop are as good as homemade ones; however, not everyone has access to a good commercial product, and here is the recipe.

To make proper cannoli, it is necessary to have cane or metal tubes 5 inches long and 1 inch wide, to be bought in hardware shops or supply houses serving Italian pastry shops. The crisp baked shells should be filled only at serving time or else they become soft. However, the baked shells, when made ahead of time, can be stored in airtight metal containers.

FOR THE PASTRY SHELLS:
1¼ cups flour
1 teaspoon powdered cocoa
½ teaspoon instant coffee powder or ground coffee
⅛ teaspoon salt
1 tablespoon sugar
1 tablespoon butter, cut into small pieces and at room temperature
⅓ cup sweet wine such as Marsala, muscat or sherry

FOR THE FILLING:
1 cup ricotta cheese
⅔ cup superfine sugar
1 tablespoon orange-flower water or sweet liqueur such as Maraschino, Strega or Amaretto
¼ cup glacé orange and citrus peels, cut into tiny dice
2 ounces sweet chocolate, chopped fine
1 tablespoon powdered cocoa

FOR ASSEMBLING:
olive oil for greasing
and deep-frying
1 egg white, slightly
beaten

⅓ cup glacé cherries, cut
into halves
confectioners' sugar

TO MAKE THE PASTRY FOR SHELLS:
Sift together the flour, cocoa, coffee, salt and sugar. Cut in the
butter with a pastry knife until the mixture resembles fine dry
bread crumbs. Add enough wine, 1 or 2 tablespoons at a time,
to moisten the dry ingredients. Stir with a fork into a ball,
adding more wine if necessary to make a medium-soft to hard
dough. Wrap the dough in plastic wrap and chill for 1 hour.

TO MAKE THE FILLING:
While dough is resting, make the filling. If ricotta is lumpy,
strain through a sieve into a bowl. Stir in the sugar and orange-
flower water or liqueur and mix well. Add the glacé peel, and
chocolate and mix well. Divide the mixture into two parts.
Keep one as is and stir the cocoa into the other. Cover and
refrigerate.

TO SHAPE AND FRY PASTRY SHELLS:
Oil cannoli tubes thoroughly with olive oil. Roll out the dough
between sheets of wax paper to a thickness of about ⅛ inch.
With a cutter, cut the dough into rounds measuring about 3½
inches in diameter. Slightly roll out these rounds between
sheets of wax paper to make them oval in shape. Place 1 oiled
cannoli tube lengthwise on each oval piece of dough. With
your finger, ease the dough around the tube with a little olive
oil. Coat the edges with beaten egg white. Fold the dough over
the tube, pressing it down in the middle. With your fingers,
enlarge the two ends to open them up; the whole cannoli
should look like a tube overlapping in the middle and opening
up toward the ends.

Heat a large amount of olive oil in a deep, heavy saucepan
to 375°F. on a frying thermometer. There should be enough oil
to submerge completely 2 cannoli at one time. Slide 2 cannoli
into the hot oil. Fry until a dark golden color. Remove carefully
with a slotted spoon and drain on kitchen paper. Cool to lukewarm. Then carefully slide the cannoli from the tubes and let
them cool completely. Before re-oiling and wrapping more

dough on the tubes, let the tubes be completely cooled. Proceed until all the dough has been used up.

TO FILL CANNOLI:

Make sure that shells are completely cold. Fill each by putting about 1½ teaspoons of the white ricotta mixture at one end and topping it with half of a glacé cherry. Fill the other end with about 1½ teaspoons of the cocoa ricotta cream and top it also with half of a glacé cherry. Sprinkle with confectioners' sugar and place on a serving dish lined with a paper or cloth doily. Serve as soon after filling as possible.

Good luck!

Génoise

one 8-inch cake

Pasta Genovese Classica

from Liguria

8 eggs	4 tablespoons butter,
1¼ cups superfine sugar	melted and cooled
1 teaspoon grated lemon	down
rind	butter and flour for pan
⅛ teaspoon vanilla extract	confectioners' sugar
2 cups flour	(optional)

Put the eggs in the top part of a double boiler or into a copper basin. Beat with a wire whisk or an electric beater until eggs are thick. Gradually beat in the superfine sugar, beating well after each addition. Over hot, not boiling, water continue beating until mixture is lukewarm. Remove from heat. Continue beating until the mixture has more than doubled in volume; with an electric beater, this will take about 10 minutes. The mixture is ready when it falls in ribbons from the beater. Beat in lemon rind and vanilla. Using a wooden spoon or a rubber scraper, fold in the flour. Gently fold in the melted butter. Generously butter and flour an 8-inch angel-food pan, individual molds or cupcake pans. Spoon the mixture into the pans no more than three-quarters full. Bake in a preheated moderate oven (350°F.) for 25 to 35 minutes in the 8-inch angel-food pan or for about 15 minutes for cupcake pans. Remove the cake or cakes from the pans as soon as they are baked. Cool on wire rack. If desired, sprinkle with confectioners' sugar.

Liguria (Camogli)

Gianduia Chocolate Cake   8 to 12 servings

Torta Gianduia   from Turin

One of the most famous Italian cakes, and the pride of pastry shops; it is seldom made at home. The word *gianduia* identifies it at once as a chocolate confection from Turin.

2 tablespoons plus 1¼
    cups superfine sugar
½ cup shelled peeled
    hazelnuts (see
    Creamy Dessert
    Icebox Cake,
    pp. 334-335)
9 eggs
1 teaspoon honey
1 teaspoon vanilla extract
12 ounces (12 squares)
    semisweet chocolate
½ cup (¼ pound) butter,
    at room temperature

1 cup sifted cake flour
1 cup sifted potato starch
    or cornstarch
    butter and flour for
    cake pan
½ cup plus 2 tablespoons
    heavy cream
2 tablespoons apricot jam
½ cup Maraschino liqueur
    or Kirsch
¼ cup brandy
8 ounces sweet dark
    chocolate, broken up
¼ cup water

Put 2 tablespoons of the sugar into a small, heavy frying pan. Melt the sugar over very low heat, stirring constantly; do not burn. Add the hazelnuts and with 2 forks move them around in the sugar to cover them completely. Turn the hazelnuts out onto a sheet of wax paper and cool completely. Grind the cooled nuts in a blender or a food processor to a fine powder, or crush them in a mortar with a pestle.

Put 6 whole eggs and 3 egg yolks into the top part of a double boiler. Stir in 1¼ cups sugar. Beat together with a wire whip. Over hot, not boiling, water continue beating the mixture until it is very thick and beginning to rise. The mixture must not be any hotter than lukewarm; if it heats up, the cake fails. Remove the pan from the heat and the top pan from the double boiler bottom. Beat in honey and vanilla. Continue beating until mixture is cold and very thick and puffy.

Grate 3 squares of the semisweet chocolate. Put them with the butter and ground hazelnuts into the top part of another double boiler. Cook, stirring constantly, over hot, not boiling, water until the chocolate has melted and is smooth. Remove the pan from the heat and the top pan from the double boiler bottom and cool thoroughly.

Meanwhile, sift together the cake flour and the potato starch or cornstarch. Fold gently into the egg mixture. Stir the chocolate mixture into the batter. Beat remaining 3 egg whites until stiff and fold them into the batter. Generously butter and flour a 10-inch springform pan. Turn the batter into the pan. Bake in a preheated moderate oven (350°F.) for 40 to 45 minutes, or until the cake tests done. Cool the cake in the pan for a few minutes, then gently release the sides and cool completely on a rack. When completely cool, remove carefully from the pan bottom and place on a sheet of wax paper.

Melt remaining 9 squares of semisweet chocolate in the top part of a double boiler over hot, not boiling, water. Stir until smooth. Stir in ½ cup of the cream. Cook, stirring constantly, until the chocolate mixture starts boiling. Remove the pan from heat and the top pan from the double boiler bottom and cool completely. Stir frequently to prevent a skin forming on top. When the chocolate mixture is cooled, stir in the apricot jam. Beat with a wire whip as if you were beating heavy cream. Combine the Maraschino liqueur and the brandy.

Now trim off all loose crumbs from the cake. Cut cake with a sharp knife horizontally into 2 equal layers. Sprinkle half of the liqueur mixture on the cut side of each half of the cake.

Reserve 4 tablespoons of the chocolate-apricot mixture. Spread the remaining part smoothly and evenly on one cake half, on the side sprinkled with the liqueur. Top with the other half, liqueur-sprinkled side on the filling. Brush off any remaining crumbs. Spread the top of the cake with the reserved 4 tablespoons of chocolate-apricot mixture, smoothing it with a metal spatula dipped into cold water.

TO MAKE THE GLAZE AND GLAZE THE CAKE:
Melt the sweet dark chocolate in the water and stir until smooth. Cool. With a metal spatula dipped into cold water, spread the top and sides of the cake with the melted chocolate, making as smooth a surface as possible. Transfer the cake to a cake plate. Whip remaining 2 tablespoons of cream and put into a pastry bag fitted with a writing tip that has a small, round hole. Hold the tip of the bag about ½ inch above the top of the cake. Working quickly and smoothly, write: *GIANDUIA* on the cake. Or trace the word first with a toothpick, and then write. Refrigerate before serving.

Ladyfingers

about 4 dozen

Savoiardi

All-Italian

The basic Italian cookie, made throughout the country. The name indicates a Piedmontese origin. Piedmont was the home of the Savoia, Italy's former royal family.

butter and flour for
    baking sheets
3 eggs, separated
½ cup granulated sugar

⅛ teaspoon salt
1 cup sifted cake flour
    superfine sugar

Lightly butter and flour 2 or 3 baking sheets. Beat the egg yolks with 6 tablespoons of the granulated sugar until very thick and lemon-colored. Stir in the salt. Gently fold in the flour, sifting it in a light, steady stream into the egg mixture. Beat the egg whites until frothy. Gradually beat in remaining 2 tablespoons of granulated sugar. Beat until stiff, but do not overbeat. Fold the egg whites into the batter. Force through a pastry tube with a small round tip in the shape of strips, ½ inch wide and 4 inches long, onto the baking sheets. Allow 2 inches of space between the cookies for expansion during baking. Sprinkle each cookie with about 1 teaspoon of superfine sugar. Let stand at room temperature for 10 minutes, or until the dough has absorbed the sugar. Sprinkle each cookie again with another 1 teaspoon superfine sugar. Let stand at room temperature for 2 minutes. Bake in a preheated moderate oven (350°F.) for 5 to 10 minutes, or until cookies are pale golden. Cool on baking sheets for a minute or two. Then remove carefully with a spatula and cool on racks or on a marble surface.

Macaroons
about 5 dozen

Amaretti
All-Italian

In pre-blender and pre-food processor days, nuts used to be crushed in a mortar with a pestle, which gives an ideal, paste-like consistency, also releasing the flavor oils. Today, nuts can be ground more easily in a blender or food processor. The latter method is quite satisfactory in this recipe, but there is a slight flavor difference in the cakes made in the old-fashioned way: they are more fragrant and smoother.

1¼ cups very dry whole blanched almonds, ground fine	2 to 3 egg whites, approximately sifted confectioners' sugar
1 cup superfine sugar	
¾ teaspoon almond extract	

Put the almonds into a bowl. With a wooden spoon, gradually work in the superfine sugar, crushing the sugar and almonds together. When the paste is smooth, work in the almond extract. Stir in the egg whites, 1 tablespoon at a time, mixing well after each addition. The mixture should have the consistency of stiffly whipped heavy cream. Put the dough into a pastry bag with a small round nozzle. Line baking sheets with aluminum foil, shiny side up. Force the dough through the nozzle into 1½-inch rounds. Sprinkle each macaroon with about ¼ teaspoon of confectioners' sugar. Let stand at room temperature for 4 hours to dry out. Bake in a preheated slow oven (300°F.) for about 30 minutes, or until macaroons just turn golden. Cool, and store in a tightly closed container.

Fruit Bread from Siena

one flat 10-inch cake

Panforte di Siena

from Tuscany

A famous and rather hard fruit bread that dates back to the Middle Ages, just like the lovely city it comes from. It is the best of the old fruitcakes found throughout Italy.

2¼ cups blanched shelled almonds, chopped into coarse pieces
2 cups blanched shelled walnuts, chopped into coarse pieces
1¼ cups blanched shelled hazelnuts, chopped into coarse pieces
5 ounces dried figs, chopped fine
1½ cups glacé citron, diced small
1½ cups glacé lemon or pumpkin (the latter is occasionally available in Italian grocery stores), diced small

1½ cups preserved watermelon rind or glacé citron or glacé pineapple, diced small
½ cup sweet cocoa mix
2 teaspoons each of ground cinnamon, ground cloves, ground white pepper, ground mace and ground coriander, mixed together
½ cup honey
1 cup superfine sugar
butter and flour for pan

In a large bowl, combine the almonds, walnuts, hazelnuts, figs, glacé citron, glacé lemon and watermelon rind, and mix well. Sprinkle with the cocoa and half of the spice mixture; mix well. Pour the honey into a saucepan and add ¾ cup of the sugar. Cook over medium heat, stirring constantly, until the mixture reaches the hard-ball stage or registers 250°F. on a candy thermometer. Remove from the heat and stir into the fruit mixture. Mix thoroughly. Butter and flour a 10-inch springform cake pan. Turn in the dough and smooth out the top with a metal spatula dipped into cold water. Bake in a preheated slow oven (300°F.) for about 30 minutes. Cool the cake in the pan before unmolding it. Sift together remaining ¼ cup sugar and remaining spice mixture and sprinkle over the cake. Keep in a cool, dry place until serving time.

Paradise Torte

one 8-inch cake

Torta Paradiso

from Lombardy

A delicious, delicate cake.

	butter and flour for pan	1½	cups flour
1½	cups (¾ pound) unsalted butter	⅞	cup potato starch or cornstarch
	grated rind of 1 lemon	3	egg whites
1½	cups superfine sugar		confectioners' sugar
8	egg yolks		

Butter and flour an 8-inch springform pan. Cream ¾ pound butter with a wooden spoon or in an electric mixer until very soft. Beat in the lemon rind. Gradually beat in the superfine sugar. Beat in the egg yolks, one by one, beating well after each addition. Sift together the flour and potato starch. Return to sifter. Sprinkle gently and gradually onto the butter-egg mixture, folding it in as you sprinkle. Beat the egg whites until stiff and fold them into the batter. Spoon the batter into the springform pan; it should no more than half-fill it. Bake in a preheated moderate oven (350°F.) for 45 to 55 minutes, or until the center of the cake tests done. Remove the cake from the pan and cool it on a cake rack or on a clean kitchen towel. Sift confectioners' sugar over the top. The cake will keep for several days if wrapped in plastic wrap or aluminum foil.

NOTE: The dough may also be dropped by tablespoons onto a greased and floured cookie sheet, allowing room for spreading. Bake in a preheated moderate oven (350°F.) for 10 minutes. Remove from sheet and cool.

Creamy Dessert Icebox Cake

8 to 10 servings

Zuccotto

from Tuscany

The most famous Tuscan dessert cake, so called because its original shape resembles that of a *zucca*, a pumpkin. It is found in all pastry shops and restaurants.

butter and flour for
cake pans
6 eggs, separated
1⅓ cups superfine sugar
1 teaspoon honey
1 teaspoon vanilla extract
⅔ cup flour
½ cup potato starch or
cornstarch
2 tablespoons brandy
2 tablespoons
Maraschino, Grand
Marnier or other
sweet liqueur
1 pint (2 cups) heavy
cream

½ cup blanched shelled
almonds, chopped
into coarse pieces
½ cup peeled shelled
hazelnuts, chopped
into coarse pieces (see
Note)
6 ounces semisweet
chocolate bits,
chopped
½ ounce (½ square)
unsweetened
chocolate, melted
confectioners' sugar
2 tablespoons powdered
cocoa

Butter and flour two 10-inch layer-cake pans. Beat together the egg yolks, ¾ cup of the superfine sugar, the honey and vanilla until very thick and pale. Beat the egg whites until stiff. Fold them gently into the first mixture. Sift together the flour and potato starch. Sift gradually into the egg mixture, folding it in gently with a rubber spatula. Spoon the dough into the 2 cake pans. Bake in a preheated moderate oven (350°F.) for 20 minutes. Cool for a few minutes, then remove from the pan and cool on a clean kitchen towel. Brush any crumbs off the cakes and remove or trim off any hard edges. Combine the brandy and the liqueur. Brush half of the mixture on one of the layers.

Line an 8- or 9-inch round-bottomed bowl with strips of wax paper. Gently fit 1 cake layer into the bowl and press against the sides to make room for the filling.

Whip the cream until stiff, but do not overwhip. Stir in the almonds, hazelnuts and chopped chocolate bits, and mix well. Divide the cream mixture into 2 parts. Leave one as is and stir the melted chocolate into the other. Mix well. Spoon the white cream into the cake in the bowl, and press it with a spoon against the sides of the cake so as to leave a hollow in the middle. Spoon the chocolate cream into this hollow. Top with the remaining cake layer, fitting it into the bowl so as to cover the filling completely. Brush with the remaining liqueur mixture. Chill for a minimum of 4 hours or, even better, overnight.

At serving time, unmold the *zuccotto* on a serving platter. Carefully peel off any wax paper that may cling to it. Cut a sheet of wax paper into a round the size of the cake. Fold the paper 4 or 5 times. Cut it into 1-inch strips from the edges, leaving the strips attached in the middle for a 1-inch length. Pull the strips apart, and cut off every other strip, leaving a star-shaped round of paper. Sift a light layer of confectioners' sugar over the top of the cake. Lay the star-shaped round over the cake. Sift together 2 tablespoons confectioners' sugar and the cocoa and sift the mixture over the cake. Carefully remove the wax-paper round so as not to disturb the pattern of the cake. Chill until serving.

NOTE: The cake is just as good, though possibly not as authentic-looking, with a single layer of confectioners' sugar.

To peel hazelnuts, place them on a baking sheet. Bake in a preheated slow oven (300°F.) for about 15 minutes. Remove and place in a kitchen towel. Rub the nuts against each other and the brown skin will come off. Wipe clean before using.

Sweet Christmas Pies   about 30 pieces

Nepitelle   from Calabria

FOR THE DOUGH:
4 cups flour
¾ cup sugar
⅔ cup lard
3 eggs
grated rind of 1 lemon

FOR THE FILLING:
1¾ cups currants, soaked
    in lukewarm water
    for 15 minutes,
    drained and
    squeezed dry
¼ cup blanched almonds,
    chopped
1½ ounces (1½ squares)
    semisweet chocolate,
    grated
⅛ teaspoon ground
    cinnamon
¼ cup sweet wine such as
    Marsala, Muscatel,
    Sherry, approximately
    confectioners' sugar

TO MAKE THE DOUGH:
Sift together the flour and ¼ cup of the sugar. Cut in the lard until the mixture resembles fine dry bread crumbs. Stir in the eggs and lemon rind. Stir with a fork to make a ball; you may have to use your hands at the end. Wrap the dough in plastic wrap and refrigerate for 1 hour. Roll out the dough between sheets of wax paper to the thickness of ⅛ inch. Cut it into 4-inch rounds.

TO MAKE THE FILLING:
Combine the currants, almonds, remaining ½ cup sugar, the chocolate and cinnamon, and mix well. Stir in just enough sweet wine to bind the mixture. Put 1 tablespoon of the filling in the middle of each pastry round, leaving a ½-inch border. Cover with another round, pinching the edges together as when making pie. Prick the top with the tines of a fork. Place the pies on a greased baking sheet. Bake in a preheated hot oven (400°F.) for about 20 minutes. Cool before serving, sprinkled with confectioners' sugar.

Christmas Fruit Bread

one 9-inch loaf

Il Certosino

from Emilia-Romagna

A traditional cake, originally made by the monks of the Certosa in Bologna.

½ cup honey
¾ cup superfine sugar
½ teaspoon baking soda
1½ tablespoons aniseed
1 cup boiling water
2 cups flour
1 cup currants, plumped
in warm water and
squeezed dry
¾ cup blanched almonds,
coarsely chopped

½ cup glacé citron,
chopped fine
⅔ cup pine nuts (pignoli)
3 ounces sweet chocolate,
chopped
butter and flour for pan
glacé cherries for
decoration

Put the honey into a large bowl. Stir in the sugar, baking soda and aniseed. Gradually stir in the boiling water. Mix thoroughly, making sure the sugar is dissolved. Cool to room temperature. Gradually stir in the flour and mix well again. Add the currants, almonds, citron, pine nuts and chocolate, and mix well into a smooth dough. Butter and flour a loaf pan, 9 × 5 × 3 inches. Spoon in the dough and smooth the top with a metal spatula dipped into cold water. Decorate with glacé cherries. Bake in a preheated moderate oven (350°F.) for about 1 hour. Cool completely before cutting; the cake is better after ripening for a day or more. It will keep fresh for several months in an airtight container.

Spongecake
one 10-inch cake

Pan di Spagna   All-Italian

This cake is eaten plain, or is used as the basis for *petits fours*.

butter and flour for pan	1 cup superfine sugar
⅔ cup flour	½ teaspoon vanilla
6 tablespoons potato	extract, or grated rind
starch	of ½ lemon
6 eggs, separated	

Generously butter and flour a 10-inch springform pan. Shake off any excess flour. Sift together ⅔ cup flour and the potato starch. Beat the egg yolks. Gradually beat in the sugar, beating well after each addition. This is best done with an electric beater or a wire whip. Beat until very thick and light-colored. Beat in vanilla or lemon rind. Beat the egg whites until stiff. Fold alternately tablespoons of flour mixture and egg whites into the batter; add the flour by sprinkling it over the batter. Blend thoroughly, but with a light hand. Spoon into the springform pan. Bake in a preheated moderate oven (375°F.) for 35 to 40 minutes, or until the cake shrinks from the sides of the pan and tests done. Cool on a rack before unmolding.

Sweet Easter Bread   1 or 2 breads

Ciambella di Pasqua   from Sicily

One of many similar Italian breads, with whole hard-cooked eggs baked on.

4 cups flour	1 cup milk,
4 teaspoons baking	approximately
powder	2 hard-cooked eggs, not
¾ cup sugar	shelled, preferably
2 whole raw eggs	colored for Easter
½ cup (¼ pound) lard, cut	butter and flour for
into small pieces	baking sheet
1 teaspoon vanilla extract	1 raw egg yolk, beaten

Sift together the flour, baking powder and sugar into a bowl. Make a well in the middle. Put the raw eggs, lard and vanilla into the well, and stir together with a fork. Add just enough milk, a little at a time, to make a dough that is soft but not runny. Knead the dough with lightly floured hands until smooth. Let it rest at room temperature for 15 minutes. Roll out the dough to a thickness of ¼ to ½ inch. Cut stiff paper or cardboard into the shape of one or two doves, lambs or hearts. These shapes must be big enough to accommodate 1 or 2 hard-cooked eggs. Put the cutout shape on top of the rolled-out dough and trace it with a pastry cutter or the tip of a sharp knife. Cut out carefully, and, using a pancake turner, transfer the cutout dough to a greased and floured baking sheet. Roll out the dough that remains from the cutouts into ½-inch wide strips. Dip the hard-cooked eggs into cold water and shake off excess water. If you are using a single cutout, place the hard-cooked eggs side by side in the middle of the cutout. If you are using 2 cutouts, place one egg on each. Place a strip of dough diagonally over each egg and press it down on egg and dough base, to secure the egg during baking. Coat the surface of each bread (the dough, not the egg) with beaten egg yolk. Bake in a preheated hot oven (400°F.) for 10 to 15 minutes. Cool on baking sheets. Remove breads carefully so as not to break them.

Easter Fruitcake

1 large roll

Presnitz

from Trieste

4 cups flour
1 cup sugar
1¼ cups (12 tablespoons) butter, at room temperature, cut into pieces
3 eggs
1½ cups currants
6 tablespoons Marsala, Muscatel or Sherry wine
6 tablespoons rum
¾ cup blanched almonds
1½ cups shelled walnut halves
⅓ cup pine nuts (pignoli)

½ cup glacé citron, cut into tiny dice
½ cup glacé orange, cut into tiny dice
½ teaspoon ground cloves
1 teaspoon grated nutmeg
1 teaspoon ground cinnamon
1 teaspoon salt
1⅓ cups fine dry bread crumbs
butter and flour for baking sheet
2 tablespoons melted butter

Sift together the flour and the sugar. Cut in the butter with a pastry cutter to the size of small peas. Add 2 whole eggs and 1 egg white. Mix quickly and lightly with a fork just to hold the dough together so that it can be shaped into a ball. Wrap the dough in plastic wrap and chill for 1 hour. Soak the currants in the wine and rum. Coarsely chop together the almonds, walnuts and pine nuts. Put into a bowl and add the citron, orange, cloves, nutmeg, cinnamon, salt ˋand bread crumbs; mix. Stir in the currants and their liquid; mix thoroughly.

Roll out the dough between sheets of wax paper into a rectangle measuring about 12 × 36 inches and ⅛ inch thick. Spoon the filling lengthwise onto the middle of the dough, leaving a 1-inch edge on either side and at the ends. Fold over these edges, seal and roll to make a sausage. Fold over the ends so that dough sausage is completely sealed to prevent the filling oozing out during baking. Place the roll seam side down on a greased and floured baking sheet. Beat the melted butter into the remaining egg yolk. Paint the cake top and sides with the mixture. Bake in a preheated moderate oven (350°F.) for 40 to 50 minutes, or until golden brown. Cool and let stand at room temperature for 2 to 4 hours for easier slicing.

Sweet Pastry Dough
one 10-inch pie

Pasta Frolla
from Campania

This rich dough requires a minimum of handling, or else it will be crumbly.

4 egg yolks	¼ cup lard, creamed
½ cup sugar	grated rind of 1 lemon
2 cups flour	1 tablespoon brandy
¼ cup butter, creamed	

Cream egg yolks with sugar. Beat in ¼ cup flour. Cream together butter and lard and beat into egg mixture. With a fork, stir in remaining flour, lemon rind and brandy. Stir only until dough is smooth and clears the sides of the bowl in a ball. Shape into a ball. Wrap in wax paper. Chill for 1 hour or longer before using. Roll out quickly, with a minimum of handling.

Easter Pie from the Naples Region   one 10-inch pie

La Pastiera di Grana   from Campania

This is an adaptation of an archaic confection well worth making because of its interesting flavor. There are different versions, made with different grains such as rice, cracked wheat (as in this recipe) or whole-wheat kernels. The grains symbolize fertility at Easter.

1 quart water	½ cup pine nuts (pignoli)
½ cup cracked wheat	½ cup raisins, plumped in
1 cup milk	warm water and
¾ cup granulated sugar	drained
2 tablespoons butter	½ cup minced glacé citron
2 cups (1 pound) ricotta	¼ teaspoon ground
cheese	cinnamon
grated rind of 2 lemons	1 recipe Sweet Pastry
grated rind of 1 orange	Dough (p. 341)
1 tablespoon rosewater or	2 egg whites, lightly
orange-flower water	beaten
or brandy	confectioners' sugar
4 eggs, beaten	

Put the water into a saucepan, add the wheat, and soak for 10 minutes. Then bring to the boiling point and simmer for 10 to 15 minutes, or until wheat is soft. Drain. Combine wheat, milk, granulated sugar and butter in a large saucepan. Bring to the boiling point, reduce heat, and cook without a cover, stirring frequently, for 10 minutes. Drain off any excess liquid. Beat ricotta with lemon and orange rinds and rosewater until fluffy. Beat in the eggs, a little at a time, beating well after each addition. Stir in pine nuts, raisins, citron and cinnamon. Break off about two thirds of the Sweet Pastry Dough, reserving remaining third. Roll it into a 12-inch round. Grease and flour a deep 10-inch pie pan or springform pan. Spread the round of Sweet Pastry Dough carefully on the bottom of the pan and up the sides for about 2 inches, the way you line a pan for pie. Spoon in the filling and smooth the top. Roll out the remaining third of Sweet Pastry Dough to a thickness of about ½ inch, and cut it into ¾-inch strips. Arrange the strips in a lattice pattern over the filling. With a pastry brush, coat the strips with the beaten egg whites. Bake in a preheated moderate oven (350°F.) for 50 to 60 minutes, or until the filling is set and the crust golden brown. Cool but do not chill. Sprinkle with confectioners' sugar before serving.

All Souls' Day Cookies

about 8 dozen little cookies

Fave dei Morti

from Lombardy

In Catholic Latin countries, it was customary to bake cookies with nuts for All Souls' Day (November 2) and leave them on the tombstones for the souls of the departed. The nuts symbolize bones.

2¼ cups very dry blanched almonds, chopped into coarse pieces
⅓ cup pine nuts (pignoli)
1¼ cups flour
¾ cup superfine sugar
grated rind of 1 lemon
⅛ teaspoon ground cinnamon

2 eggs
2 tablespoons grappa, brandy or Kirsch liqueur
butter and flour for baking sheets
1 egg white, lightly beaten

Combine all the ingredients except the beaten egg white in a large bowl. Mix and toss thoroughly, first with a spoon, then with your hands, until the nuts are well distributed throughout the dough. Place the dough by measuring teaspoons on greased and floured baking sheets, leaving space between the cookies. With your finger, make a small indentation in the middle of each cookie, and paint the top of the cookie with a little of the egg white. Bake the cookies in a preheated slow oven (325°F.) for about 20 to 25 minutes, or until light golden.

Aniseed Cookies   about 24 cookies

Anicini   from Sardinia

These simple, dry cookies may be served with a sweet dessert wine or, as in Sardinia, with a glass of the famous powerful dry Vernaccia wine of Orestano, not to be confused with the Vernaccia of Tuscany.

1 cup superfine sugar	1 tablespoon aniseed
6 eggs, separated	butter for baking pans
1 cup flour	
½ teaspoon baking powder	

Reserve 2 tablespoons of the sugar. Beat remaining sugar and the egg yolks until very thick. Beat in the flour and the baking powder, beating well after each addition. Beat in the aniseed. Beat the egg whites until stiff, and fold them gently into the mixture. Line a baking sheet with brown paper and lightly butter it. Or use 2 lightly buttered 8-inch-square baking pans. Spoon the dough onto the paper or into the pans, and smooth it with the back of a knife dipped into cold water or a metal spatula dipped into cold water. Sprinkle with the reserved sugar. Bake in a preheated moderate oven (375°F.) for about 20 minutes, or until light gold. Remove from the oven. Cut the baked dough into strips 1 inch wide and 4 inches long. Return the strips to the baking sheet or pans, placing them side by side. Bake for 5 to 10 minutes longer, or until the cookies are very crisp.

Almond Cookies

about 3 dozen cookies

Fregolata

from Venice

2¼ cups blanched almonds
1½ cups sugar
2½ cups flour
⅛ teaspoon salt
　 grated rind of 1 lemon
2 eggs, lightly beaten
4 tablespoons butter, at
　 room temperature,
　 cut into small pieces

2 tablespoons light or
　 heavy cream
　 butter and flour for
　 · baking sheets

Chop the almonds coarsely in a blender, adding sugar as you go along. This is best done by dividing the almonds into 8 batches and chopping each batch with 1 tablespoon of sugar— 8 tablespoons in all. In a bowl, combine the almonds, flour, salt and lemon rind, and mix well. Stir in remaining 1 cup sugar, the eggs and butter. Mix with a spoon, then knead the dough with your hands, adding 1 tablespoon of cream at a time to make the dough easy to handle. Break off pieces of dough and roll them with your hands into ¾-inch-thick rolls. Cut these rolls into 1½-inch-long pieces. Place the cookies on buttered and floured baking sheets. Bake in a preheated moderate oven (350°F.) for 20 to 25 minutes, or until barely golden. Do not overbake or the cookies will be hard.

NOTE: The almonds can be chopped separately, without sugar, and mixed with all of the sugar. But chopping them with sugar gives a different flavor to this cookie.

Christmas Spice Cookies

about 6 dozen cookies

Mustaccioli di Natale

from Campania

Traditional cookies that are found throughout Italy south of Rome.

3½ cups flour
1⅔ cups superfine sugar
1 teaspoon ammonium carbonate (see p. 348), or baking powder
½ teaspoon ground cloves
½ teaspoon grated nutmeg

1 teaspoon ground cinnamon
1 teaspoon vanilla extract
about ¼ cup water
butter and flour for baking sheet

FOR THE GLAZE:
⅔ cup apricot jam
1¾ cups confectioners' sugar
½ cup water

1 tablespoon white corn syrup or glucose
⅔ cup powdered cocoa

Sift together the flour, sugar, ammonium carbonate or baking powder, cloves, nutmeg and cinnamon into a bowl. Stir in the vanilla and just enough water to make a stiff dough. Knead the dough until the ingredients are well blended. Shape the dough into a ball, wrap in plastic wrap, and chill for about 1 hour. Break off pieces of dough and roll out between sheets of wax paper to a thickness of ⅛ inch. Cut the rolled-out dough into 4-inch strips. Cut each strip diagonally into 1-inch widths. Place on a greased and floured baking sheet. Using a pastry brush or your finger, coat each cookie with water. Bake in a preheated moderate oven (350°F.) for about 8 minutes. Cool on racks or on a marble surface.

TO MAKE THE GLAZE:
Put the apricot jam into a small saucepan. Stir in ¼ cup confectioners' sugar and ¼ cup water. Cook over low heat, stirring constantly, for about 5 minutes. Remove from the heat. In another saucepan, combine remaining 1½ cups confectioners'

sugar, the corn syrup or glucose and remaining ¼ cup water. Mix well. Cook over low heat, stirring frequently, for about 5 minutes. Cool slightly. Using a pastry brush, coat each cookie with the sugar glaze. Let dry. When the glaze has dried, top with a layer of apricot jam and let dry again. Then top the apricot jam with another coat of sugar glaze. Dry again thoroughly at room temperature. Store in an airtight container.

Marzipan Cookies from Siena   3 to 4 dozen cookies

Ricciarelli di Siena   from Tuscany

One of the traditional almond cookies found throughout Italy.

3 cups blanched almonds	2 teaspoons vanilla
2 cups superfine sugar	extract
2 egg whites, slightly	1 cup sifted
beaten	confectioners' sugar

Grind the almonds as fine as possible, or whirl them in a blender or a food processor. Do not use a meat grinder or the almonds will be oily and unsuited for the purpose. Combine ground almonds with the superfine sugar. Strain through a coarse sieve into a bowl to get rid of any lumps. Add the egg whites by the tablespoon to the almond mixture, and mix well after each addition. Add vanilla. Knead the paste with your hands until it is smooth and stiff. Sprinkle a pastry board with confectioners' sugar. Snipping off a little paste at a time, shape it into diamonds 1½ inches × 3½ inches. With a sharp knife dipped into more confectioners' sugar, trim the cookies to make a neat shape. Place cookies on baking sheets. Let stand overnight at room temperature to dry out. Bake in a preheated very slow oven (250°F.) for 30 minutes; they must not brown at all. Turn off the heat, open the oven door, and cool the cookies in the oven. Sprinkle with confectioners' sugar before serving.

Fruited Cornmeal Cookies   about 3 dozen cookies

Gialletti or Zaletti   from Venice

A famous Venetian cookie. The ammonium carbonate in the recipe is a leavening agent that was used before the days of commercial baking powder. It is the hirschhorn salt of old recipes. It gives an especially crisp texture to a cookie. Ammonium carbonate can be bought in drugstores. It comes in small lumps and should be crushed with a rolling pin just before being used. Equal quantities of baking powder may be substituted for the ammonium carbonate.

1 cup plus 2 tablespoons fine yellow cornmeal	⅓ cup melted butter, cooled
1¼ cups flour	1 cup currants, plumped in warm water, drained and dried
1 teaspoon crushed ammonium carbonate	
½ teaspoon salt	butter and flour for cookie sheets
3 egg yolks	
½ cup superfine sugar grated rind of 1 lemon	confectioners' sugar

Sift together the cornmeal, flour, ammonium carbonate and salt. Beat the egg yolks and gradually beat in the superfine sugar, beating well after each addition. Beat in lemon rind and butter; mix thoroughly. Gradually beat in the cornmeal mixture, beating until smooth. Stir in the currants and mix them through the batter. The batter should be on the stiff side, but not too stiff (and cornmeal varies in the absorption of liquid). Put the dough by heaping tablespoons on greased and floured cookie sheets, leaving a space of 2 inches between cookies. Pat the cookies into diamond shapes. Bake in a preheated moderate oven (375°F.) for about 15 minutes, or until crisp. Cool on the baking sheets for a few minutes, or until crisp. Cool on the baking sheets for a few minutes, then transfer to racks or kitchen counter to cool completely. Sprinkle with confectioners' sugar.

Spicy Nut Bread Cookies   about 18-20 little loaves

Pan Pepato   from Umbria

These cookies are hard and dry.

½ cup currants, plumped in warm water and squeezed dry

⅓ cup chopped shelled walnuts

⅓ cup chopped blanched almonds

⅓ cup chopped shelled hazelnuts

½ cup mixed glacé fruits, chopped fine

1½ ounces semisweet chocolate, shredded

½ teaspoon salt

¼ teaspoon freshly ground pepper

½ teaspoon grated nutmeg

⅓ cup honey, approximately

¼ cup warm water, approximately

2 cups flour, approximately

2 teaspoons double-action baking powder

butter and flour for baking sheets

Combine the currants, walnuts, almonds, hazelnuts, glacé fruits, chocolate, salt, pepper and nutmeg in a bowl. Mix thoroughly, using your hands. Stir the honey into the warm water. Stir into the fruit mixture and blend thoroughly. Combine flour and baking powder and sift it over the fruit-honey mixture to make a dough with the consistency of bread dough. You may have to adjust the flour, adding a little more, since different honeys absorb flours differently. Knead the dough with lightly floured hands until it is smooth. Shape it into little round loaves approximately 3½ inches in diameter and about 1½ inches high. Place them on a greased and floured baking sheet. Glaze the top of the loaves with a little more honey. Bake in a preheated hot oven (400°F.) for about 25 to 30 minutes, or until golden brown. Do not overbake or cookies will be too hard.

Chocolate Nougat   4 to 5 pounds candy

Torrone al Cioccolato   from Abruzzi

An all-Italian favorite, probably of Arab origin, that is made in many parts of the country. In Italy *torrone* is made commercially so that there is no reason to make it at home. However, *torrone* is seldom available except in Italian pastry shops and groceries in America; hence the following recipe.

6½ cups shelled peeled   9 ounces semisweet
    hazelnuts (see p. 335   chocolate, grated
    for peeling   1 cup honey
    instructions)   3 egg whites
  2 cups sugar   thin wafers
¾ cup water

Make sure the hazelnuts are free of their inner skins. If very large, cut into halves. Put ¼ cup of the sugar and ¼ cup water into a heavy saucepan. Cook over moderate heat, stirring constantly, for 5 minutes, or until the sugar and water have become a medium-thick syrup. Stir in the chocolate and continue stirring until chocolate has melted. Remove from heat. Pour the honey into another heavy saucepan. Heat it over medium heat, taking care that it does not turn dark. The honey is ready when a drop of it, dropped into cold water, forms a soft ball, or when it registers 238°F. on a candy thermometer. Remove from heat. Put remaining 1¾ cups sugar into another heavy saucepan and stir in ½ cup water. Cook over medium heat for 8 to 10 minutes, or until the sugar has become a light caramel color. Stir in the honey, mix well, and remove from heat. Put the egg whites into the top part of a double boiler. Over, not in, hot, but not boiling, water beat until egg whites are very stiff. Pour the hot honey mixture over the egg whites, beating continually. Add melted chocolate and hazelnuts and mix well. Spread the wafers on a baking sheet or on a marble slab. Pour the candy over the wafers to the thickness of about ¾ inch. Smooth out the top with a metal spatula dipped into cold water. Cover with more wafers and cool. When *torrone* is lukewarm, cut it into rectangles, using a sharp knife dipped into cold water. Wrap the individual candy pieces in aluminum foil. Store in a tightly covered container, but do not refrigerate. Let ripen for a day or two before eating.

NOTE: Thin wafers are sold in pastry shop supply houses or under the name of *Karlsbader Oblaten* in stores carrying German delicacies. They are widely used in German baking. Or else, using buttered hands, press the *torrone* to the thickness of ¾ inch into well-buttered shallow pans or baking sheets. Cover loosely with wax paper and let stand in a cool place but do not refrigerate. Then proceed as above for cutting and storing.

Almond Brittle   about 2 pounds candy

Croccante di Mandorle   from Liguria

---

olive oil
3¾ cups blanched almonds
2½ cups superfine sugar

4 tablespoons water or rosewater

Lightly brush a marble top or a serving platter with olive oil. Arrange the almonds in a single layer on a baking sheet. Bake in a preheated slow oven (275°F.) for about 20 minutes, or until almonds are very dry but still white; they must not brown. Cool the almonds. Chop them into coarse pieces. Put the sugar in a heavy saucepan. Stir in 2 tablespoons water or rosewater. Place over very low heat. Stirring constantly with a wooden spoon, dissolve the sugar without browning it. If necessary, add 1 or 2 more tablespoons water. Stir in the chopped almonds. Cook, stirring constantly, for about 3 minutes, or until the almonds are thoroughly coated with sugar. Pour the candy onto the prepared oiled surface to the depth of ¼ inch, smoothing it with a metal spatula dipped into water. Cool completely. Then cut the candy into strips or diamonds, wrap each piece in metal foil, and store in an airtight container. It will keep for months.

Orange Rind Candy

about 1 pound candy

Aranciata di Nuoro

from Sardinia

rind of 8 oranges,
yellow part only, cut
very thin (use a
swivel vegetable
peeler)
⅞ cup honey,
approximately

⅓ cup slivered blanched
almonds, lightly
toasted
¼ cup sugar
silver shot

Cut orange rind into julienne strips. Soak in cold water to cover for 2 days, changing water twice. Drain the rind and dry it very thoroughly in a clean kitchen cloth. Pour the honey into a heavy saucepan. Over very low heat, cook until honey is liquid. Add orange rind. Cook, stirring constantly with a wooden spoon, for about 20 minutes, or until rind is thoroughly coated and imbued with the honey. Add the almonds and cook, stirring all the while, for 5 more minutes. Stir in the sugar and remove from heat. Turn the mixture onto a slightly moistened large flat serving dish or cookie sheet. Cool for a few minutes, then turn into desired shapes. Or, while still warm, sprinkle with silver shot. The cooled candy may be wrapped in foil, but it should be eaten within a few days.

Index